2.

HE'S DANGLED BY HIS FEET.

C: "CHARLES, MUST YOU?" 7B

...TO [...] CATHERINE MAMEY + KATEY.
MAMEY WALKS TOWARDS DICKENS.

HIS UPSIDE DOWN P.O.V. OF DICKENS.
STATION ROOF IN B/G.

REVERSE. MAMEY HAND DICKENS THE SPECTACLE CASE.

PLORN IS SPUN AROUND.

C/U SPECS CASE. DICKENS TAKES IT.

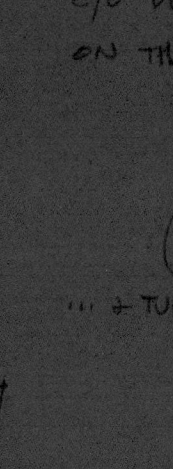

PLORN'S MOVING P.O.V. OF THE PASSENGERS.

10A

C/U DICKENS KISSES MAMEY ON THE FOREHEAD...

AS FR. 4) ~ MARBLES FALL OUT OF HIS POCKETS + BOUNCE ON THE GROUND.

D: "YES, DEAR." 10B

... + TURNS BACK TO CATHERINE.

WIDER ~ DICKENS + PLORN ARE BESIDE THE WHEEL ARCH OF THE ENGINE. DICKENS HAULS PLORN UP.
TRACK ROUND...

11

DICKENS' L/L P.O.V. ~ CATHERINE TURNS AWAY + DEALS WITH THE PORTERS.

THE ART OF
MOVIE STORYBOARDS
VISUALISING THE ACTION OF THE WORLD'S GREATEST FILMS

4.

12/ D: "I AM ENTRUSTING YOU..."

DICKENS PLACES PLORN ONTO A PLATFORM ON THE ENGINE.
(PLAY WHOLE SEQUENCE HERE).

13/ D: "I AM ENTRUSTING YOU..."

CUTAWAYS—
DICKENS ADDRESSES PLORN.

14/

REVERSE — O.T.S. DICKENS FOR PLORN'S REACTIONS.

15A/ SAME SHOT

(AS FR. 13)
DICKENS DOES HIS MARBLE TRICK...

15B/

... & PRESENTS IT TO PLORN.

16/

(AS FR 14 (ISH))
PLORN TAKES IT, DELIGHTED.

THE ART OF
MOVIE STORYBOARDS
VISUALISING THE ACTION OF THE WORLD'S GREATEST FILMS

Fionnuala Halligan

ILEX

THE ART OF MOVIE STORYBOARDS

First published in the United Kingdom in 2013 by
ILEX
210 High Street
Lewes
East Sussex
BN7 2NS

Distributed worldwide (except North America)
by Thames & Hudson Ltd., 181A High Holborn,
London WC1V 7QX, United Kingdom

Copyright © 2013 The Ilex Press Limited

Publisher: Alastair Campbell
Creative Director: James Hollywell
Executive Publisher: Roly Allen
Managing Editor: Nick Jones
Senior Editor: Ellie Wilson
Commissioning Editor: Zara Larcombe
Picture Manager: Katie Greenwood
Art Director: Julie Weir
Designer: Grade Design

Any copy of this book issued by the publisher is sold subject to the condition that it shall not by way of trade or otherwise be lent, resold, hired out, or otherwise circulated without the publisher's prior consent in any form of binding or cover other than that in which it is published and without a similar condition including these words being imposed on a subsequent purchaser.

British Library Cataloguing-in-Publication Data

A catalogue record for this book is available from the British Library.

ISBN: 978-1-78157-105-7

All rights reserved. No part of this publication may be reproduced or used in any form, or by any means – graphic, electronic or mechanical, including photocopying, recording or information storage-and-retrieval systems – without the prior permission of the publisher.

All images © their respective copyright holders.

Cover image courtesy of Universal Studios Licensing LLC
© 1960 Shamley Productions, Inc.

Printed and bound in China

Colour Origination by Ivy Press Reprographics

10 9 8 7 6 5 4 3 2 1

Contents

Preface — 06
Introduction — 08

MENZIES, DALI, HITCHCOCK — 20

Gone with the Wind (1939) — 22
Spellbound (1945) — 26
Psycho (1960) — 30
The Birds (1963) — 32

THE GOLDEN AGE OF HOLLYWOOD — 34

Man Hunt (1941) — 36
The Magnificent Ambersons (1942) — 40
The Big Sleep (1946) — 46
Rebel Without a Cause (1955) — 48
A Farewell to Arms (1957) — 52

THE ARCHERS: HEIN HECKROTH, IVOR BEDDOES, AND THE RED SHOES — 54

The Red Shoes (1948) — 56
The Inn of the Sixth Happiness (1958) — 62
Lawrence of Arabia (1962) — 68

SAUL BASS AND THE SIXTIES — 70

Spartacus (1960) — 72
West Side Story (1961) — 74
The Longest Day (1962) — 78
To Kill a Mockingbird (1962) — 80
Who's Afraid of Virginia Woolf? (1966) — 84

FRESH FORCES IN AMERICAN FILMMAKING — 86

Star Wars (1977) — 88
Apocalypse Now (1979) — 96
Raging Bull (1980) — 104
Raiders of the Lost Ark (1981) — 114
Rain Man (1988) — 124
The Crow (1994) — 126

GREAT ECCENTRICS — 130

The Boy Friend (1971) — 132
Brazil (1985) — 138
Caravaggio (1986) — 142
The Adventures of Baron Munchausen (1988) — 148

STORYBOARDING ANIMATION — 150

Animal Farm (1954) — 152
Who Framed Roger Rabbit (1988) — 154
The Wrong Trousers (1993) — 160

INTERNATIONAL PERSPECTIVES — 168

Pather Panchali (1955) — 170
Ran (1985) — 176
Amélie (2001) — 180
Oldboy (2003) — 184
Pan's Labyrinth (2006) — 188

DRAWING THE TWENTY-FIRST CENTURY — 194

Gladiator (2000) — 196
Cold Mountain (2003) — 198
Harry Potter and the Goblet of Fire (2005) — 206
Land of the Dead (2005) — 212
The Chronicles of Narnia: The Voyage of the Dawn Treader (2010) — 218
Anna Karenina (2012) — 222
The Invisible Woman (2013) — 226
The Crossing (2014) — 230

Glossary — 234
Picture Credits — 236
Index — 237

of the fact that storyboards are, for the most part, executed on pencil and paper, they can seem very ephemeral. Someone tells you about an amazing set of boards they've seen or heard about. They appear to be in a certain archive, but it turns out that's not the case. You find a box; it's empty. You see some storyboards online, but they turn out to be illegal reproductions.

The sad truth is that many of the great storyboard artists of Hollywood's golden age have passed away and most of their work is probably lying in a box in an attic (that's if it survived the studio clear-outs of the 1970s, which saw much irreplaceable material consigned to the bin). Very few storyboard artists hold the copyright to their material and many of the entities involved are now defunct.

Storyboards are also, by their very nature, progressive artworks. An artist will go through hundreds of roughs before they get to the final boards, and even then the scene may be excised from the finished film, or the film may not even be made at all.

The intention with this book is to show as many styles as possible, across the widest timeframe possible, and hopefully for films that hold an artistic significance in the history of cinema. Although I wanted to avoid concept art (also known as production art) or concept storyboards (which are mostly concerned with scene-setting), in the end, there are some examples that straddle the line but were too beautiful not to include.

Copyright restrictions mean that the work of the art department on a film is not widely circulated to the outside world; this book is an attempt to lift the curtain on their tradecraft. Although storyboards are, by their very nature, quick and disposable, they are very much an art form, one which goes much deeper than the strip: they work at a very profound level of the filmmaking process.

This book includes work by most of the legendary storyboard artists of the film business; omissions are most likely due to the difficulty in either locating work or obtaining permissions to publish it. Likewise, every effort has been made to find and credit the storyboard artists featured. In the rare event that they are not named, it is because typically more than one artist will work on a film and it was not possible to determine who drew the work in question—there is a fuzzy line between production illustrator, concept artist, and storyboard artist when it

RIGHT Mary Costa with storyboards for Disney's *Sleeping Beauty*.

comes to an incomplete credit list. I've also tried, where possible, to include examples of the craft from an international perspective.

This book clearly isn't a how-to title. I couldn't have done anything at all without the help of people who know "how to." So thank you to Dean Tavoularis, Alex McDowell, Sarah Greenwood, and Jim Bissell for pointing me in the right direction; to the cheerful Tina Mills and Chris Holm at Lucasfilm, and James Mockoski at American Zoetrope; to Marianne Bower and Martin Scorsese; Arthur Sheriff and Anna Harding at Aardman; Terence Chang, Annie Pressman, Guillermo del Toro, Terry Gilliam and his daughter Holly, Jean-Pierre Jeunet, Tamia Marg, Gaby Tana, Louise Tutt, Mike Goodridge, Carlo Dusi, Jennifer Lim, Rhonda Palmer, Daniel O. Selznick, Annie Pressman, and everyone else I've begged for a favor along the way. And, of course, to Justin Knight, Aidan, and Xavier.

Archivists at the Academy of Motion Picture Arts and Sciences have been unflaggingly helpful—in particular Anne Coco—alongside those at the British Film Institute, Albert Palacios and Steve Wilson at the Harry Ransom Center at the University of Texas, and Mr. Masahiko Kumada at the Kurosawa Archive. Without the help of Yoko Shimada in Japan we would not have the beautiful work of Akira Kurosawa and I am again grateful for her help. Katie Greenwood is an untiring and dedicated picture editor and part responsible for the finished product.

But overall the debt of gratitude is to the artists whose work is represented on this pages. They have their own debts to the past masters, which they acknowledge; they helped me enthusiastically and were generous with their time. So, in order, thank you David Allcock, Ed Verreaux, David Russell, Christopher Hobbs, Martin Scorsese, Michael Salter, Jane Clark, Rob McCallum, Temple Clark, Terry Gilliam, Joe Johnson, Nick Park, Raúl Monge, Sylvain Despretz, and Luc Desportes for your support. I hope the finished product sits as well with you as your work sits within it.

Fionnuala Halligan

Introduction

The art department tends to be the unsung hero of a finished film. It's easy to notice a flash camera angle or filter or a fancy costume while still taking for granted the visual fiber of a film and attributing it to the script or the direction.

A director can come late to a project; a cinematographer can start on a film the week before it shoots. But the art department must be there from the outset, deciding—collaboratively, of course—what the film will look like.

One of the first people to work on a film is the storyboard artist, charged with providing, at its essence, a blueprint for a finished feature. A storyboard is the first look at a work about to go into production that has hitherto only existed as words. Working closely with the director, storyboard artists translate screenplays, or sequences from screenplays, into the first vision of what is to come. Occasionally, they see their work directly translated onto the screen in the final film; more often, they witness the spirit of it come to life.

ABOVE A storyboard from Hein Heckroth and Ivor Beddoes's "The Red Shoe Sketches." The artists storyboarded the entire seventeen-minute ballet sequence in Michael Powell and Emeric Pressburger's *The Red Shoes* (1948).

In the early days of the storyboard, from the 1930s and throughout the "Golden Age of Hollywood," the process was widely used but not particularly esteemed as an art. Rather, it was considered a means to an end. When the studios broke up and the lots were taken apart, many valuable storyboards were sacrificed in the clear-out. Random works now survive in archives and in private collections—literally, the luck of the draw.

On the other hand, the end of the studios also signaled the rise of the director as auteur. With that, the mechanics of making a film have been pushed aside in favor of an overriding focus on its helmsman. Most directors prefer to talk about the finished product than how it came about, and storyboard artists have remained in the shade. Copyright issues abound, and ownership of the work belongs to the production. Some boards can be seen online, but they're limited and generally unauthorized.

The "disposable" nature of the storyboard artist's work doesn't help their art either. They're quick and they're reactive and page after page hits the floor. Sequences are cut; ideas aren't used. Many storyboard artists shy away from "polished" boards, believing that if too much time has been spent on them, then the point has been missed.

But storyboarding is clearly an art, and one that is rapidly gaining in reputation and recognition. In part helped by the adoption of storyboarding in other industries, appreciation has grown for the storyboard as an artwork that penetrates much further than what can be seen on the page. For all the difficulties in uncovering forgotten boards, you'll find many passionate advocates for the process and its stars, from William Cameron Menzies through to Harold Michelson, Mentor Huebner, Sherman Labby, Alex Tavoularis, and on to the crop of talented professional storyboard artists working in film today.

The "art" of the storyboard has two distinct sides: there's the beauty of the work you'll see on these pages, but that skill is only valid if it can be coupled with the ability to conceive a way for a director to visually discover his three-

All we have to do is to walk until we find civilization—

'Who's coming for a swim,' demands / Jack

They enter the jungle fringe

They gambol forward in high glee

It is pretty, mildly luxuriant country

leading up a gentle slope.

Strung out in a widish front the / children move forward

There is no path, but the grass & plants / are low & easily negotiable

Across the sun-speckled landscape the / children play without restraint

a joyous cavalcade of innocence

dimensional film. These artists are a bridge between the director's internal take on the script and the externalized execution of it. They're on board before the wheels of the production even lock into the cogs, and will be gone by the first or second week of shooting. When you look at a payroll, often they're "Employee No. 3 or 4" on a film whose workforce can later grow into the hundreds.

Storyboard artists take the clues provided in the script and, working in very close collaboration with the director, collate all these ideas in one "cartoon-strip" image that appears magically three-dimensional. Sometimes directors will hand the storyboard artist their rough sketch; sometimes the artists will come up with this themselves in a "rough" and refine it until it fills the boards you see on these pages. These will often have written instructions regarding camera angles and dialogue to further pinpoint the scene.

Apart from helping directors clarify what they want to achieve, storyboards work across all departments to allow the heads to conceive and develop what is required for everything from camera and lighting set-ups to stunts, prosthetics, CGI, and even set dressing. Even when a director knows precisely what he wants from the get-go, storyboards work as a reminder and a template.

When talking about storyboards, however, it's important to draw a line between stick figure sketches on the one hand, and what is known as "production art," or "concept art," on the other. Production art/concept art, which is almost entirely computerized across the industry today and is executed in color, is an artistic impression, a scene-setting tool to provide visual keys and inspiration. Stick figures are often what a storyboard artist is handed to work with.

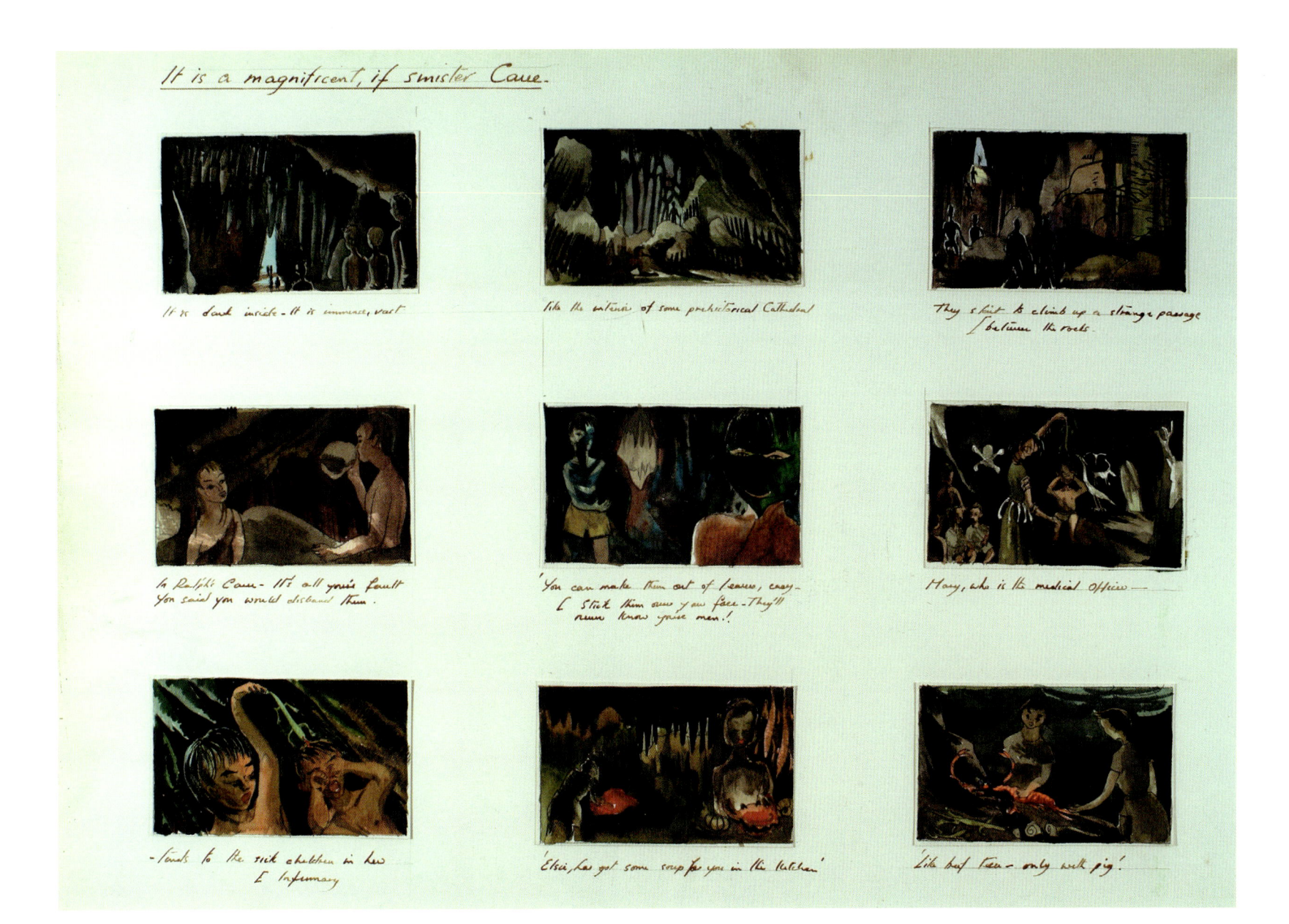

OPPOSITE AND ABOVE Attributed to British art director Wilfred Shingleton (1914–1983), it's unlikely that these *The Lord of the Flies* storyboards were produced for Peter Brook's 1963 big screen adaptation of William Golding's novel, which was filmed on location in Puerto Rico in black and white, without an art department or even a script. Instead, it's possible they were made for an earlier, abandoned Ealing Studios production.

12 INTRODUCTION

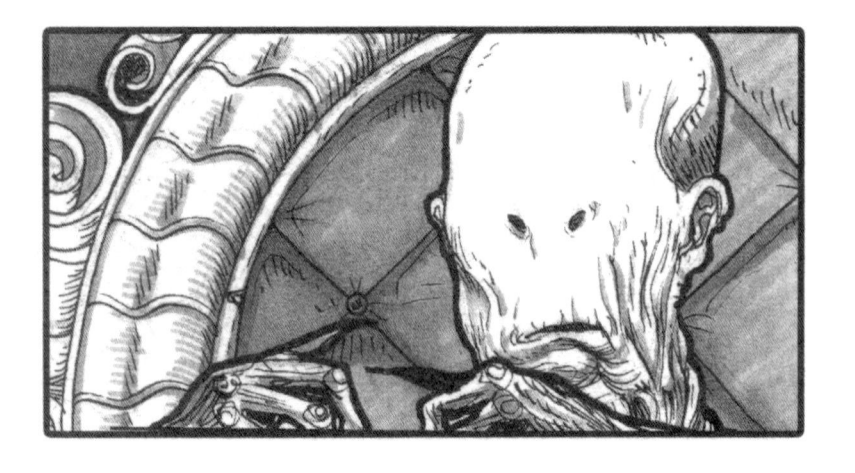

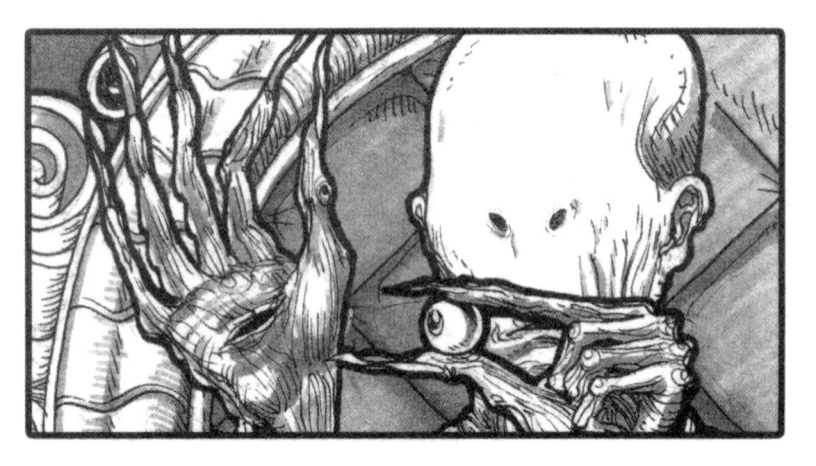

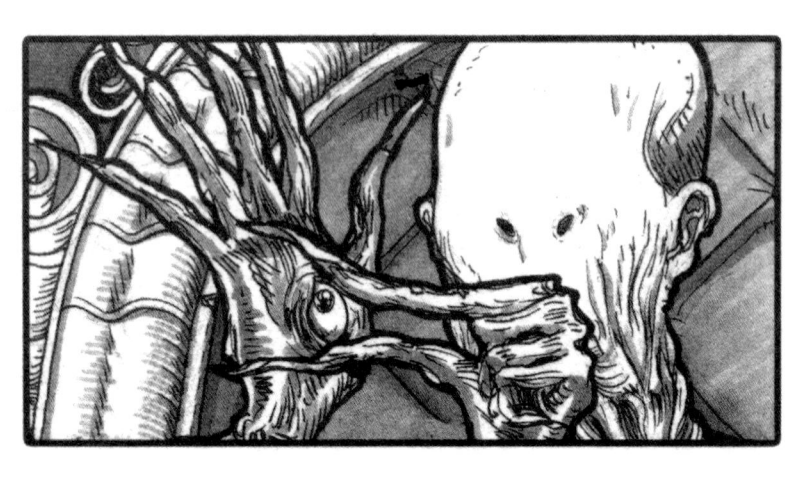

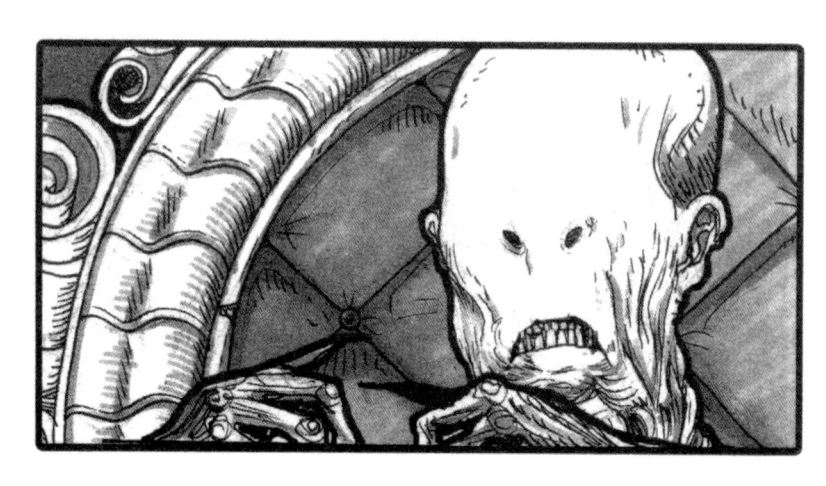

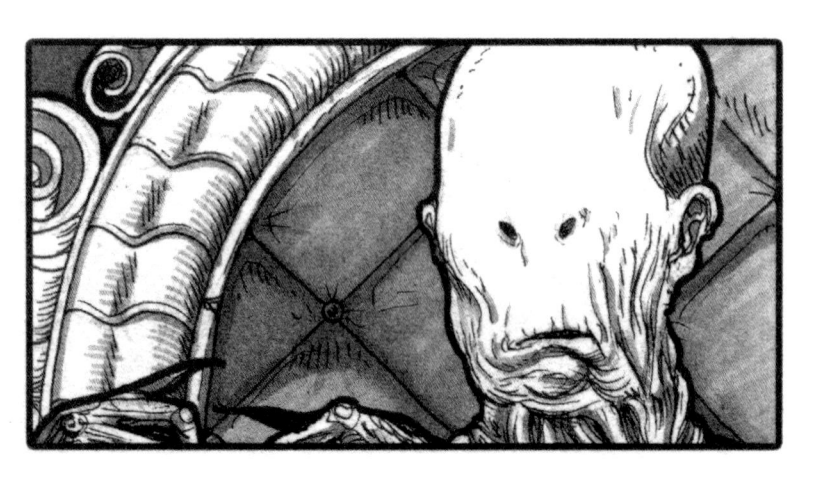

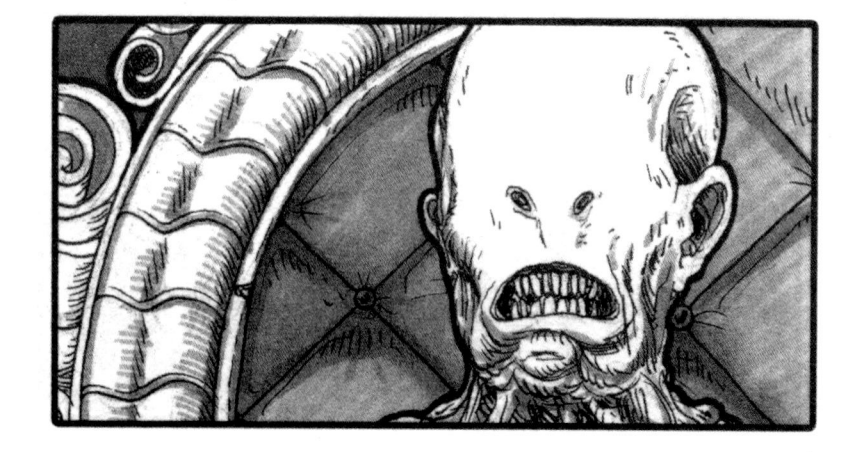

OPPOSITE This extract from Raúl Monge's boards for Guillermo del Toro's *Pan's Labyrinth* (2006) demonstrates how a storyboard can prefigure an iconic movie moment—in this case the waking of the memorable "Pale Man."

That said, this book does include some storyboards that could possibly be classified as "concept art," in particular those most unusual boards painted by Akira Kurosawa over a decade for *Ran* (1985, pages 176–179), while the inclusion of a single set concept by John Box for *Lawrence of Arabia* (1962, pages 68–69) is simply intended to illustrate the craft as practiced in Britain at that time. Other unusual work comes from the British artist Christopher Hobbs, who, working with Derek Jarman, planned *Caravaggio* (1986, pages 142–147) with a concept-storyboard hybrid. And despite clearly being artworks, the sequence from *The Red Shoes* (1948, pages 56–61) was also such a pure storyboarding process that Powell and Pressburger would insert live action footage into the animatic as they shot. In fact, boards such as Hein Heckroth's for *The Red Shoes* are most reminiscent of the work of William Cameron Menzies, credited with introducing the storyboard into live action filmmaking in *Gone with the Wind* (1939, pages 22–25).

All the other storyboards in this book are pure, prescriptive storyboarding incorporating clear frames. They are not used for every shot; just for those more elaborate sequences that are complicated to execute and perhaps need stunt or special effects work or multiple cameras. They're cost-effective and they can be shown to backers and studios to ease minds and open wallets. They can also be useful when it comes to jazzing up talking heads sequences—see the storyboards for the famous "Who's on First" sequence for *Rain Man* (1988, pages 124–125), repeated throughout the Barry Levinson film. Started at the very front end of production, storyboards will ultimately be pinned up on a large board on the set during the shooting day, so the entire crew has a visual reference to where they are as it relates to a particular sequence. (With movies shot in portions of scenes and out of sequence, this becomes increasingly important during production.)

As the director Terry Gilliam says of his own storyboards for *Brazil* and *The Adventures of Baron Munchausen* (1985, pages 138–141; 1988, pages 148–149), "they . . . are the thing I can hang onto as chaos descends around me. With them, I know what I have to do in the shot. I can see through the disorder."

As film has become digitized, there are many more tools available to storyboard artists, and unsurprisingly the outside perception is that the storyboard artist now generally uses computer programs to ply his or her trade. In reality, most still prefer to work with pencil and paper, using the old-fashioned trick of photocopying their work to get a higher contrast. Nothing, they say, works better when it comes to speed and precision. These drawings are then scanned into a computer, refined, and used to form the basis of programs such as Previz, which is a computerized rendering of a film's setting used heavily throughout the industry today, particularly when it comes to effects and larger-budget productions.

So, despite technological advances, the art very much lives on as it always has.

Being a storyboard artist requires special talents. The first is clearly an ability to draw, but the second is equally as important—to have good ideas and to be able to communicate and execute them in a close collaborative setting. A good storyboard artist has to be able to see the film in his or her mind's eye, and that includes visualizing how it might be shot. Consequently, an understanding of how the camera works is essential, alongside composition, continuity, the mechanics of effects shots, and stunt work. Artists need to be able to analyze the script and break it down. It's a unique craft, and often a precarious existence, given that storyboard artists are freelance workers with no job security and generally don't have agents.

It is believed that storyboarding as we know it was developed at the Walt Disney Studios during the early 1930s (although it is fairly certain that some of the larger silent films were storyboarded; no material survives). According to John Canemaker's *Paper Dreams: The Art and Artists of Disney Storyboards*, these first boards evolved from comic-book-like sketches that were used as a basis for the first cartoon shorts such as *Steamboat Willie* (1928; a seven-minute black-and-white animated short, this marked the debut of Mickey and Minnie Mouse; it was also one of the first animated films with synchronized sound). Disney animator Webb Smith has been credited with the idea of drawing scenes and pinning them up on a board to tell the story in sequence sometime after he started in Disney's story department in the early 1930s.

Storyboard artists have a special place at the core of animated filmmaking, which tends to be structured differently to live-action work. There are generally no full scripts for animated films; the story and characterization are fleshed out by heads of story and their storyboard teams before their work goes through to be animated. They have significant responsibilities when it comes to character, plot, and particularly gag development. On a big animated studio feature, up to thirty storyboard artists can work, collaboratively, on a "story crunch." Live-action filmmaking generally uses the services of two or three storyboard artists, each with their own scenes to develop, scaling up according to the size of the production and the amount of stunt work or CGI involved.

This book features examples from different styles of animated film, in particular David Russell's storyboards for

RIGHT Walt Disney (back) at a storyboard conference with staff in the early 1930s.

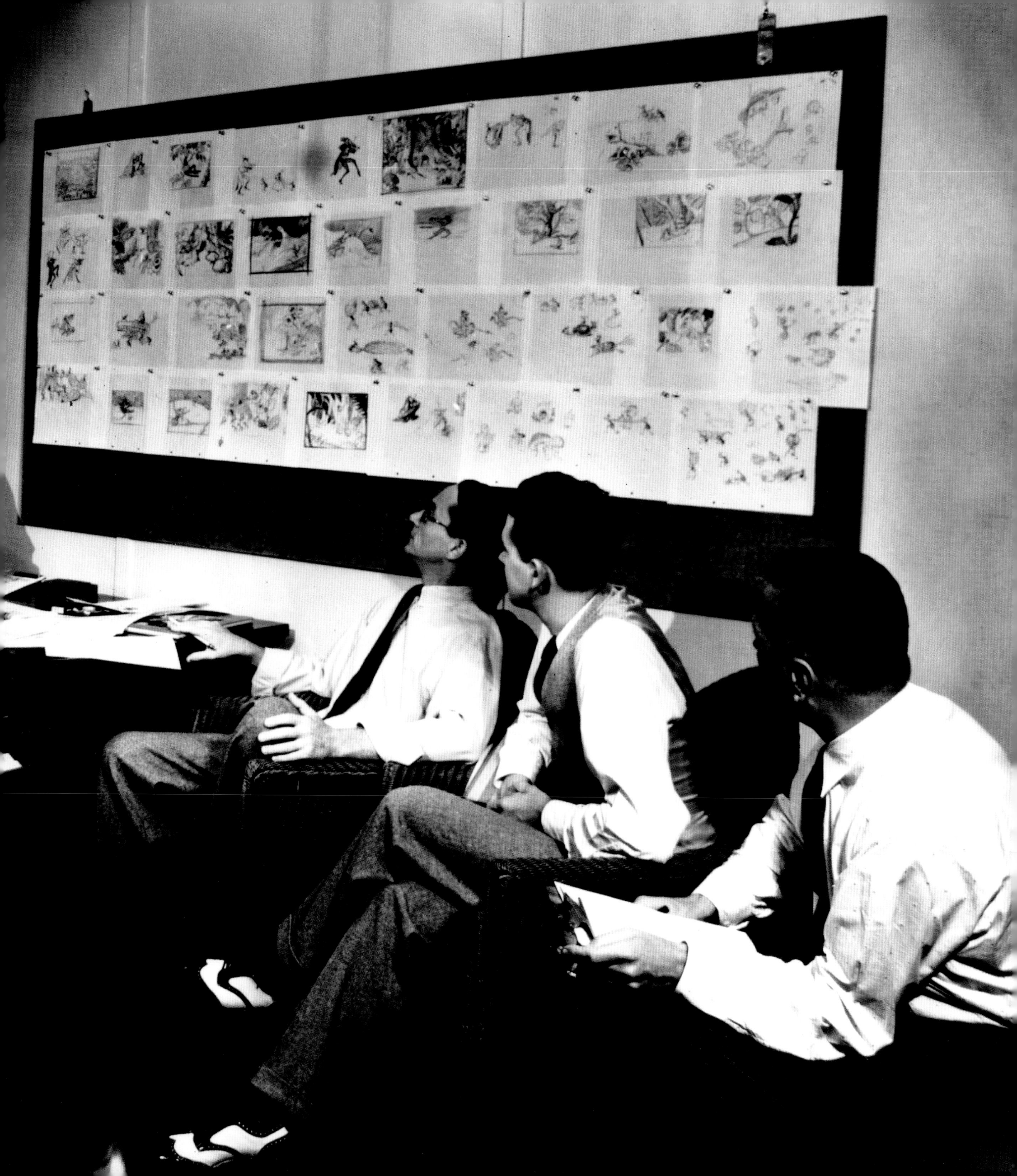

LEFT Director Bryan Singer and actor Tom Cruise looking at boards for *Valkyrie* (2008).

16 INTRODUCTION

the revolutionary live action/animated hybrid *Who Framed Roger Rabbit* (1988, pages 154–159), credited with turning around the fortunes of the animated feature. Nick Park's gripping climax for *The Wrong Trousers* (1993, pages 160–167) speaks for itself: it's all there, on the page. Even more remarkable is the fact that Park produced that entire sequence by himself.

So effective was the system dreamed up by Webb Smith and his fellow artists at Disney that the other big Hollywood studios were quick to adopt this new idea. By 1939, the giant and expansive *Gone with the Wind*, the largest and most lavish production Hollywood had yet produced—shot in revolutionary Technicolor and starring Clark Gable and Vivien Leigh—was considered too valuable for producer David O. Selznick to leave to chance. He hired (and invented the job description "production designer" for) William Cameron Menzies to design the look of the film, and Menzies storyboarded the key sequences including the burning of Atlanta, which he also directed. It is thanks to Selznick's determined preservation of his papers that this, and the unique visuals for *Spellbound* (1945, pages 26–29), survive.

After the war, storyboarding became accepted practice, with storyboard artists working within the art departments throughout the Golden Age of Hollywood. Hollywood art departments in the "big five" studios—Fox, RKO, MGM, Paramount, and Warners—were enormously powerful. Legend has it that directors merely showed up on set and pointed the camera where they were told, although it's hard to imagine Frank Capra or Billy Wilder ever obeying the orders of a gaffer. Examples of this distinctive, noirish work can be seen on pages 36–47 in storyboards for *Man Hunt* (1941), *The Big Sleep* (1946), and the poignant boards for *The Magnificent Ambersons* (1942), Orson Welles's "lost" masterpiece (although it can be seen, it will never be shown as he intended it).

The "master of suspense" Alfred Hitchcock wasn't overly fond of suspense when it came to his sets. He relied heavily on the storyboard, so much so that he earned a reputation for never looking through the viewfinder on the day. That is clearly not the case: the boards for his films seen on these pages are an accurate representation of what was shot. Hitchcock's *Spellbound* is possibly the most famous example of storyboarding as art, with the producer David O. Selznick drafting in the Spanish surrealist Salvador Dali to provide what we would call "concept art" for the film's significant dream sequences. (Hitchcock and Selznick had a contentious relationship, however, and William Cameron Menzies worked over those "boards.")

By the time of *Psycho* in 1960 (pages 30–31), "visual consultant" Saul Bass was providing shot-by-shot instructions for the shower sequence. Bass, most famous for his revolutionary work on film credit sequences, also storyboarded scenes from *Spartacus* and *West Side Story* (1960, 1961, pages 72–77). Another great Hollywood art director, Harold Michelson, worked on Hitchcock's *The Birds* (1963, pages 32–33). And further greats are represented by the work of Mentor Huebner ("the king of the storyboards") in *The Longest Day* (1962, pages 78–79), alongside Henry Bumstead's redolent boards for *To Kill a Mockingbird* (1962, pages 80–83).

All storyboard artists are precisely that—artists. There is no typical career route to the job, although common themes include working as illustrators, graphic artists, graphic novelists, or animators. They will mostly have trained in art school, although many are self-taught. Talented and expressive, they will almost always be outgoing people, drawn to filmmaking due to the collaborative nature of the work as opposed to other ways of working in fine art. They can't be upset, either, when good work is passed over, scenes are completely cut, or sketch after sketch simply isn't deemed to be right.

George Lucas's *Star Wars* (1977, pages 88–95) is believed to mark the start of the modern blockbuster (although Steven Spielberg's *Jaws* had cleared the waters in 1975). The artists Ralph McQuarrie and Joe Johnston famously provided a mixture of concept art, storyboards, and character designs for Lucas's universe as executed by Industrial Light and Magic (ILM), and Johnston's boards are shown in this book, providing a guide to the opening sequence of Lucas's space opera. This ushered in a period of enormous invention and creativity in American film-making, which produced films as varied but equally as exciting as *Apocalypse Now* (1979, pages 96–103), *Raging Bull* (1980, pages 104–113), and the *Indiana Jones* series, beginning with *Raiders of the Lost Ark* (1981, pages 114–123).

Later sections of this book open the storyboard internationally to countries such as France and Korea, where storyboards have not traditionally been used until recently—but are now being enthusiastically adopted as a communication (and often money-saving) tool. The directors who have been quick to adapt them as a directing tool have also been those most predisposed to larger-scale visions, such as France's Jean-Pierre Jeunet (pages 180–183) or Mexico's Guillermo del Toro (pages 188–193), who has switched between making films in Spain and Hollywood. And as cinema moved into the new century, with ambitious, seemingly impossible artistic visions to achieve, the storyboard became more needed than ever. Artist Jane Clark laid the visual foundations for Harry Potter's expansive sweep (pages 206–211); likewise David Russell with *Narnia* (pages 218–221), and Temple Clark for the late Anthony Minghella and *Cold Mountain* (2003, pages 198–205).

Before going much further into this book, it's worth noting the words of Aardman's senior storyboard artist, Michael Salter: "It's tempting to be impressed by beautiful boards but it's a discipline to not get drawn into the detail too much, to grasp space, angles, keep it loose and rough." Others caution that the skill is not about looking good in an "art of" book—such as this—but being at the service of the director and his film. Many Blu-ray and DVD special editions will show storyboards side-by-side with the finished frame, which is always a feature worth looking for, and helps to form a deeper appreciation of the "art."

The final set of storyboards in this book are for a film that hasn't, at time of writing, been made: a lavish John Woo production titled *The Crossing*, to be shot throughout 2013. Budgeted at $30m—a huge amount for an Asian film set in Shanghai and Taiwan—it will recreate battles from the Second World War and the Chinese Civil War and the famous sinking of a ship in the China Sea. The storyboards here have been produced for the famously non-computer-compliant Woo. He has used them—as with many of the boards on these pages—to drum up financing and communicate a vision not just to the crew but also to its potential backers. Thus, just as the art of the storyboard goes beyond what you see on these pages, its uses are more fundamental than might previously be imagined. In other words, and despite their origins: not at all "Mickey Mouse."

OPPOSITE TOP Director Chris Wedge looking at boards for *Ice Age* (2002).

OPPOSITE BOTTOM Director Alexander Witt working on storyboards for *Resident Evil: Apocalypse* (2004).

INTRODUCTION 19

The production of live-action filmmaking took a giant leap with *Gone with the Wind* in 1939, one of the first major films to be entirely storyboarded, by William Cameron Menzies (1896–1957). Shot in Technicolor and produced by the famously "hands-on" David O. Selznick, *Gone with the Wind* churned through directors and cinematographers, but the one steady hand on the artistic tiller throughout production was Menzies. So great was his contribution to the look, color, and staging of the film that producer Selznick declared in a memo that Menzies was "the final word . . . responsible for all the physical aspects of the production and for the color values of the production and any difference [of opinion] should be settled by him."

Selznick invented the term "production designer" for Menzies, who also directed several scenes in the film, most notably the burning of Atlanta. So when Selznick encountered artistic difficulties on the set of *Spellbound* (1945), it was naturally Menzies he called upon to help realize the famous dream sequences designed by Spanish surrealist artist Salvador Dali for director Alfred Hitchcock.

Selznick had, with great fanfare, brought Hitchcock over from England in 1939 on a seven-year contract that began with the film *Rebecca* (1940) and was followed by several loan-outs. Selznick and Hitchcock's relationship was often fraught, however, with the director chafing under his producer's control. Thus Menzies was brought in to supervise the storyboarding and filming of the key dream sequence with the film's art director, James Basevi, working from Dali's paintings. The film had come about because of Selznick's own preoccupation with analysis, which was very fashionable at the time—Freud died a mere four years before *Spellbound* went into production. Although the film's star, Ingrid Bergman, later claimed that twenty minutes of Dali's highly Freudian sequence was shot, no record remains of the cut footage.

Having trained as a draftsman and started his film career designing title cards for silent movies for Famous Players-Lasky, Alfred Hitchcock was known for his extensive pre-production work and reliance upon the art of storyboarding. Just how much has been disputed—he

RIGHT William Cameron Menzies working up storyboards for the Sam Wood–directed melodrama *Kings Row* (1942).

may have been more flexible than was previously his reputation. He generally shot in sequence, a tricky and expensive way of filming, and he made sure to work with the great storyboard artists of the Hollywood golden age.

Saul Bass (1920–1996), in particular, enjoyed an artistically memorable collaboration with Hitchcock, most famously on the shower sequence for *Psycho* (1960; he was credited as "visual consultant" on that film, and also designed the title sequence). Later, the legendary graphic artist claimed to have directed it, and although that has been contested, his contribution to Janet Leigh's cinematic demise would appear to have been extensive. Hitchcock made use of Bass's considerable talents for his poster work as well, most notably on the dizzying spiral block graphics for *Vertigo* (1958).

The storyboard artist and production designer Harold Michelson (1920–2007) was also one of Hitchcock's favorite illustrators, providing the boards for *The Birds* (1963) and *Marnie* (1964). Having started out as a storyboard artist on films including *The Ten Commandments* (1956) and *Ben-Hur* (1959), Michelson spent most of the 1960s working as an illustrator and storyboard artist on films such as *Cleopatra* (1963), *Who's Afraid of Virginia Woolf?* (1966), and *The Graduate* (1967, those last two for director Mike Nichols). Like many storyboard artists, who need to hold the film's entire technical ambition in their heads before conceiving a board, Michelson found the move to production design a natural progression and he was nominated twice for an Academy Award for his work on *Star Trek: The Motion Picture* (1979) and *Terms of Endearment* (1983).

Gone with the Wind 1939

DIRECTOR Victor Fleming
STORYBOARDS William Cameron Menzies

BELOW William Cameron Menzies's storyboards for one of the best-known sequences in *Gone with the Wind*, the burning of the city of Atlanta.

Production designer William Cameron Menzies won an honorary Oscar in 1940 for his work on *Gone with the Wind*, awarded "for outstanding achievement in the use of color for the enhancement of dramatic mood." He storyboarded the film and also directed several scenes in it, most notably the burning of Atlanta, storyboarded here (see below and pages 24–25). Menzies, born in Connecticut to Scottish parents, was already a highly experienced art director and director by the time he shot *Gone with the Wind*. He joined Famous Players-Lasky (later Paramount) in 1919, first finding renown in adopting the angular drama of German expressionism for black-and-white studio fare such as Mary Pickford's *Rosita* (1923, directed by Ernst Lubitsch) and several Douglas Fairbanks films, notably *The Thief of Bagdad* (1924). As seen in these storyboards, Cameron Menzies loved slashing diagonals, overreaching shadows, the low horizon, and worm-eye views. He believed that each shot had to have "one forceful, impressive idea." It is hard to overestimate his impact on the craft of motion picture filmmaking as it developed.

22 MENZIES, DALI, HITCHCOCK

GONE WITH THE WIND **23**

3 shots of
Hooligans.

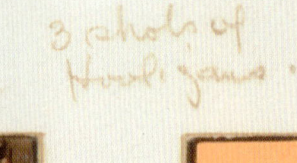

LEFT Not only did Cameron Menzies storyboard the burning of Atlanta sequence in *Gone with the Wind*, he directed it as well.

GONE WITH THE WIND 25

Spellbound 1945

DIRECTOR Alfred Hitchcock
STORYBOARDS Salvador Dali, William Cameron Menzies, James Basevi

Spellbound's famous, visually-stunning dream sequence was designed by art director James Basevi and set director Emile Kuri from sketches and paintings by the Spanish surreal artist Salvador Dali, supervised by William Cameron Menzies (who was brought in by producer David O. Selznick). Director Alfred Hitchcock praised Dali because of the "architectural sharpness of his work," although not all of the shot sequence was used and none of the discarded footage survives.

In *Spellbound*, Ingrid Bergman plays Dr. Constance Peterson, the only female psychiatrist at the Green Manors insane asylum where the amnesiac John "JB" Ballantyne (Gregory Peck) is sent, believing himself to be the murdered hospital chief Dr. Edwards. He has dreams quite unlike anything seen in Hollywood before, with the smoke and mirrors replaced by spatial distortions and terrifyingly empty landscapes. Dr. Peterson must try to analyze the clues in his dreams to provide the key to his identity.

The first dream sequence pictured here, a segment of the *Spellbound* rooftop storyboards in which a mysterious man falls to his death (see right), is a photograph of a Dali painting with William Cameron Menzies's sketching over the top. Another key dream sequence (below and overleaf) is set in a "gambling house." As Dr. Peterson describes in the film: "It was full of odd people playing with blank cards. One of the people in the place went around cutting the drapes in half . . . there were eyes painted on the curtains around the walls." These boards are original paintings by James Basevi, again, from Dali. The idea of eyes being cut by scissors refers, of course, to Dali's work with the Spanish director Luis Buñuel on the short film *Un Chien Andalou* (1929).

26 MENZIES, DALI, HITCHCOCK

OPPOSITE BELOW A James Basevi board for the dream sequence set in a gambling house, inspired by Salvador Dali, and in turn owing a debt to Dali and Luis Buñuel's work on *Un Chien Andalou* (1929).

BELOW The rooftop dream sequence—a photograph of a Dali painting sketched over by William Cameron Menzies.

SPELLBOUND 27

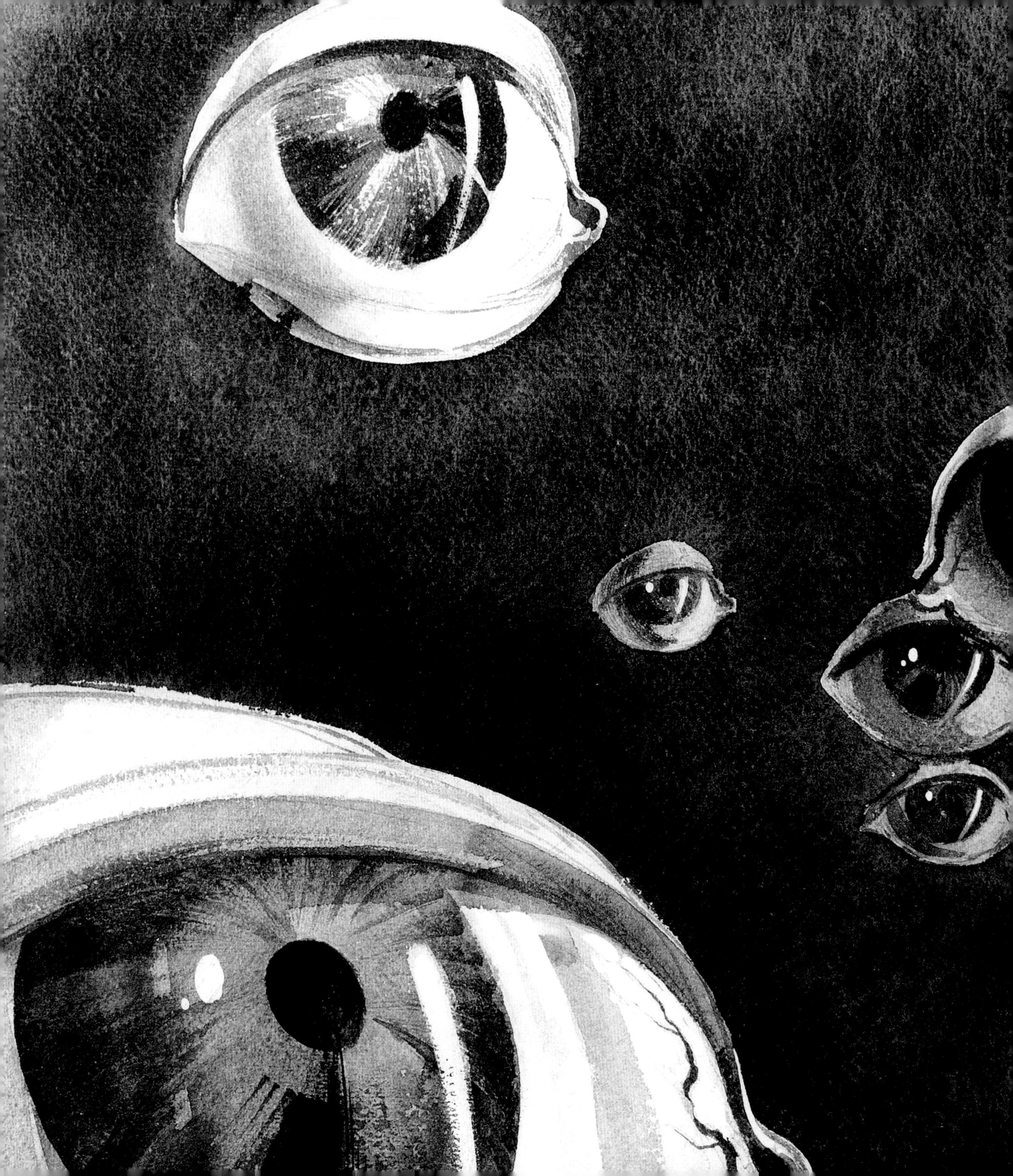

LEFT AND ABOVE James Basevi's boards—working from Salvador Dali's artwork—for the gambling house dream sequence, with eyes painted on the walls and on the drapes.

SPELLBOUND 29

Psycho 1960

DIRECTOR Alfred Hitchcock
STORYBOARDS Saul Bass

The shower sequence from *Psycho* is one of the most memorable, and most debated, sequences in film history, featuring as it does fifty cuts, many in extreme close-up. It was comprehensively storyboarded by Saul Bass after extensive discussions with Alfred Hitchcock; much later, Bass claimed that he himself had directed the sequence. The film's star, Janet Leigh, disagreed: "Absolutely not!" she exclaimed. "I was in that shower for seven days, and believe me, Alfred Hitchcock was right next to his camera for every one of those seventy-odd shots."

Looking at the forty-eight storyboards provided by Bass, however, proves the contribution of the visual consultant and storyboard artist (who also designed the credits). Key aspects of the final scene appear here, including Marion Crane's outstretched arm, the close-up of the knife as it is being thrust, and the move from the drainage hole to Marion Crane's dead eyes. The "controversy" will undoubtedly preoccupy fans for years to come, but clearly Bass and Hitchcock's work together was characterized by creative genius; previously, Bass provided the British director with the title sequence and uncanny poster for *Vertigo* (1958).

RIGHT The *Psycho* shower scene, storyboarded by Saul Bass. Panels run top to bottom, left to right.

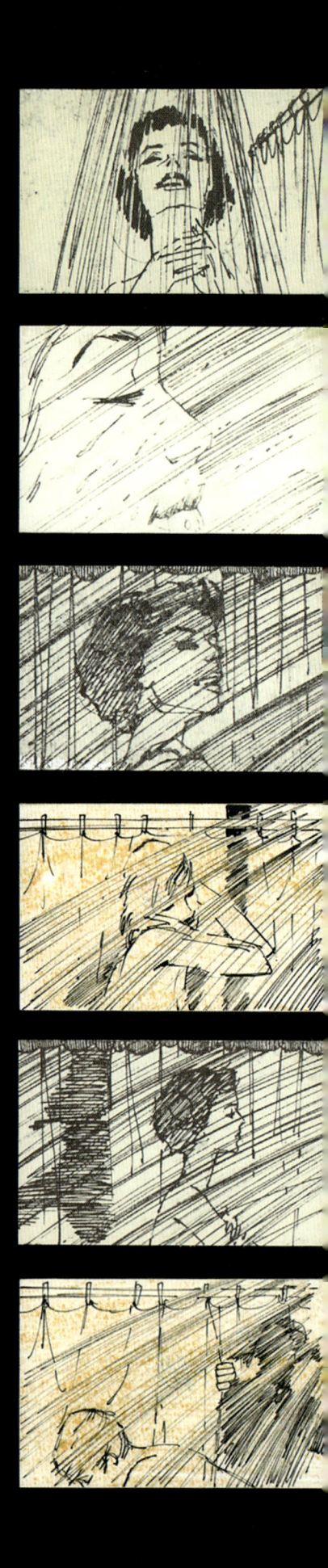

30 MENZIES, DALI, HITCHCOCK

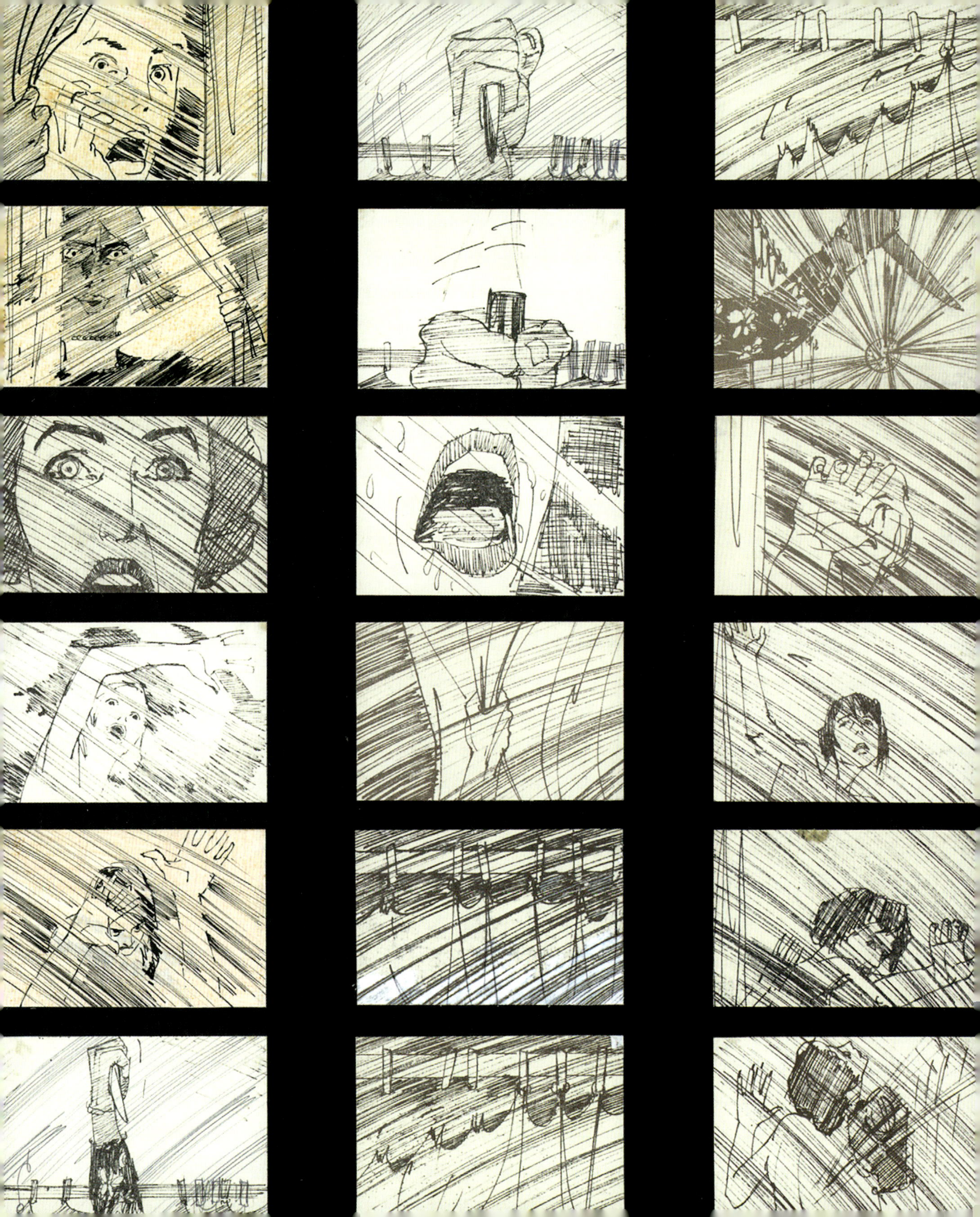

The Birds 1963

DIRECTOR Alfred Hitchcock
STORYBOARDS Harold Michelson

Harold Michelson was known as "the industry's greatest illustrator" and his storyboards for *The Birds* give some indication as to why. The film was one of the trickiest attempted at that time due to the live-action avian component and Hitchcock's insistence on using the cumbersome "sodium vapor process" for effects shots, of which there were many. Michelson storyboarded the entire shoot and once again, as with Saul Bass's boards for the *Psycho* shower sequence, the level of detail is exacting and extensive enough to almost resemble an animated version of the final film.

Michelson worked from production designer Robert Boyle's "roughs"—charcoal sketches—to provide a precise shooting guide. Nowhere is the meticulousness of Hitchcock/Boyle/Michelson's work more clear than in the bird attack sequences, which cover just seconds of screen time. While minor details may have changed, Hitchcock never deviated from the storyboards' master plan.

THE BIRDS 33

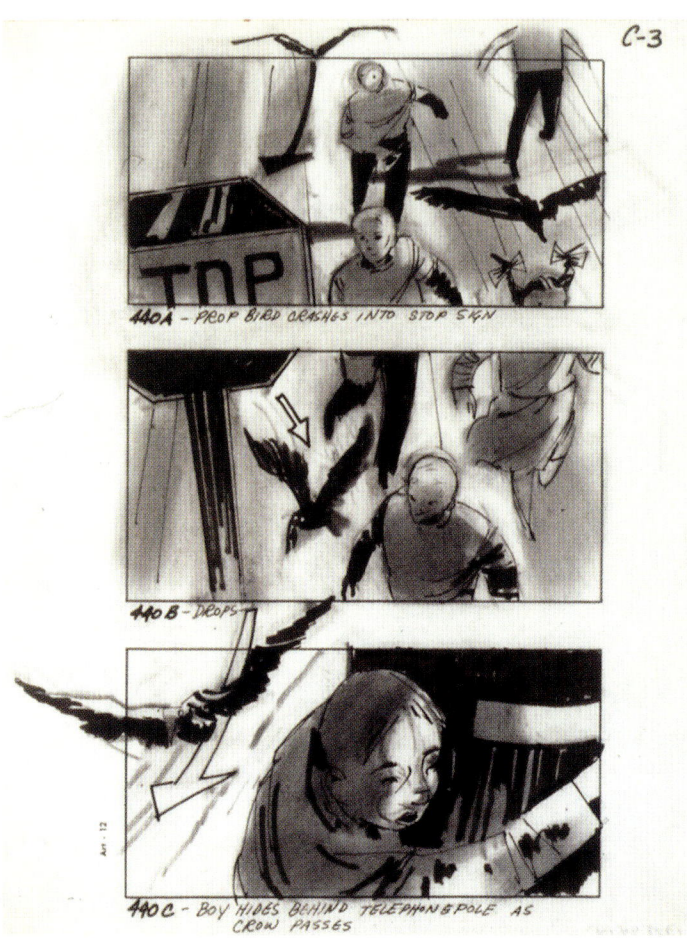

The Golden Age of Hollywood

Hollywood's "Golden Age" refers to the era of the studio system, from the late 1920s and the first talkies, to the late 1950s, when the power of the "big five" studios—MGM, Warners, 20th Century Fox, Paramount, and RKO—began to wane. The studios controlled both production and distribution of cinema (through their own network of theaters); not only did they keep stars under contract but they employed thousands of people on payroll—vast art departments that facilitated a production schedule not easily replicated today. Art directors and storyboard artists would work within a studio, and while actors and directors were usually contracted to a studio, they were often "loaned out."

These art departments were tight-knit, ultra-professional units of craftsmen (often Russian and German émigrés) who often worked on several features at once. Cedric Gibbons, perhaps the most famous studio art director, lived the art deco dream outside the studio, marrying the silent screen beauty Dolores del Rio. He is credited with art directing 1,500 films and creating the look of MGM movies from when the studio started in 1924 to his retirement in 1956. Gibbons was known to be particularly autocratic; over at Paramount, German émigré Hans Dreier was thought to be more relaxed, and enjoyed personal collaborations with Josef von Sternberg and Ernst Lubitsch, and later with Preston Sturges and Billy Wilder.

It was an era of great power and professionalism for the art departments; many still rue their demise. Giant backlots used revolving sets that were cataloged, stored, and recycled. Stories abound of directors turning up on the day to point the camera where the art department showed them to. It was not an era of the auteur director, even though it is hard to imagine directors such as William Wyler or Frank Capra accepting art department diktats.

Artistically, the classic noir titles of this era have remained highly influential, as the boards for *The Big Sleep* and *Man Hunt* illustrate. Orson Welles may be most revered for *Citizen Kane* (1941) but the tragic tale of *The Magnificent Ambersons* and RKO Studio is the most redolent illustration of where power lay in Hollywood during this time; the storyboards have a poignant sense of a vision that was never fully realized.

ABOVE Silent screen star Dolores del Rio poses with her husband, famed art director Cedric Gibbons.

Man Hunt 1941

DIRECTOR Fritz Lang
STORYBOARDS Wiard B. Ihnen

BELOW AND OPPOSITE Wiard B. Ihnen's boards, with their bold use of chiaroscuro, prefigure the expressionistic feel of Lang's film, which was based on Geoffrey Household's classic 1939 thriller, *Rogue Male*.

The great Austrian Expressionist director Fritz Lang fled his homeland in the late 1930s (rather than make propaganda films for Joseph Goebbels), and *Man Hunt* was the first of four anti-Nazi films he made in the U.S. The director of *Metropolis* (1927) worked with art director Wiard B. Ihnen on this production, which starred Walter Pidgeon as Captain Alan Thorndike, an American soldier and big game hunter who happens upon Hitler's lodge while hunting in Bavaria and takes aim. Captured, Thorndike is tortured and left for dead by a river—but he finds a rowboat and attempts to navigate it to port without being discovered by the Nazis, who rake the water's surface with a searchlight.

The boards shown here, in graphite pencil, are classic film noir, with large parts of the page left in the dark. Thorndike ("Thorndyke") must turn in order to avoid the lights before reaching port where he can stow away on a ship to Britain. Ihnen, who was born in New Jersey, trained as an architect and worked for over three decades as a Hollywood art director. He was married to the legendary costume designer Edith Head.

36 THE GOLDEN AGE OF HOLLYWOOD

56c THORNDYKE TURNS BOAT
AFTER LIGHT ~~LEAES~~ LEAVES
HIM IN DARKNESS AND

MAN HUNT

ABOVE Captain Thorndike attempts to avoid detection in his rowboat in this panel from Wiard B. Ihnen's evocative boards.

38 THE GOLDEN AGE OF HOLLYWOOD

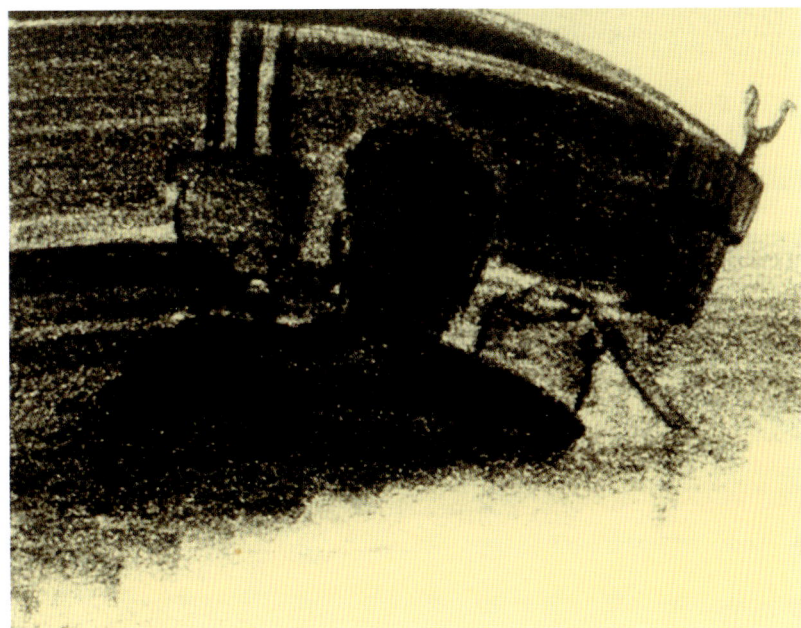

ABOVE Thorndike is forced to abandon his vessel when a patrol boat nears.

MAN HUNT

The Magnificent Ambersons 1942

DIRECTOR Orson Welles
STORYBOARDS unattributed

The Magnificent Ambersons is Orson Welles's tragic masterpiece, his much-hyped follow-up to *Citizen Kane* (1941). It featured an extravagant set constructed at RKO's studios—the Ambersons' mansion, with its moving walls, which provided the setting for Welles's beloved central ballroom sequence and extensive tracking shots (drastically cut in the theatrical release).

Audacious and daring, *The Magnificent Ambersons* suffered one of Hollywood's most traumatic post-production periods. The writer-director had negotiated away his final cut and was working in Brazil on another project when he delivered a (second edit) 131-minute film. It received poor responses from a test audience and RKO took control.

"Everybody they could find was cutting it," recalled Welles later. It is believed the film went from 131 to 88 minutes, and many sequences were reshot, without Welles's approval, by the film's editor, Robert Wise. It was also given a new, more optimistic ending. The edited footage was later destroyed and the original cut has disappeared; all that remains is Welles's script and some storyboards, unattributed.

The Magnificent Ambersons left Welles with a poor reputation in Hollywood and he struggled to find work after it, yet the film is beloved by critics and cineastes and considered to be one of the greatest movies ever made, its tortured history providing a poignant backstory to the action onscreen.

RIGHT Albert S. D'Agostino was RKO's art director and supervised the glossy look of all the studio's films, including *The Magnificent Ambersons*; he would certainly have had control over the Amberson Mansion, as constructed in RKO's Gower Street Studios.

40 THE GOLDEN AGE OF HOLLYWOOD

MAKE MATTE

38-B ISABEL - "THOSE WERE TERRIBLE WORDS FOR YOU TO USE, DEAR

38
No caption

38-A GEORGE - "HE'S AN OLE LIAR!"
38A

38-B

38-C
No capt.

38 D
No capt.

BELOW AND OPPOSITE In the unusual closing credits of *The Magnificent Ambersons*, Welles credits Mark-Lee Kirk with the film's set design, and it would certainly appear that the film's look was a close collaboration between the director and Kirk.

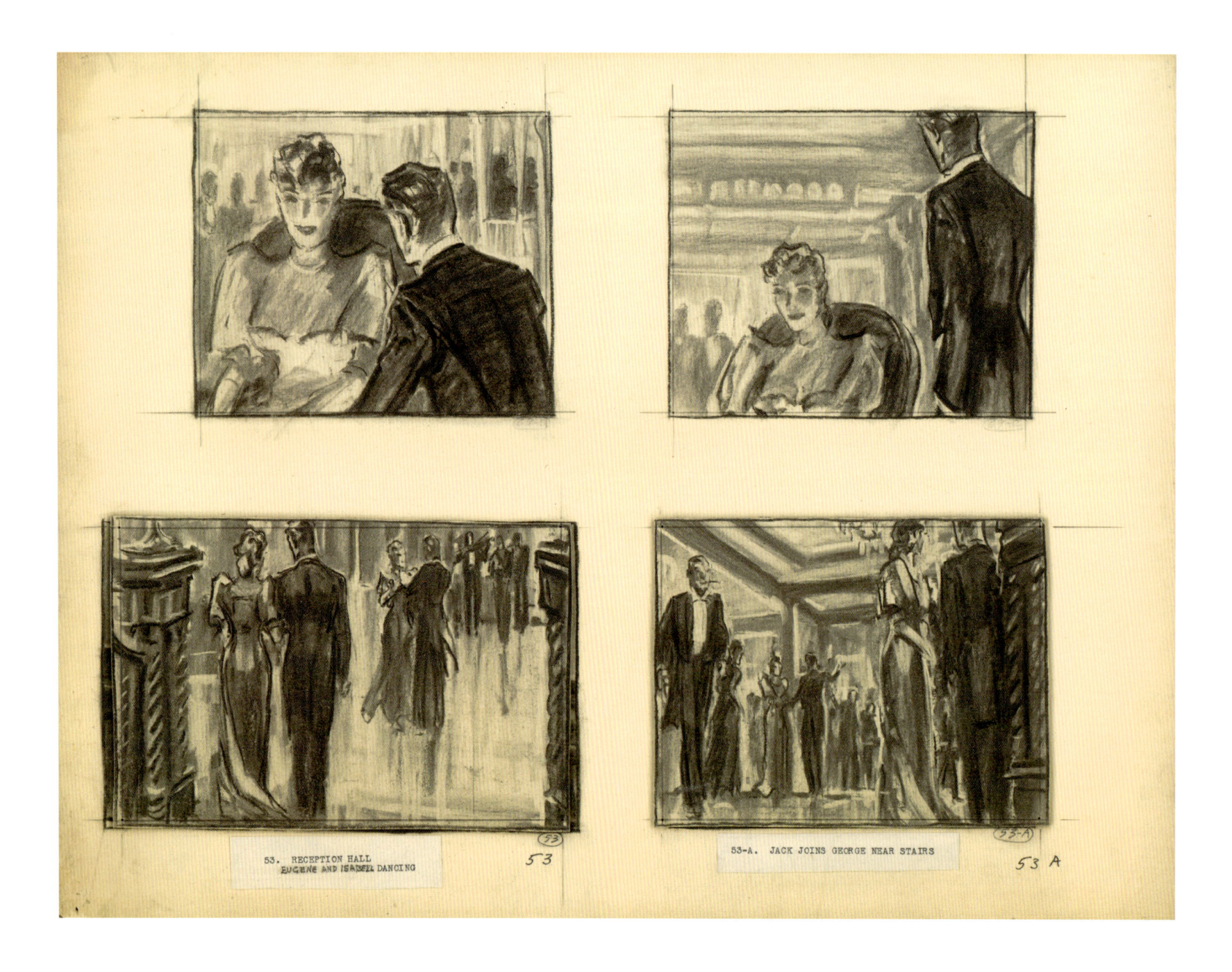

53. RECEPTION HALL
EUGENE AND ISABEL DANCING

53-A. JACK JOINS GEORGE NEAR STAIRS

42 THE GOLDEN AGE OF HOLLYWOOD

54. GEORGE TURNS AND SEES ISABEL

54-A. GEORGE - "WELL, OLD LADY, WHAT'S THE MATTER?"

54-B. ISABEL - "YOU'RE GOING AWAY SO SOON?"

54-C. ISABEL - "AND I'M A LITTLE BOTHERED ABOUT YOUR FATHER, TOO?"

THE MAGNIFICENT AMBERSONS

BELOW AND OPPOSITE One of the film's most celebrated sequences shows George and Lucy in a horse-drawn sleigh, speeding past the motor-carriage (a 1905 Model Sears in the film) that has stalled in the snow. George shouts, "Get a horse, get a horse!"

72-C GEORGE – "SOMEBODY OUGHT TO KEEP THOSE STATUES CLEAN!"

72-D GEORGE – "WHAT ARE YOU LAUGHING AT NOW?"

72-E LUCY – "LOOK – IT'S FATHER'S CAR" (SLEIGH STOPS AND RETURNS)

72-F GEORGE – "GIT A HOSS!"

44 THE GOLDEN AGE OF HOLLYWOOD

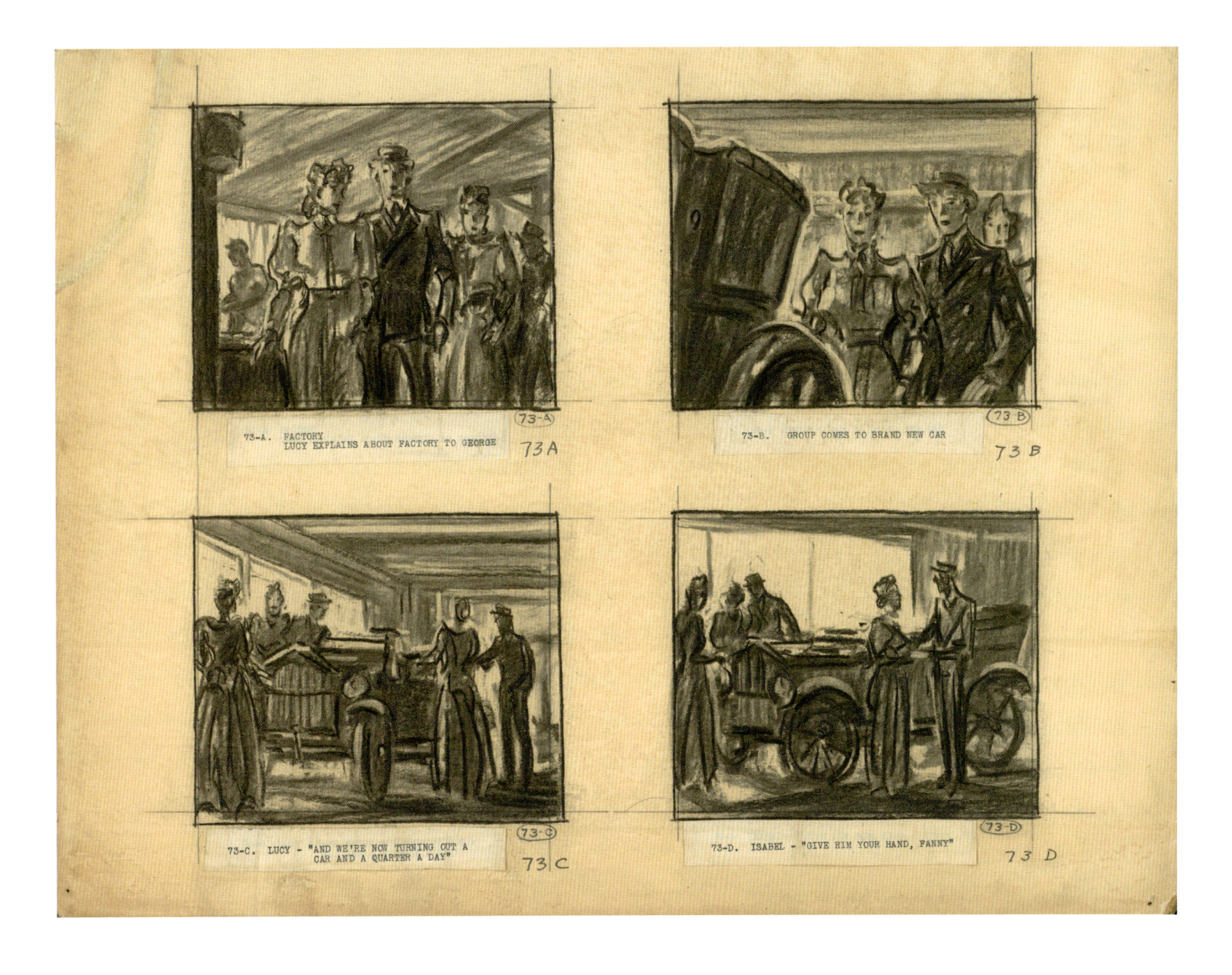

73-A. FACTORY
LUCY EXPLAINS ABOUT FACTORY TO GEORGE

73-B. GROUP COMES TO BRAND NEW CAR

73-C. LUCY - "AND WE'RE NOW TURNING OUT A CAR AND A QUARTER A DAY"

73-D. ISABEL - "GIVE HIM YOUR HAND, FANNY"

THE MAGNIFICENT AMBERSONS

The Big Sleep 1946

DIRECTOR Howard Hawks
STORYBOARDS Bill Herwig

This Warner Bros. production is *the* Hollywood noir classic; an adaptation of Raymond Chandler's 1939 novel directed by Howard Hawks, co-written by William Faulkner, and starring Humphrey Bogart as hardboiled gumshoe Philip Marlowe, with Lauren Bacall as Vivian Rutledge.

Although the plot is somewhat convoluted, *The Big Sleep* is still considered one of the greatest movies of that era. The look of the film in particular is spectacular; moodily shot by Sid Hickox, its claustrophobic interiors (with exteriors almost always characterized by rain) were art directed by the renowned German émigré Carl Jules Weyl. As an architect, Weyl designed the Hollywood playhouse (now Avalon Hollywood); under contract at Warner Bros. until 1947, he also designed *Casablanca* (1942).

The storyboards shown here are credited to Bill Herwig, a former Disney animator of the 1930s, and are a clear indication of the mood of the piece. The original cut of the film in 1945 was re-edited and released in 1946.

OPPOSITE This page from Bill Herwig's boards, drawn in pencil, depicts Carol Lundgren—the chauffeur of Arthur Gwynn Geiger, the rare book dealer who is blackmailing Philip Marlowe's client, General Sternwood—preparing to shoot the gambler Joe Brody outside Brody's apartment.

BELOW Humphrey Bogart as Philip Marlowe with Lauren Bacall as Vivian Rutledge in *The Big Sleep*.

46 THE GOLDEN AGE OF HOLLYWOOD

LUNDGREN RUNS ACROSS STREET,
WHIRLS TO FIRE

REVERSE TOWARD
RANDALL ARMS

Rebel Without a Cause 1955

DIRECTOR Nicholas Ray
STORYBOARDS Nicholas Ray

BELOW In this alternative ending for *Rebel Without a Cause* that was never shot, Plato (Sal Mineo) climbs to the top of the Planetarium at Griffith Park Observatory with Jim (James Dean) in pursuit. Plato is brandishing his gun. We see a police marksman take aim...

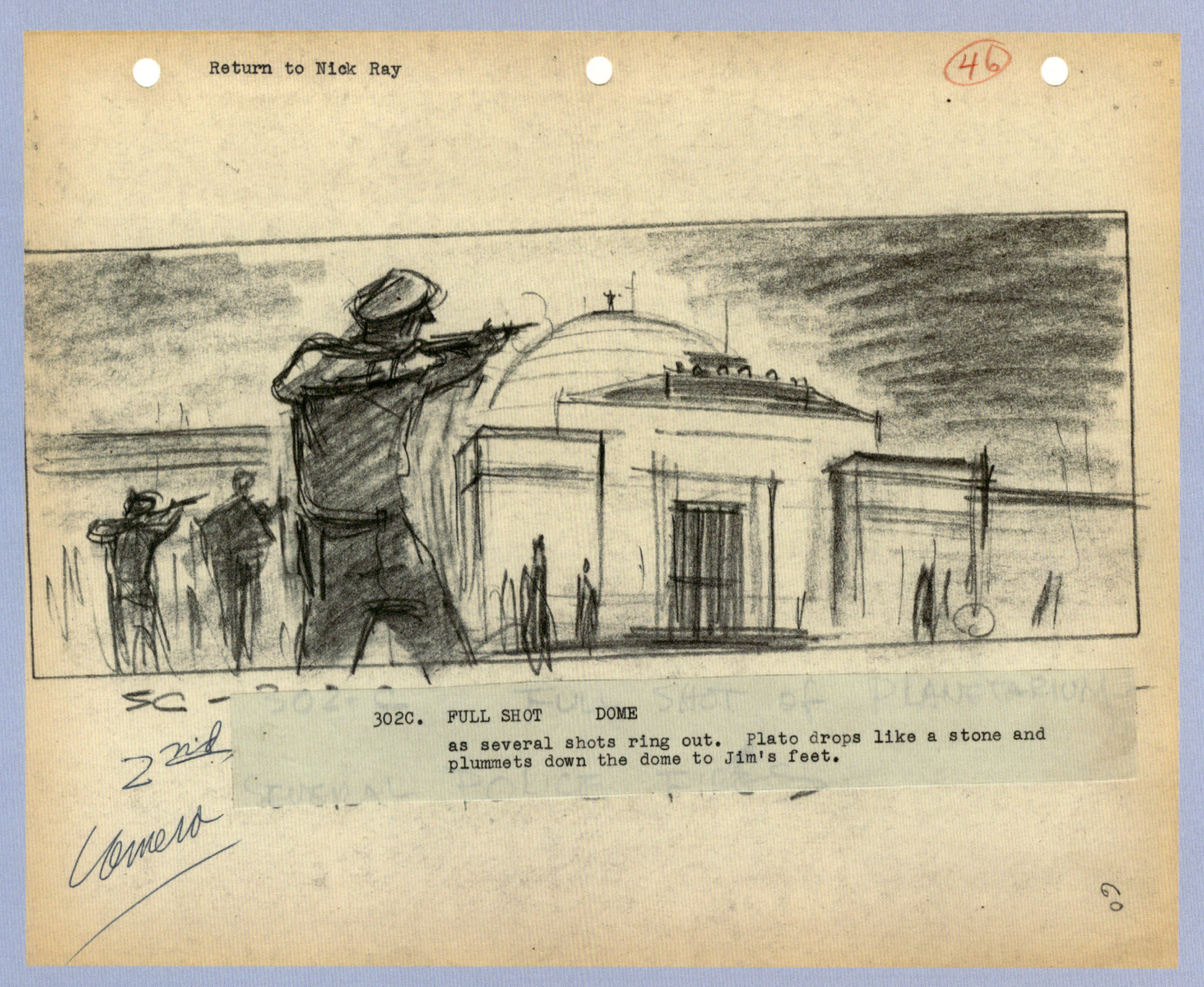

When it came out in 1955, shortly after the death of its star, James Dean, in a car crash, Nicholas Ray's *Rebel Without a Cause* was hailed as the voice of a new postwar generation of alienated "teenagers," or, as the film calls them, "juvenile delinquents." Enormously influential at the time and an iconic piece of filmmaking today, it was Ray's most successful film and bears most of his trademarks: daring use of color (there's that famous red jacket) and architecture (the Griffith Observatory, used in several major sequences) alongside heightened drama and emotions.

Starring Dean as Jim Stark, alongside Natalie Wood, and Sal Mineo as the confused Plato, *Rebel Without a Cause* was adapted from Ray's own treatment. The Wisconsin-born director was a greatly admired filmmaker even before

48 THE GOLDEN AGE OF HOLLYWOOD

the movie's release, hailed as highly influential on the French New Wave, in particular Jean-Luc Godard.

These working storyboards, complete with edit marks by Ray himself, measure 8.5 x 11 in, and clearly indicate dialogue changes and camera positions as well as matte shots. They are highly unusual in that they reveal an alternative ending for the film—one that was planned but never shot.

Rebel Without a Cause is about three "outsider" friends played by Dean, Wood, and Mineo. After Jim (Dean) is goaded into a high-speed "chicken" car race in which one of his High School taunters dies, the stakes escalate dramatically for all concerned. (This scene was to gain an added poignancy after Dean's death in a car crash the month before the film was released.) Plato (Mineo) becomes increasingly unhinged, brandishing his mother's gun and shooting one of the bullies before himself being shot at the Planetarium.

The boards clearly indicate how Ray planned for a much more dramatic final sequence, with Plato climbing to the top of the building and being shot by a police marksman. The camera instructions show a close-up of Jim's horrified face as Plato's body falls past him to the ground.

It is thought that Ray's original sequence would have been much more expensive and complicated to set up, and he changed his plans at the last moment—with Plato instead simply running out of the building brandishing his gun and being shot by a policeman.

BELOW . . . and Plato is hit by the marksman's bullet, crumpling and beginning to fall from the dome.

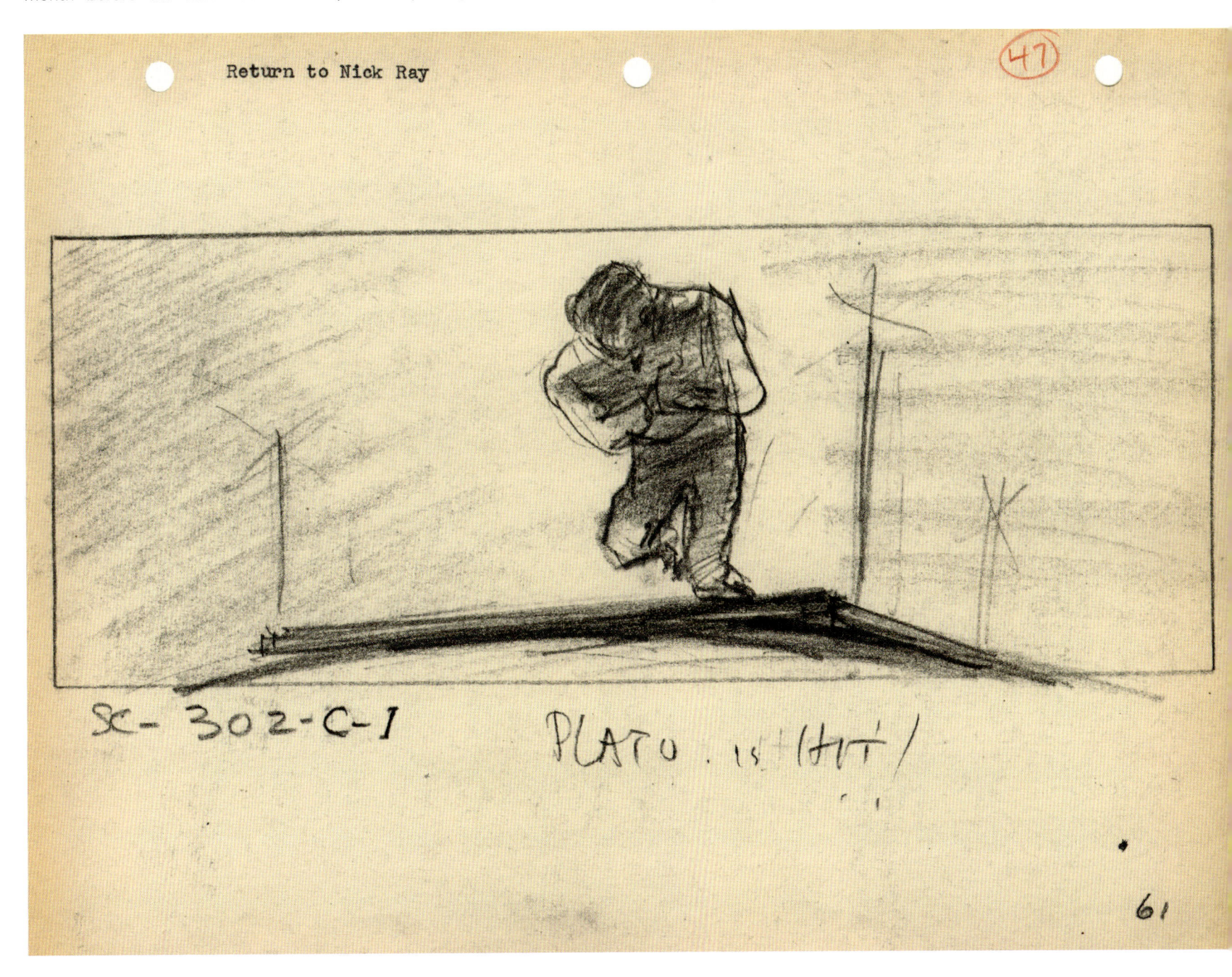

BELOW AND OPPOSITE Realizing what has happened, a horrified Jim (Dean) exclaims, "But I've got the bullets!" Other panels in director Nicholas Ray's storyboards (not shown) cut away to the crowd forming below, including the police chief, Plato's nanny, and Jim's parents. In essence, the ending is similar to that which was eventually shot and does not change the outcome—it was a matter of logistics, with Ray deciding to dispense with Plato climbing the planetarium and falling off, in particular the shot where "Plato plummets down past Jim." The sequence then cuts to Plato's nanny and ends with Jim holding Plato in his arms. The film was released one month after Dean's death in a car crash and was immediately hailed as the voice of a generation, becoming one of Hollywood's most iconic movies.

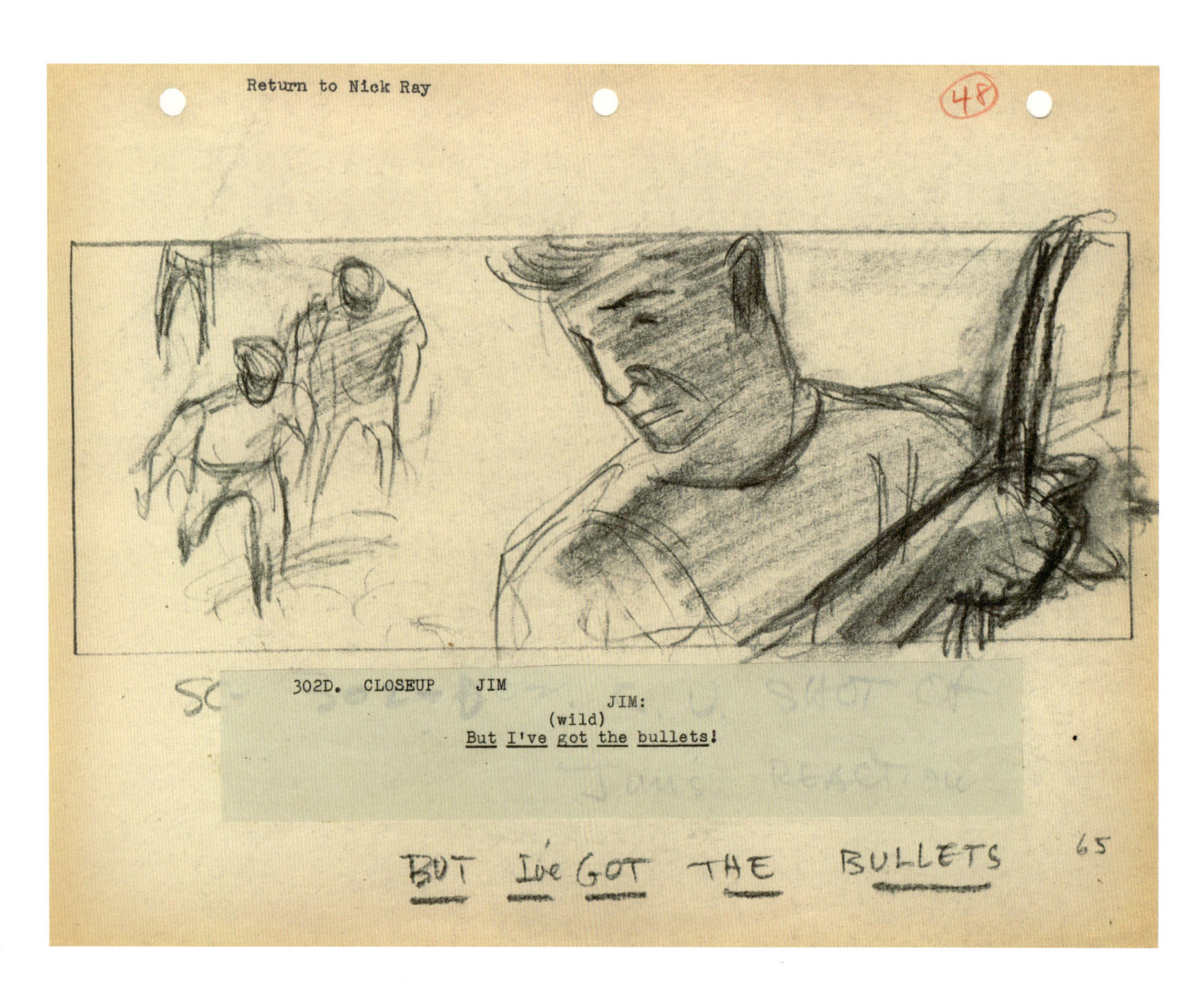

50 THE GOLDEN AGE OF HOLLYWOOD

Return to Nick Ray

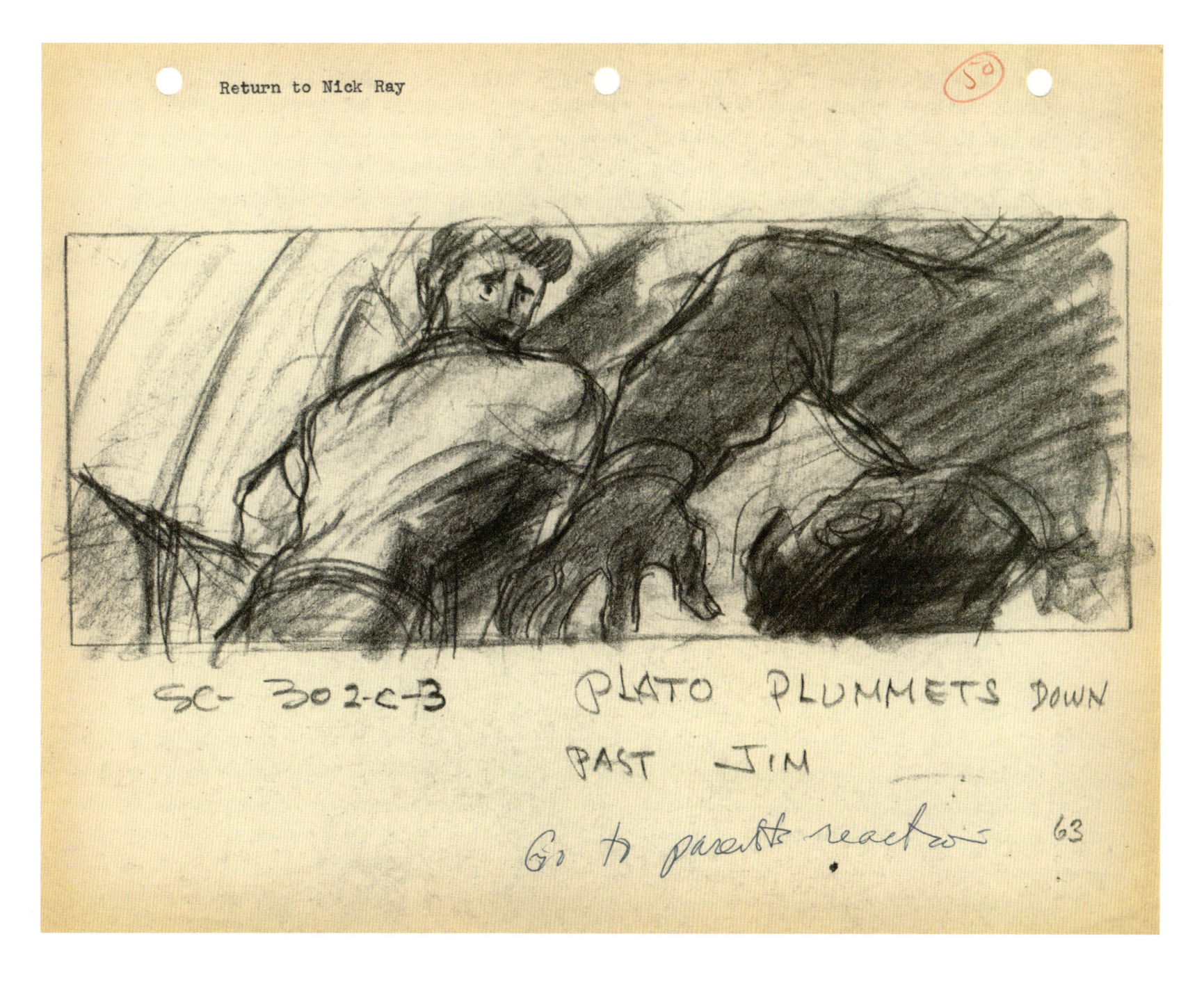

SC-302-C-B   PLATO PLUMMETS DOWN
                PAST JIM

                Go to parents reaction   63

REBEL WITHOUT A CAUSE 51

A Farewell to Arms 1957

DIRECTOR Charles Vidor
STORYBOARDS Alfred Junge

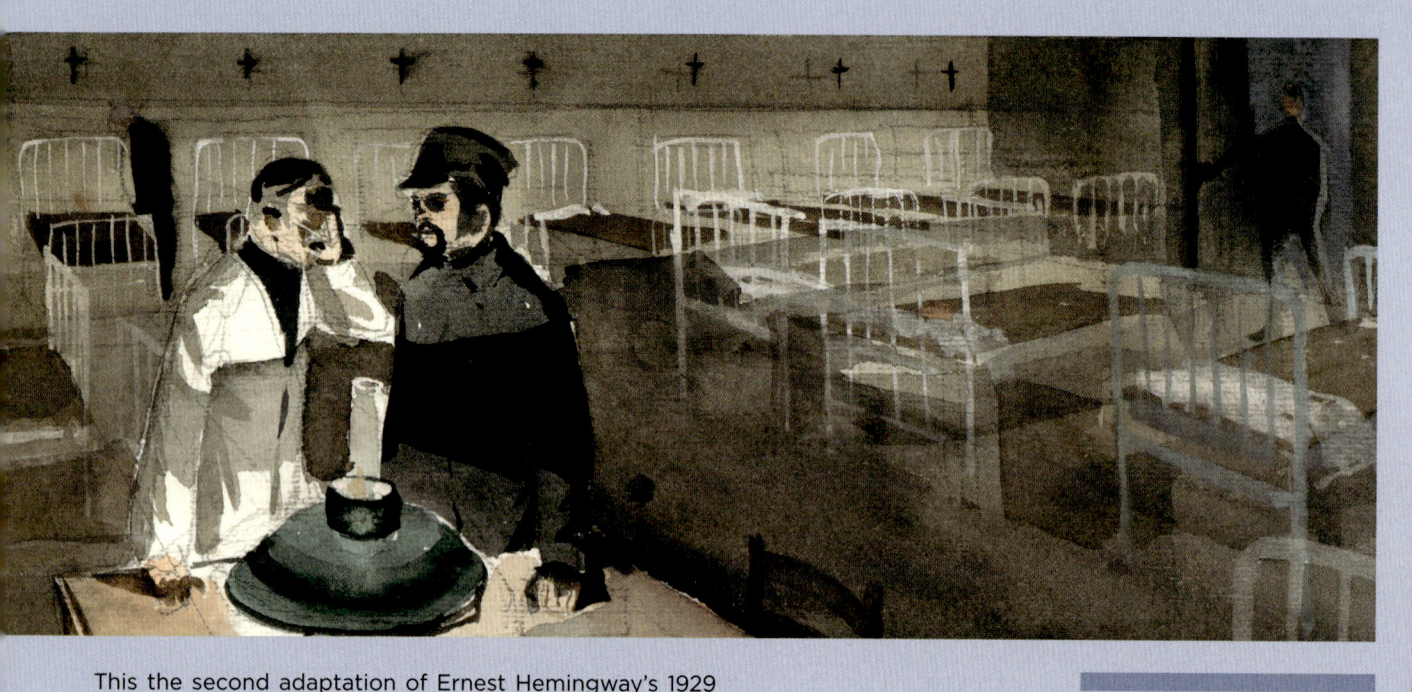

This the second adaptation of Ernest Hemingway's 1929 novel, filmed in 1957 and starring Rock Hudson as the American ambulance driver Lt. Frederic Henry and Jennifer Jones as the Red Cross nurse he meets on the Italian front during the Second World War. The film—which followed a 1932 version with Gary Cooper and Helen Hayes—was designed by Alfred Junge, the German émigré who, as a pivotal member of the Archers team (see pages 54–55), designed ten films for British duo Powell and Pressburger, and spent most of his career in the UK.

A Farewell to Arms was producer David O. Selznick's last feature, and not an entirely happy affair; original director John Huston left the project at a late stage and was replaced by Charles Vidor. Shot entirely in Italy, it was not liked by Ernest Hemingway, who disapproved of Selznick's decision to cast his thirty-eight-year-old wife Jones as the ingénue.

ABOVE AND RIGHT Painted in watercolor by production designer Alfred Junge, these boards depict the Italian field hospital at the center of the film's early sequences.

52 THE GOLDEN AGE OF HOLLYWOOD

A FAREWELL TO ARMS 53

The Archers:
Hein Heckroth,
Ivor Beddoes,
and *The Red Shoes*

ABOVE Hein Heckroth, paintbrushes in hand (and mouth), stands before "The Red Shoe Sketches."

The surrealist artist Hein Heckroth, a German émigré to the UK, designed sets and costumes for opera and ballet in both countries before he joined Michael Powell and Emeric Pressburger's film company the Archers under production designer Alfred Junge, working on costumes and designs for *A Matter of Life and Death* (1946) and *Black Narcissus* (1947).

He ascended to the rank of production designer on *The Red Shoes* (1948) after Powell and Junge fell out; the film could have been dreamed up specifically for Heckroth's talents and he rose to the occasion, working with art director Arthur Lawson and his close collaborator, the British sketch artist and matte painter Ivor Beddoes.

While Salvador Dali had worked on the dream sequence for *Spellbound* in 1945 (see pages 26–29), and Picasso and Matisse had designed for Serge Diaghilev's Ballets Russes, *The Red Shoes* was, according to Powell, "I think the first time a painter had been given the chance to design a film, including the titles, and it was a triumph of work and organization." The film centers on an unknown ballerina (Moira Shearer) who joins the famous Lermontov Ballet and becomes its lead dancer in a new version of Hans Christian Anderson's cautionary tale *The Red Shoes*.

For this seventeen-minute ballet-within-a-film (choreographed by Robert Helpmann, who plays the lead male dancer) Powell edited 120 of Heckroth and Beddoes's paintings into a sequence scored by Brian Easdale, now called "The Red Shoe Sketches." This rough film was used by cinematographer Jack Cardiff to replicate camera angles and lighting indicated by Heckroth's expressionistic paintings. Over six weeks, the dancers' performance was shot and, day by day, inserted into the animated film, replacing the sketches. Through this unique and daring process, the Archers were able to see their extraordinary ballet come alive.

Ivor Beddoes could hardly have been better suited to the film, either: prior to the war, Beddoes had danced with Ninette de Valois and worked at the Windmill Theatre, London, as a singer and dancer. He was also hired by Junge and worked (with Heckroth) on *Black Narcissus* before designing *The Red Shoes*. It was during this film that Beddoes learned his craft as a matte painter (painting onto glass) at Technicolor; he would later join the company as its in-house art director.

Hundreds of sketches for costumes and production impressions survive, for which Beddoes and Heckroth are often jointly credited, although Heckroth was always the artistic driver. Beddoes sheds light on their process in a note reproduced here accompanying a sketch by Heckroth: "He was never a one to use words when a drawing told me EVERYTHING he had in his mind's eye."

Heckroth and Beddoes worked together for five years; Beddoes also enjoyed a long collaboration with the revered production designer Ken Adam on several Bond films and Kubrick's *Barry Lyndon* (1975), and created storyboards for *Star Wars: The Empire Strikes Back* in 1980. Hein Heckroth, meanwhile, continued to paint and work for Powell and Pressburger—later for Powell alone—and returned to Germany in the 1950s. One of his last creations was a German television adaptation of Béla Bartók's *Bluebeard's Castle* opera, for which he enlisted his old collaborator Powell as director.

The Red Shoes 1948

DIRECTORS Michael Powell & Emeric Pressburger
STORYBOARDS Hein Heckroth & Ivor Beddoes

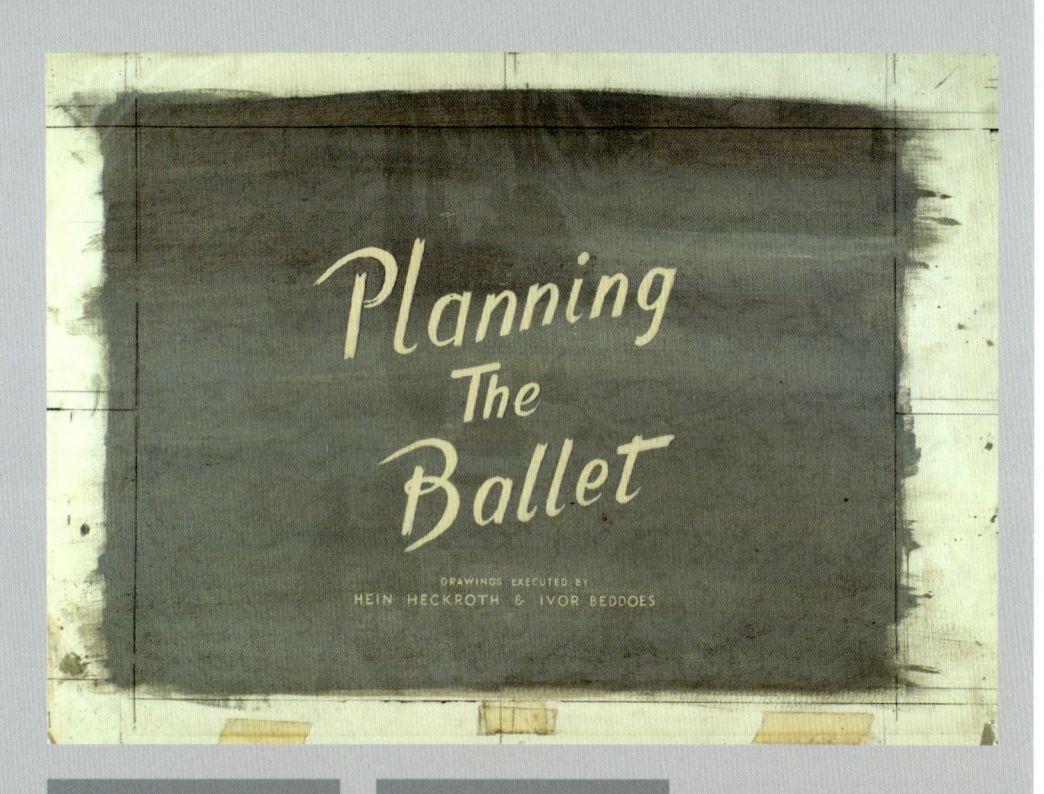

ABOVE Opening credits for "The Red Shoe Sketches," created by Michael Powell as a blueprint on which the production would base the seventeen-minute ballet-within-a-film. The sequence credits "drawings sketched by Hein Heckroth and Ivor Beddoes."

RIGHT An early design for the animated film, signed by Hein Heckroth.

56 THE ARCHERS: HEIN HECKROTH, IVOR BEDDOES, AND *THE RED SHOES*

THE RED SHOES 57

RIGHT Two stretched heads in vivid colors form part of *The Red Shoes* animation sequence. All the sketches are executed in gouache, pencil, and some oils.

RIGHT A male figure holding red shoes in *The Red Shoes* animation sequence.

58 THE ARCHERS: HEIN HECKROTH, IVOR BEDDOES, AND *THE RED SHOES*

RIGHT A head and shoulders with large spectacles sketch for the ballet animation sequence.

RIGHT Carousel detail for the animation sequence.

THE RED SHOES 59

ABOVE Credited to Heckroth and Beddoes, this board, executed in pencil, gouache, and some oils, depicts "the theatre transformed into the sea with the impresario sitting on a rock." Powell and Pressburger attached great importance to Heckroth's vision of how the film should look. During principal photography, which started in June, 1947, the entire company waited in the south of France while the writer-directors searched the coastline between Monte Carlo and Nice for a place that looked like Heckroth's sketches of ballet impresario Lermontov's villa, eventually choosing the Villa Leopolda, Villefranche.

60 THE ARCHERS: HEIN HECKROTH, IVOR BEDDOES, AND *THE RED SHOES*

RIGHT In this note accompanying a charcoal sketch by Heckroth, Beddoes explains how the artist passed on instructions. "He was never one to use words when a drawing told me EVERYTHING he had in his mind's eye . . . He used to rail (in private!) at Mickey [Michael Powell] and Emeric because they always jumped to using a piece of explanatory lettering on screen. As Hein says, never use caption inserts when you can convey it in images. They break the continuity of shape and color. He was right."

THE RED SHOES 61

The Inn of the Sixth Happiness 1958

DIRECTOR Mark Robson
STORYBOARDS Olga Lehmann; production design by John Box

Without a vast studio system and endless backlots on which to build, the postwar British film industry was required to be inventive. The great British production designer John Box was known for the geographic trickery of his work. He recreated China in Snowdonia; the deserts of Aqaba in Spain for David Lean's *Lawrence of Arabia* (1962); even the frozen glamor of *Doctor Zhivago* (1965) was shot in the height of summer using candlewax for ice in the parched deserts of Almeria.

Directed by Mark Robson, *The Inn of the Sixth Happiness*, an adaptation of the memoirs of British missionary Gladys Aylward, was Box's most blatant cinematic confection, working as ever with cinematographer Freddie Young. The tall Swedish actress Ingrid Bergman played the short Cockney heroine, and Box chose Snowdonia in Wales to double for China's remote Anhui province in this story of wartime heroism. Box, whose designs for Aqaba are featured on pages 68–69, drew on the considerable talents of storyboard artist Olga Lehmann to help him frame his vision.

Prior to the war, Slade graduate Lehmann had worked as a theater designer and was known for her mural work, but later she became closely associated with the British film industry. She became an art director and later a production designer, and also created costumes for films including *The Guns of Navarone* (1961) and *A Countess from Hong Kong* (1967). These images from *The Inn of the Sixth Happiness* comprise a montage sequence built around Aylward, newly arrived in Yangcheng, changing money at the local market. The film tells the story of the missionary's rescue of 100 orphans when the town comes under attack by the Japanese. Singlehandedly, Aylward leads them across the mountains into safety in a neighboring province.

Ingrid Bergman, at the time an outcast from Hollywood, won the Academy Award for Best Actress in 1956 for *Anastasia*, and *The Inn of the Sixth Happiness* (for which she was also Oscar-nominated) was her follow-up feature and part of her rehabilitation following a very public affair and marriage to the Italian director Roberto Rossellini (which had just broken up). Playing a real-life Cockney heroine called Gladys Aylward (the film was based on her memoirs), Bergman overcomes the odds of her poverty-stricken upbringing to arrive in China via the Trans-Siberian Express to the remote Northern town of Yangcheng. Here she assists a veteran missionary who has set up an inn where travelers can get a hot meal and hear stories from the Bible. When China comes under attack from the invading Japanese, Gladys refuses to leave and ends up with 100 orphans in her care.

The sequence storyboarded so colorfully here by Olga Lehmann shows Gladys arriving in Yangcheng to change her money. As *The Inn of the Sixth Happiness* was shot in Snowdonia, the Chinese orphans were brought in from Liverpool's Chinese community.

"Inn of the Sixth Happiness"
money changer montage sequence
Olga Lehmann

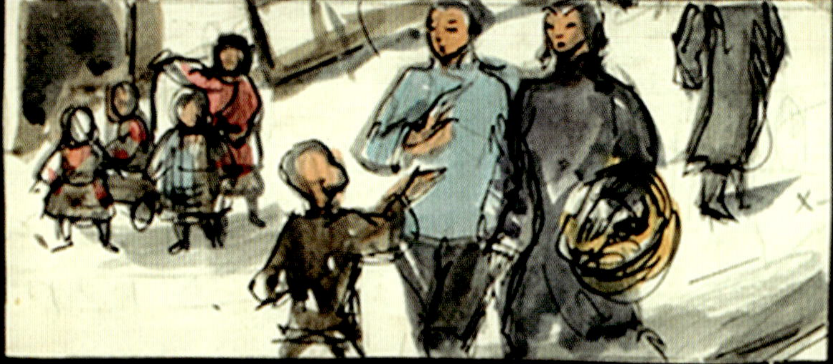
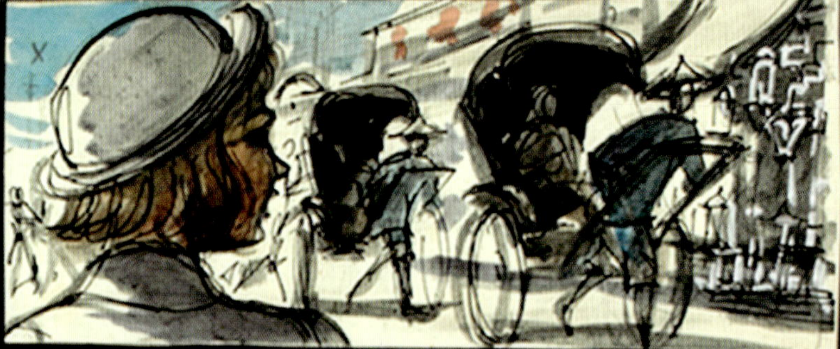
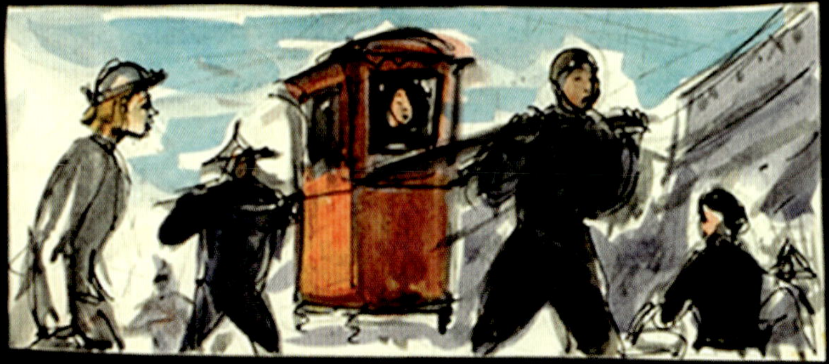
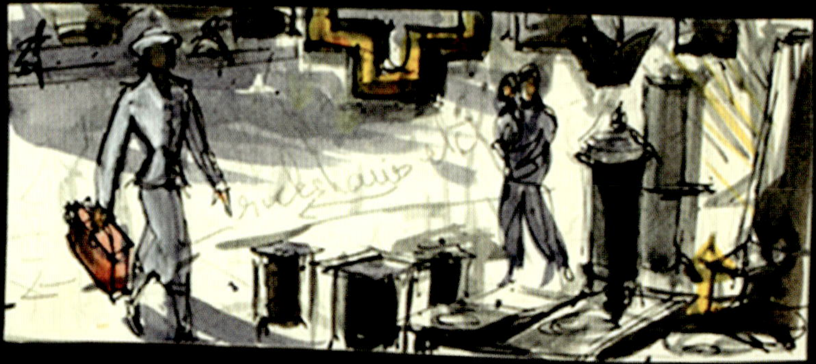
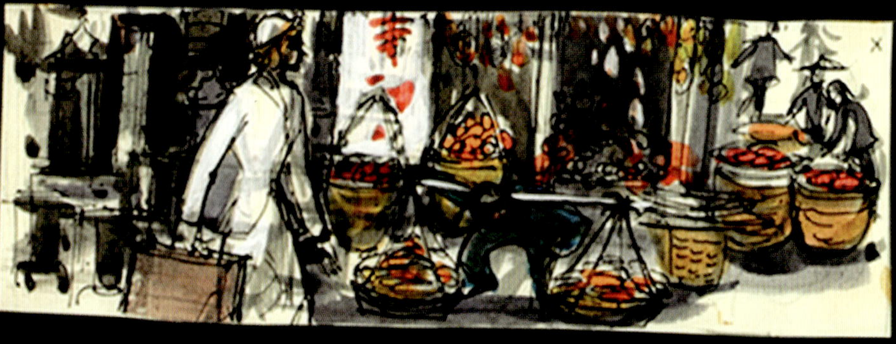
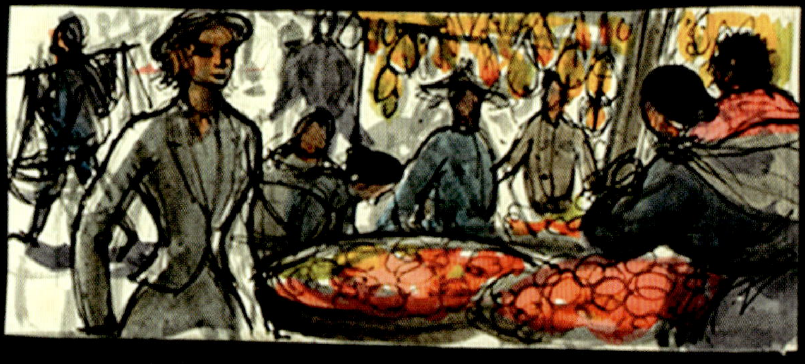
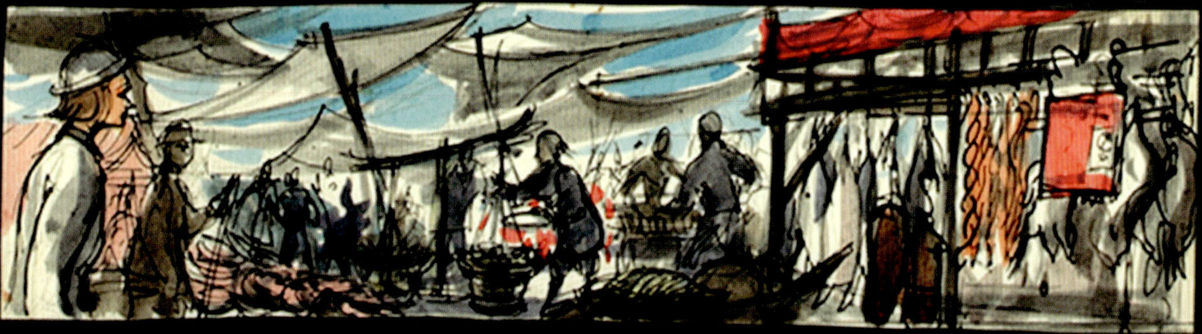

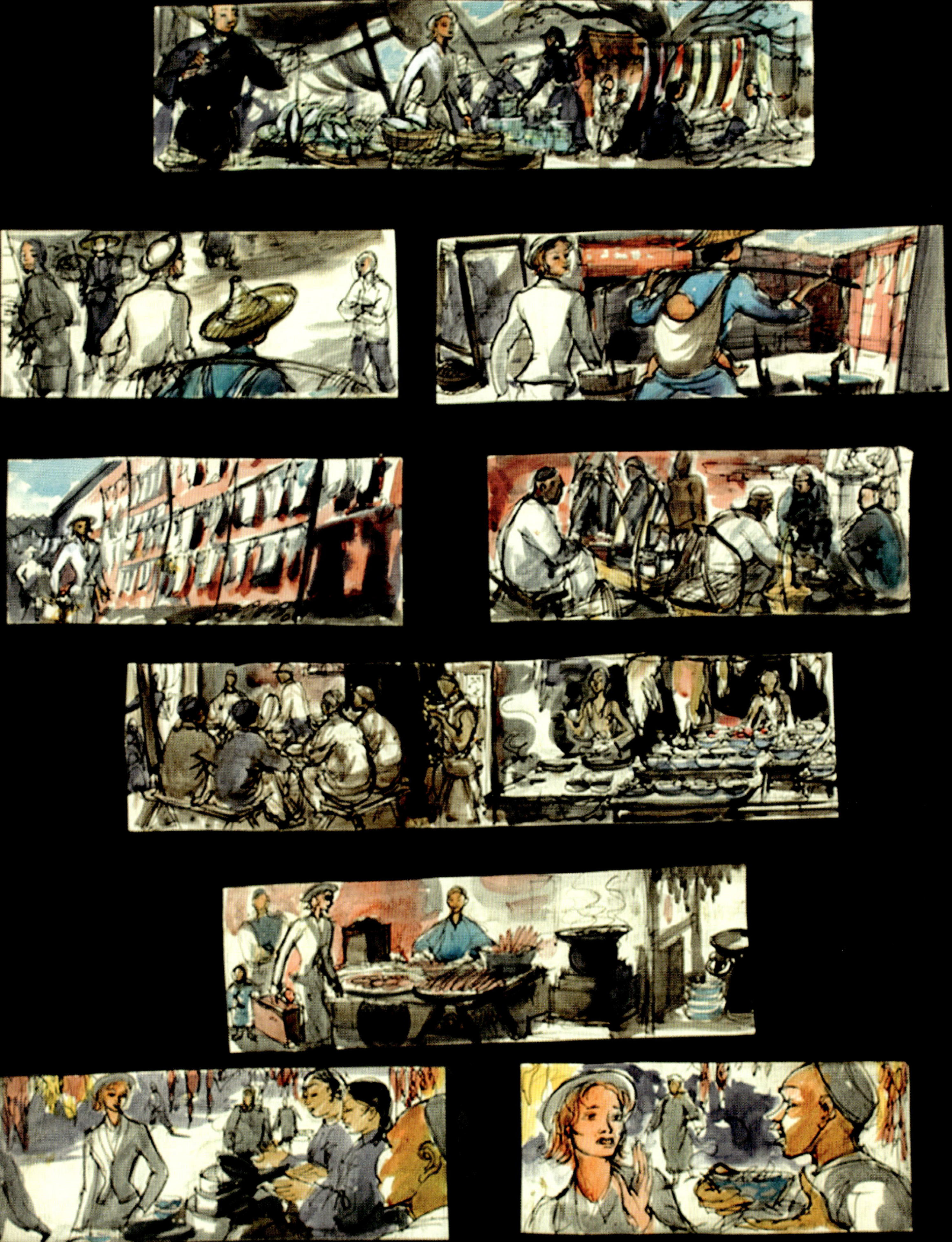

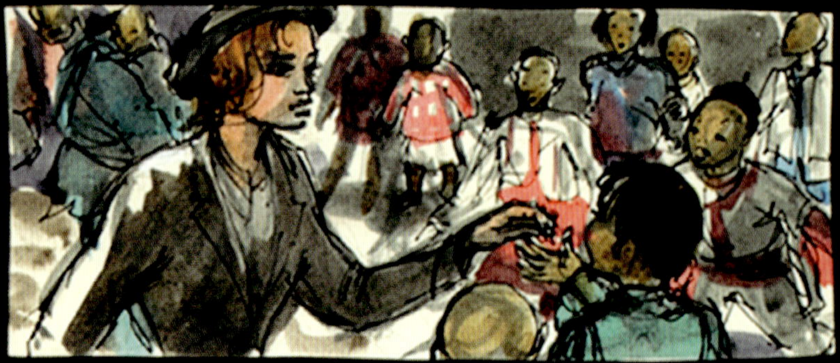
LOT

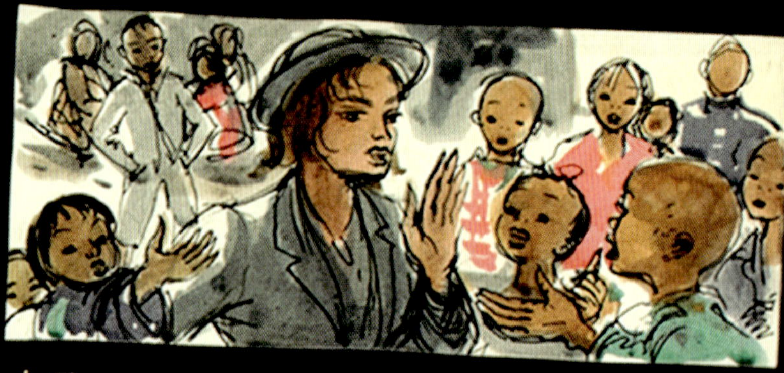
LOT

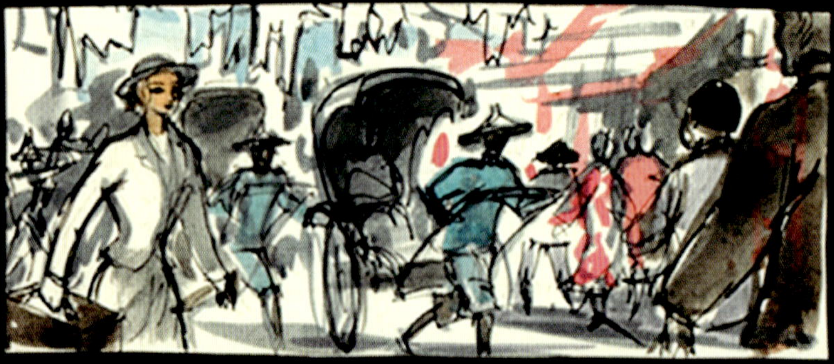
LOT

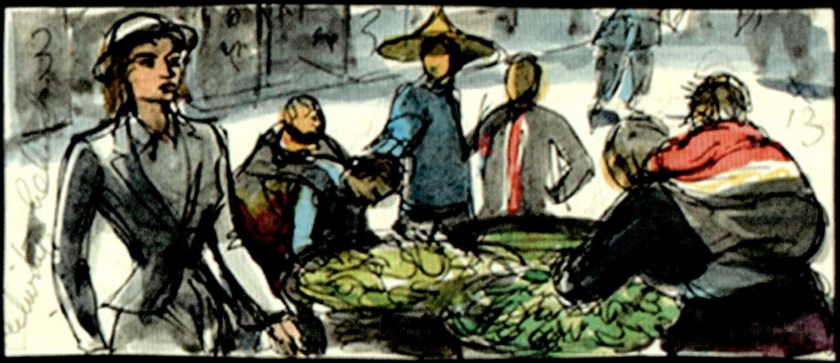
LOT

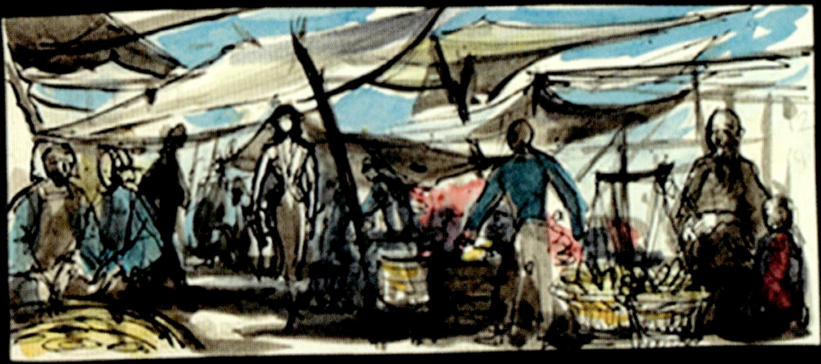
LOT

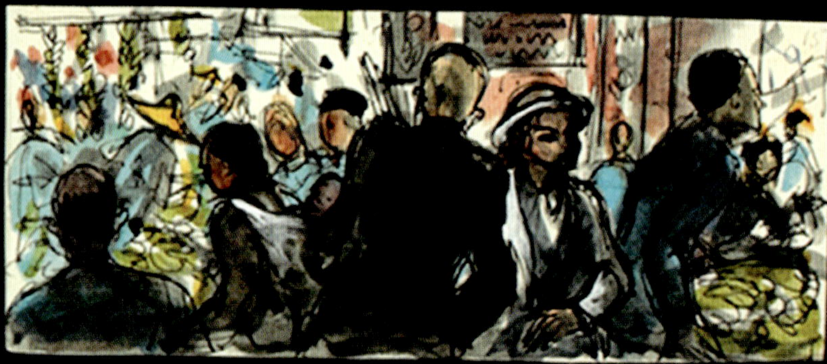
LOT

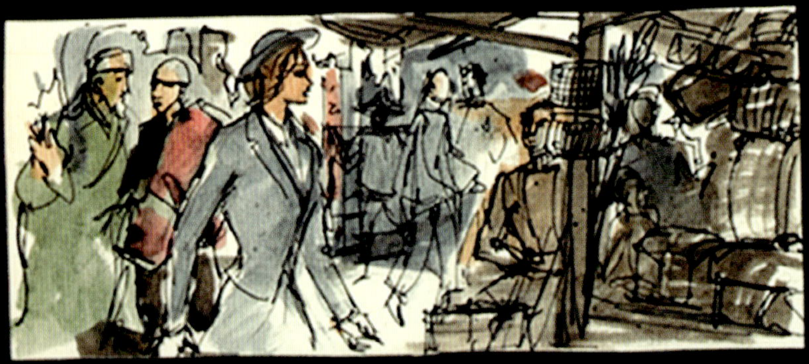
LOT

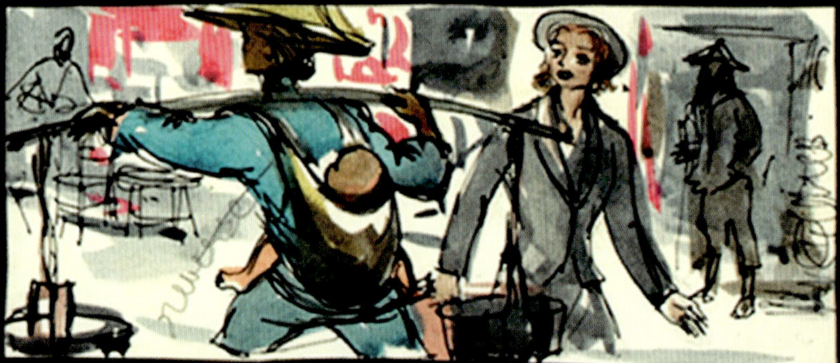
LOT

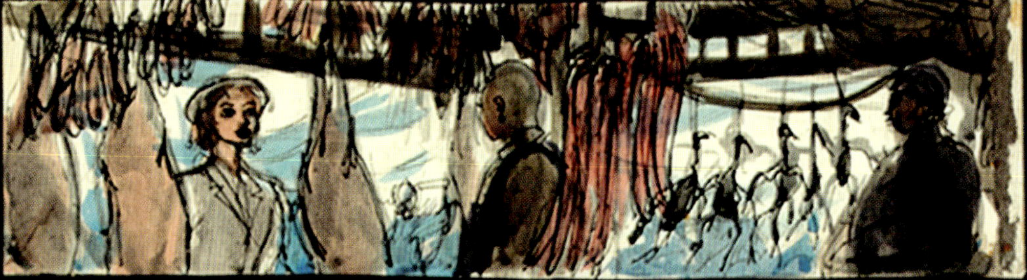

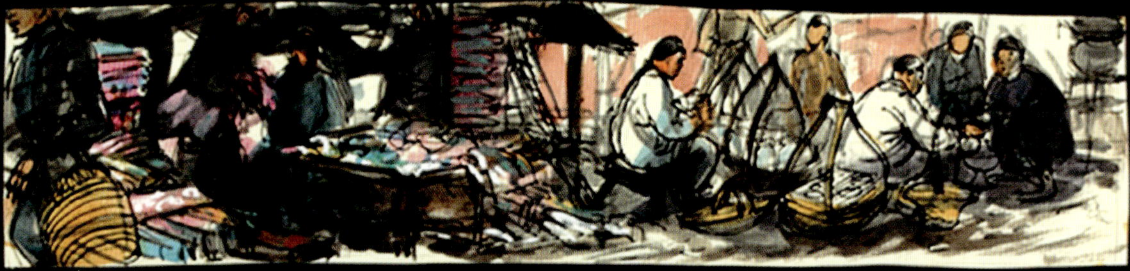

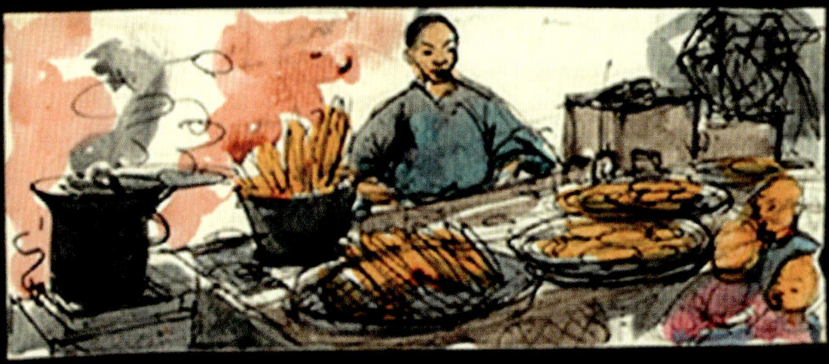

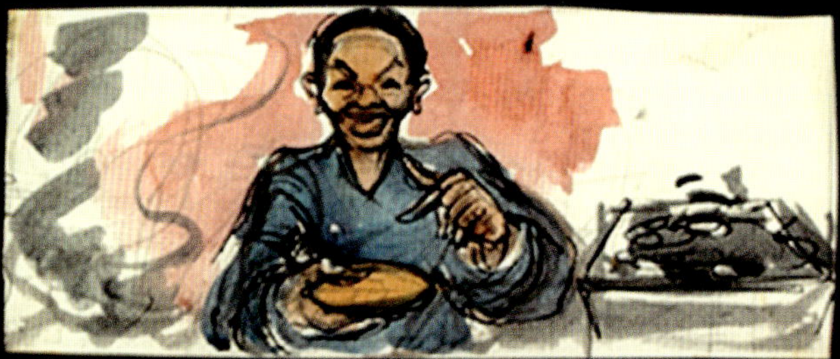

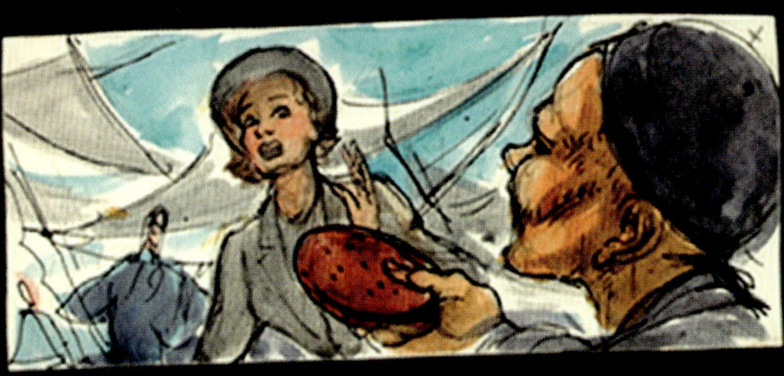

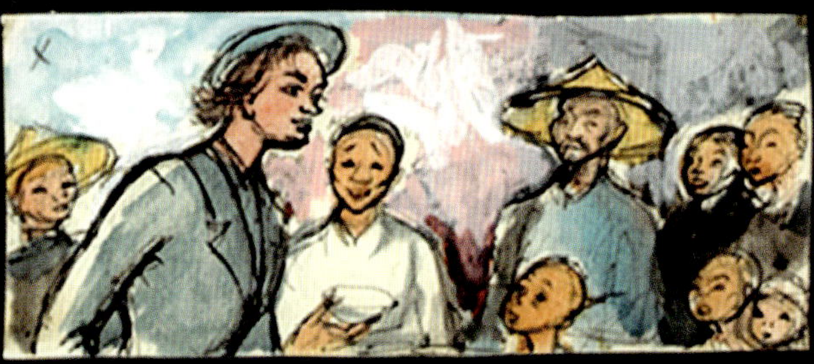

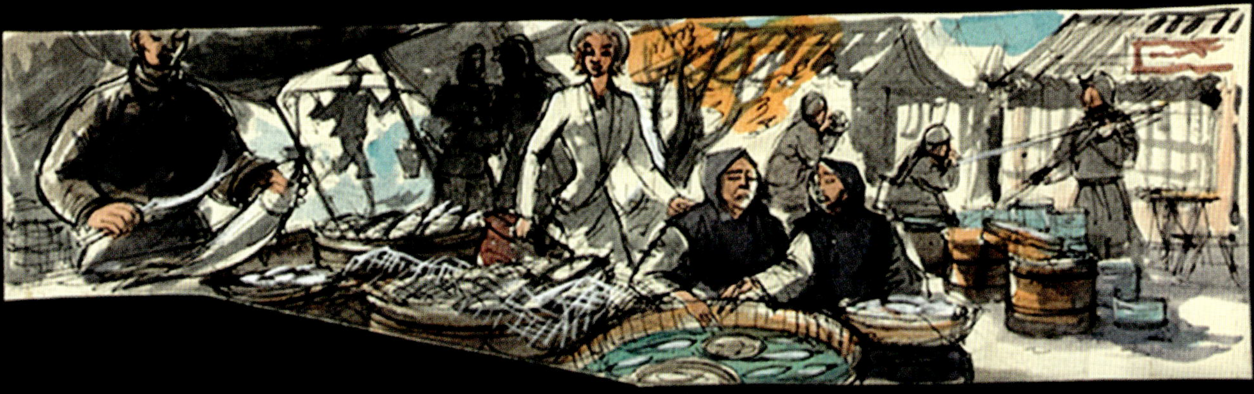

Lawrence of Arabia 1962

DIRECTOR David Lean
PRODUCTION SKETCHES John Box

Though not, strictly speaking, storyboards, John Box's production notes demonstrate his inventiveness in turning Carboneras in Almeria, southern Spain, into the Jordanian city of Aqaba on the Red Sea, setting for the Battle of Aqaba. Box's work on *Lawrence of Arabia* would win him the Academy Award for Best Art Direction.

LAWRENCE ATTACKS FROM THE DESERT — TURKISH CAMP

SKETCH SHOWING THE DESIGN FO

"AQUABA" — THE COMPLETED

68 THE ARCHERS: HEIN HECKROTH, IVOR BEDDOES, AND *THE RED SHOES*

...ing the charge—finishing on the very blue gulf of Aqaba with the gun pointing hopelessly towards the horizon.

AQABA TOWN - BIG GUNS POINTING OUT TO SEA -

THE TOWN OF "AQABA"

SET - BUILT AT CARBONERAS SOUTHERN SPAIN

GUNS FACING OUT TO SEA

LAWRENCE OF ARABIA 69

The artist Saul Bass occupies a unique space in the history of film design. His innovative title sequences—which graphically honed in on a film's key theme—and avant-garde posters were renowned. As "visual consultant" to several films, including *Psycho* and *Spartacus* (both 1960), he also designed and storyboarded key sequences, helping to set the overall "look" of the movies.

Famously, Bass storyboarded the shower sequence in *Psycho* (see pages 30–31). He designed the title and prologue for the multiple-Oscar-winning *West Side Story* (1961), as well as the race sequences in John Frankenheimer's *Grand Prix* in 1966. Three decades later he was still working, as Martin Scorsese's title designer of choice on *Goodfellas* (1990), *Cape Fear* (1991), and *The Age of Innocence* (1993). His last title sequence was *Casino* (1995), again for Scorsese. Calling to mind Bass's own work on *Ocean's Eleven* (1960), it sets a disembodied Robert De Niro spiraling through a car explosion into the neon flames of the Las Vegas Strip.

Born in The Bronx in 1920, Bass's first significant cinematic collaboration was with the director Otto Preminger on the 1954 film *Carmen Jones* (both poster and title sequence); a later collaboration with Preminger, *The Man with the Golden Arm* (1955), became one of Bass's most recognizable works.

Bass's contribution to cinema was extensive and varied. In *Around the World in Eighty Days* (1956), for example, he created an entire animated story as a prologue (one that was in many ways superior to the film that followed). He died the year after designing the titles for *Casino*. His *New York Times* obituary called him "a minimalist auteur who put a jagged arm in motion in 1955 and created an entire film genre . . . and elevated it into an art."

LEFT Saul Bass (seated) working with director Otto Preminger on advertising layouts for *Anatomy of a Murder* (1959).

Spartacus 1960

DIRECTOR Stanley Kubrick
STORYBOARDS Saul Bass (as visual consultant)

Although hugely successful, *Spartacus* was a troubled production from start to finish. The project was generated by the actor Kirk Douglas, and the original director, Anthony Mann, was fired a week into shooting. He was replaced by Stanley Kubrick, who generally avoided storyboards in his later career; the movie was filmed using the 35mm Technirama format, which was then blown up to 70mm.

Saul Bass had provided the boards shown here for Douglas as the film's visual consultant, and designed the film's quietly powerful title sequence, which still feels modern today. Stanley Kubrick shot the battle sequences depicted on the boards (the final battle between the slaves and the Romans) in Spain, but due to their ferocity many sequences were cut and do not survive today. Designs by Bass for the film's gladiator school immediately call to mind Ridley Scott's *Gladiator* (2000; see pages 196–197), shot forty years later.

RIGHT AND OPPOSITE Saul Bass's storyboards for the battle between the slave army and the Romans convey both the scale and the ferocity of the conflict, the diagonally slashing spears imbuing the artwork with an irresisitible energy. In translating these boards to the screen, director Stanley Kubrick shot for six weeks, in the process employing 8,000 extras.

72 SAUL BASS AND THE SIXTIES

SPARTACUS

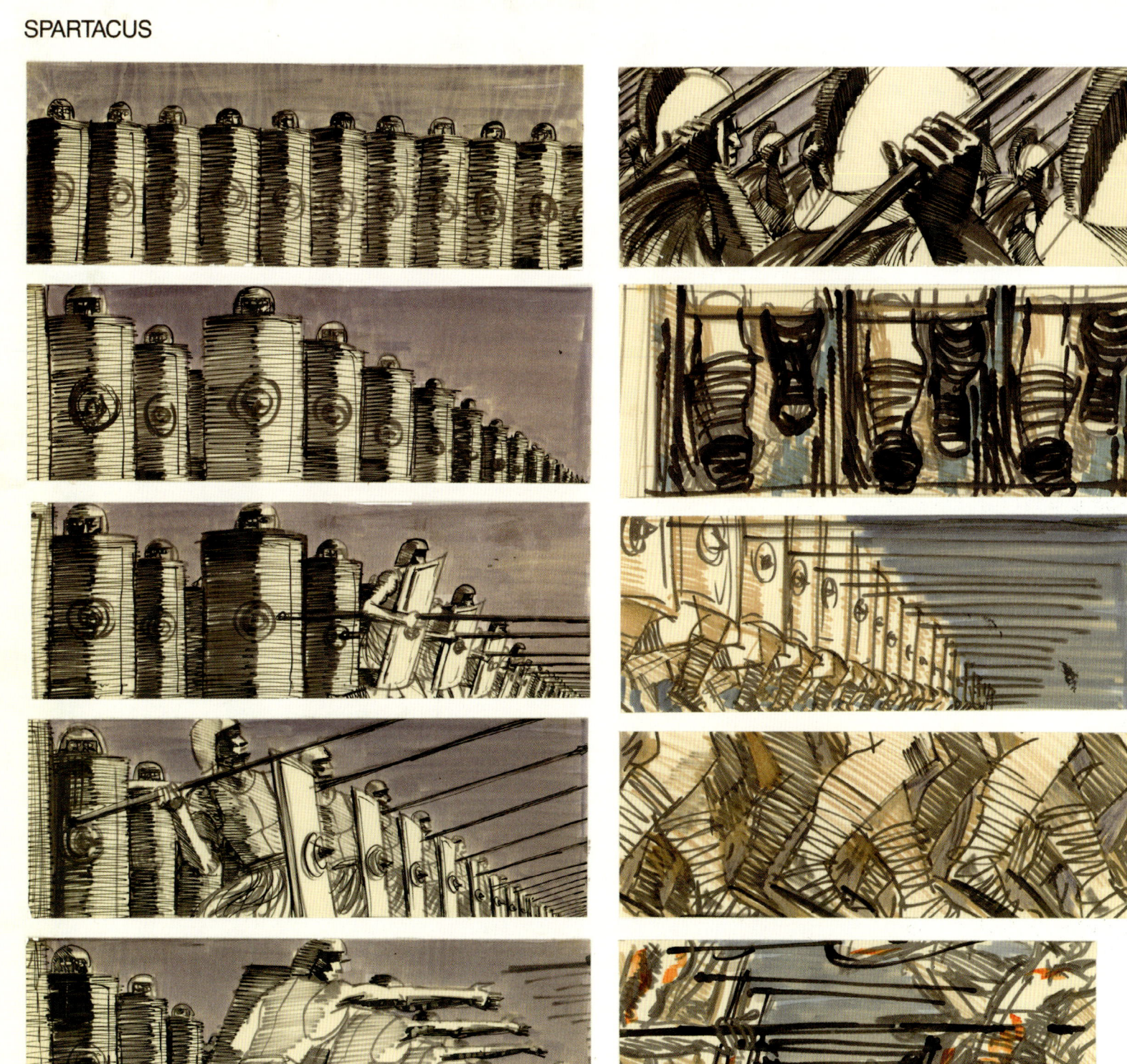

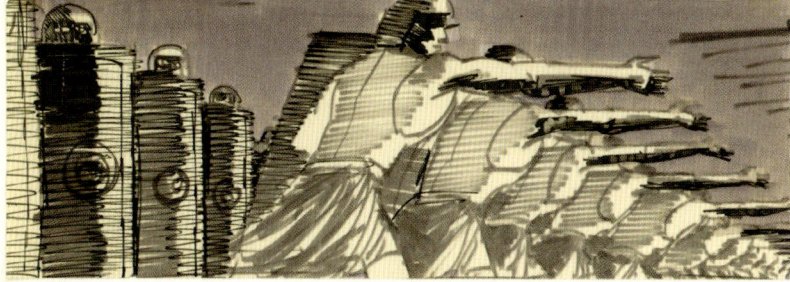

West Side Story 1961

DIRECTORS Robert Wise & Jerome Robbins
STORYBOARDS Saul Bass (as visual consultant)

As *West Side Story*'s visual consultant, Saul Bass filmed the prologue and storyboarded the key opening dance sequence as shown on these pages. (He also devised the film's end credits, which appear as graffiti.) The ink sketch of the New York City skyline dissolves into an aerial shot of Manhattan; the camera then plunges down over key landmarks until it reaches a concrete playground where a gang of street kids click their fingers to the insistent rhythm of Leonard Bernstein's score. As the frames on these pages—which devise the film's dance-fight prologue—indicate, Bass achieved his goal of immediately setting the film's tone before the conventional drama commenced.

West Side Story would go on to win ten Academy Awards (including Best Picture), the most ever won by a musical film.

RIGHT Drawn in pencil and reading top to bottom, left to right, Saul Bass's storyboards for *West Side Story*'s prologue are an intricately designed mix of choreography, signage, lighting, and directions.

74 SAUL BASS AND THE SIXTIES

WEST SIDE STORY: PARTIAL STORYBO

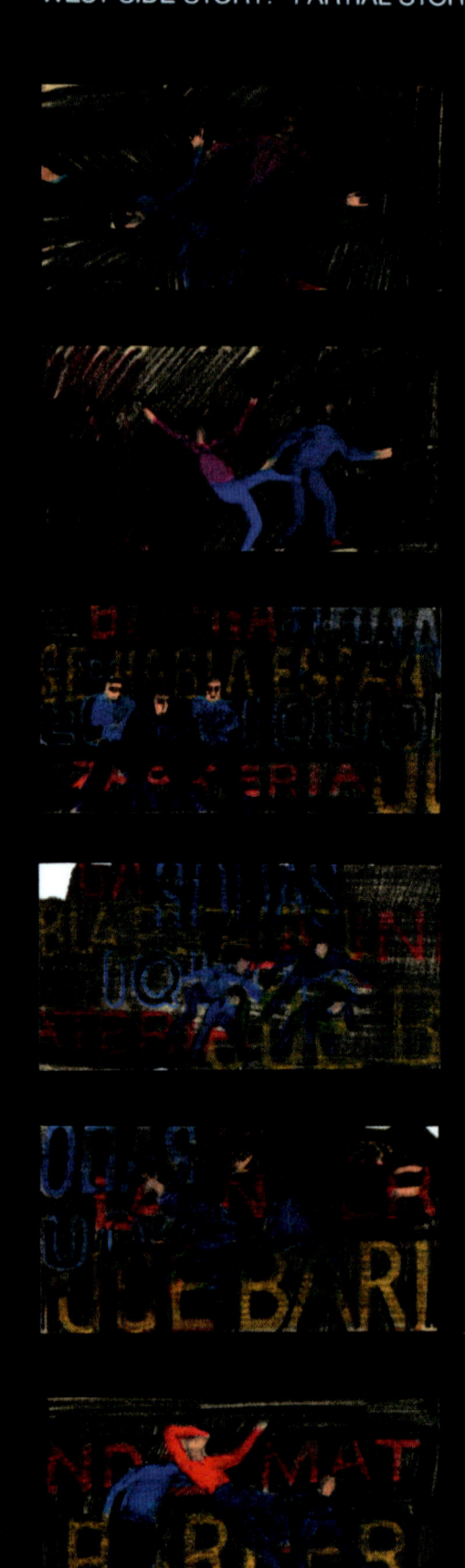

PROLOGUE "THE TIME BEFORE"

WEST SIDE STORY: PARTIAL STORYBOARD PROLOGUE "THE TIME BEFORE" (CONTINUED)

LEFT The prologue sequence for *West Side Story* continues, as rival gangs the Jets and the Sharks confront one another on the streets of Manhattan. Directional plans scattered throughout communicate how the dancers will move through the scenery.

WEST SIDE STORY 77

The Longest Day 1962

DIRECTOR Ken Annakin, Andrew Marton & Bernhard Wicki (in a Darryl F. Zanuck production)
STORYBOARDS Mentor Huebner

BELOW AND OPPOSITE Mentor Huebner's storyboards for *The Longest Day* eventually numbered up to 4,000 throughout the course of the film's production, the three evocative examples here being but a small sample.

The Longest Day was certainly one of the longest productions to employ a Hollywood storyboard artist; by all accounts, the legendary Mentor Huebner spent well over a year on the drawing board for this mammoth, all-star production, most of it on location in France.

Known as "the king of the illustrators," Huebner was revered by his colleagues as fast, accurate, and tireless, producing countless uncannily three-dimensional charcoal sketches over a fifty-year career. Easily one of the most sought-after storyboard artists in Hollywood for his tough, visceral visuals—as well as being a mentor to many illustrators working today—Huebner lost the sight in his right eye through cancer when he was still in his twenties. Despite this, he was known for being extraordinarily quick and perceptive with his sketches.

In an extensive career, *The Longest Day* was Huebner's grandest achievement: the film employed up to four directors working in the UK, the U.S., France, and Germany

78 SAUL BASS AND THE SIXTIES

(not to mention a special crew for aerial sequences), but Huebner was the only illustrator, and they all worked from his boards.

The film was legendary Hollywood producer Darryl F. Zanuck's baby, and details the events of D-Day as related from opposing sides of the conflict. Starring John Wayne, Robert Ryan, and Richard Burton—amongst a cast of hundreds, many in cameo roles, and with many real-life protagonists from the war taking part—*The Longest Day* was a monumental undertaking. Clocking in at 178 minutes it was, at $10m, the most expensive black-and-white film ever made (until *Schindler's List* three decades later in 1993), and was shot in V.O. (i.e. in the participants' original language), using subtitles where necessary.

To Kill a Mockingbird 1962

DIRECTOR Robert Mulligan
STORYBOARDS Henry Bumstead

Inspired by events in her childhood, Harper Lee's Pulitzer Prize–winning novel *To Kill A Mocking Bird* was first published in 1960 at a time of growing Civil Rights awareness in the U.S. Set in America's racially-segregated Deep South, it was quickly adapted by Robert Mulligan into the 1962 Hollywood classic starring Gregory Peck as the noble lawyer Atticus Finch in a story of prejudice, injustice, and lost childhood innocence.

The venerated Atticus, an enduring hero of American fiction, is a man who believes in justice for all, no matter what the circumstances. As witnessed through the eyes of his tomboy daughter, Scout (Mary Badham), Atticus attempts to defend the African American man, Tom Robinson (Brock Peters), who has been unjustly accused of raping a poor white girl. Although it is clear that he could not have committed this crime, Tom is found guilty and Atticus loses the case. Later, Tom is killed, and the town sets against Atticus for defending a "colored."

The courtroom scenes shown in these storyboards were pivotal to the book and form the heart of the film. To prepare for the shoot, art director and storyboard artist Henry Bumstead visited Harper Lee's hometown of Monroeville, Alabama, where the story is set. She grew up within a few blocks of the county courthouse and Bumstead personally discussed the forthcoming adaptation extensively with the publicity-shy Lee. The courthouse was completely recreated on a Hollywood soundstage for the film, alongside other sets that replicated the city at that time.

Art director Henry Bumstead was known for his accuracy, and the storyboards shown on these and the following pages indicate precisely how the action would be shown, from the full shot of the courtroom to a close-up of the "colored balcony."

80 SAUL BASS AND THE SIXTIES

SC. 235 - COLORED BALCONY - GROUP REACT.

SC. 236 - ATTICUS, JUDGE, AND MAYELLA.

SC. 237 - CLOSE UP - MAYELLA.

Sc. 237 - ATTICUS SITS DOWN - MAYELLA PASSES.

Sc. 238 - TOM TAKES OATH.

Sc. 239 - ATTICUS AND TOM.

SC. 240 CLOSE UP - TOM.

SC. 240 CLOSE UP - ATTICUS.

SC. 241 - FULL SHOT - COURTROOM

Who's Afraid of Virginia Woolf? 1966

DIRECTOR Mike Nichols
STORYBOARDS Maurice Zuberano

Mike Nichols was the most successful, sought-after stage director in America by the time he was approached by Warner Brothers to adapt Edward Albee's 1962 play *Who's Afraid of Virgina Woolf?* for the big screen. He had no film experience, but he was also unafraid—and the quality of his production team was unrivalled (from Haskell Wexler's camera to Richard Sylbert's production design).

The producer Ernest Lehman agreed to have the experienced illustrator Maurice Zuberano at Nichols's side throughout the production, which starred the powerhouse couple Elizabeth Taylor and Richard Burton as Martha and George (the scenario was thought to reflect the troubles of their own marriage). Nichols and Zuberano worked closely together, as this storyboard illustrates—it comes close to being an animated stage direction. Sylbert also worked with the storyboard artist Harold Michelson on this film. *Who's Afraid of Virginia Woolf?* was nominated for thirteen Academy Awards—including for Nichols as director—winning five, among them Elizabeth Taylor's second for acting.

Maurice Zuberano started out as a storyboard artist on the ultimate Hollywood classic, *Citizen Kane* (1941). He may well have provided the boards for Orson Welles's follow-up, *The Magnificent Ambersons* (1942; see pages 40–45), although he was not credited on the final, much-edited film. He certainly enjoyed a close relationship with Welles's editor on both pictures, Robert Wise, and they continued to work together when Wise made the jump to directing, on *Helen of Troy* (1956), *West Side Story* (1961), *The Sound of Music* (1965), and *Star Trek: The Motion Picture* (1979). Zuberano's last work was for Warren Beatty, on the director/star's *Dick Tracy* (1990).

OPPOSITE This page of Maurice Zuberano's storyboards is littered with character notes, stage directions, and snatches of dialogue, reflecting the close working relationship between Zuberano and the film's director, Mike Nichols.

LEFT Elizabeth Taylor with Richard Burton in *Who's Afraid of Virginia Woolf?*

84 SAUL BASS AND THE SIXTIES

LIVING RM ARCH.
FIGURE OF GEORGE DRAWS ASIDE REVEALING MARTHA
YES LOVE
"GEORGE"
PULL BACK
FWD.
CUT TO M FROM L.R ARCH
NEW 50?
"WHY DONT YOU-"
"WELL DEAR-"
CONT.
- FOLLOW M
"TAKE YOU
"PIG"
BACK TO MAKE ROOM FOR
CONT
"FIRSTY"
EXCLUDE G?
LOOK SWEETHEART
FWD 2 STEPS
"JESUS"
CUT
TURN + PUSH G ASIDE TO BAR THEN TOWARD DOOR

Fresh Forces in American Filmmaking

Fresh winds blew through American filmmaking in the late 1970s and early 1980s, as a generation of young film school graduates rewrote the rules of film production. With some notable exceptions, movies had previously been shot in highly controlled conditions on soundstages or studio backlots. Studio art departments functioned as conveyor belts; art directors would work on several productions at the same time, cataloging and recycling sets provided by teams of draftsmen, all working on different scenes from different films. It was a hierarchy, but many of these artists were German and Russian émigrés who brought skills to the Hollywood youngsters learning at their feet.

The legendary production designer Dick Sylbert, who would preside over the world of Mike Nichols films, including *Who's Afraid of Virginia Woolf?* (1966; see pages 84–85) and *The Graduate* (1967), as well as Roman Polanski's *Rosemary's Baby* (1968) and *Chinatown* (1974), learned his trade from William Cameron Menzies. Having been an animation "in betweener" at Walt Disney studios, Dean Tavoularis was art directing *Bonnie And Clyde* by 1967, with his brother Alex Tavoularis drawing the boards.

Godfather: Part II was hopping from Nevada to Sicily; the two-year effort that was *Apocalypse Now* (1979) shot in the Philippines, with dictator Ferdinand Marcos providing the Huey helicopters for the attack sequence storyboarded by Alex Tavoularis.

Brash and busy, the new directors were spearheaded by George Lucas with his Industrial Light & Magic in Van Nuys, and Francis Ford Coppola with his filmmaking collective, American Zoetrope, in San Francisco. Steven Spielberg, a child of Hollywood, made films including *Close Encounters Of The Third Kind* (1977), *E.T.: The Extra-Terrestrial* (1982), and *Poltergeist* (also 1982, directed by Tobe Hooper; Spielberg co-wrote and produced) as a filmmaker on the edge of the system, his characters perched on the outskirts. In New York, Martin Scorsese powered in with *Mean Streets* in 1973, a story of small-time hoods trying to make it in Little Italy.

They all relied on the storyboard as an indispensible visual reference and communication tool within the teams who worked for them—although occasionally they would also use boards to convince potential backers to put their

THE RAGING BULL
87B
4
MARTIN SCORSESE
MICHAEL CHAPMAN
INT/DAY CAM: A

Star Wars 1977

DIRECTOR George Lucas
STORYBOARDS Joe Johnston

A long time ago in a galaxy far, far away, a Rebel Alliance blockade runner carrying Princess Leia is pursued by Darth Vader's Star Destroyer in the stunning, game-changing opening sequence for George Lucas's space opera *Star Wars*. These initial dramatic moments pull the audience immediately into the complex *Star Wars* galaxy and introduce Industrial Light & Magic model-making never before seen by audiences. The Imperial Destroyer that hones in on the rebel ship was conceived as a mile in length and constructed as a three-foot model; the droids R2-D2 and C-3PO (the latter a clear tribute to Fritz Lang's creation in *Metropolis*) were the first concept visualizations by production artist Ralph McQuarrie; the storyboards shown here were drawn by his colleague, Joe Johnston.

Much of the production art was produced to help budget the film—it was thanks to Alan Ladd at Fox that the film was eventually made. The boards shown on these pages were collated by George Mather into an all-important storyboard bible as technicians at the newly-set-up ILM in Van Nuys grappled with the scale of it all. Johnston later went on to become an A-list Hollywood director on films such as *The Rocketeer* (1991) and *Jurassic Park III* (2001), but it all began when he was recruited by Lucasfilm. Johnston worked his way up to head storyboard artist and effects supervisor (winning an Academy Award for *Indiana Jones and The Temple of Doom*, 1984) before Lucas put him through film school.

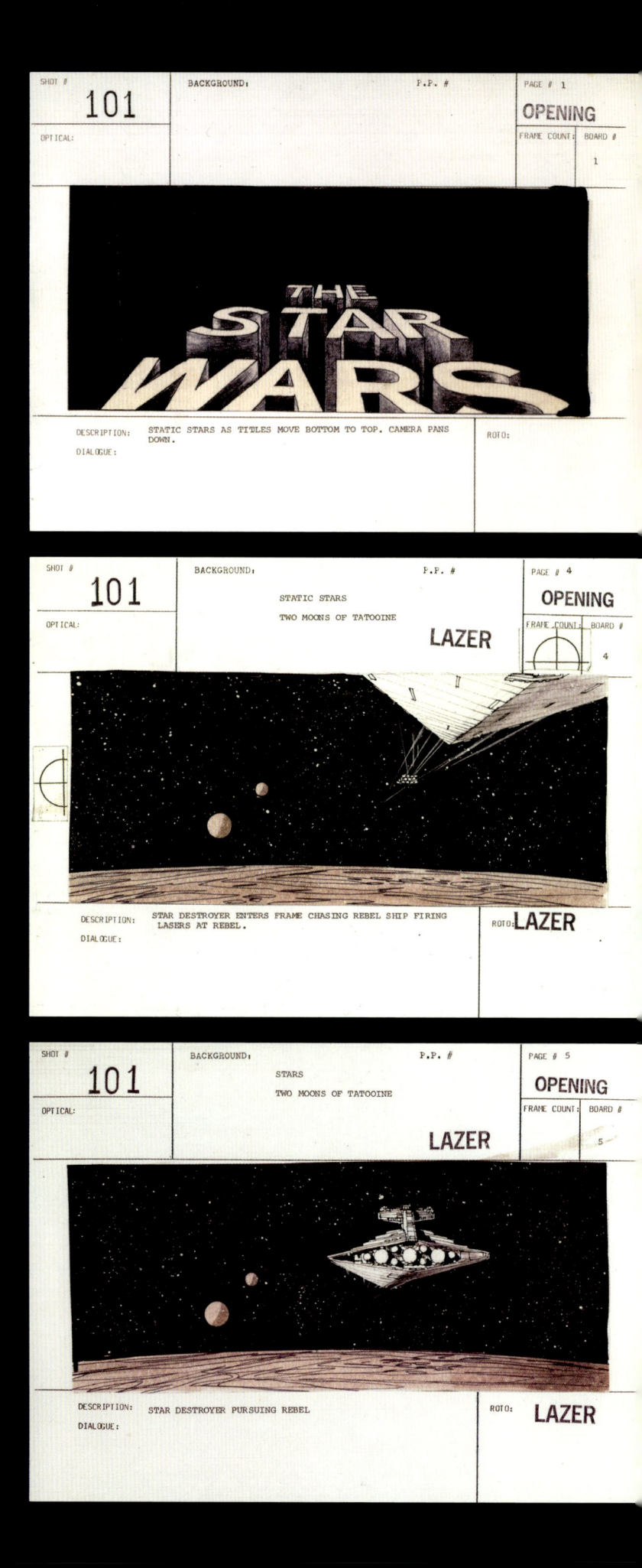

88 FRESH FORCES IN AMERICAN FILMMAKING

SHOT #	BACKGROUND:	P.P. #	PAGE # 6
102	STARS		**OPENING**
OPTICAL:			FRAME COUNT:	BOARD #

DESCRIPTION: REBEL SHIP AND IMPERIAL SHIP TO CAMERA ABOVE TATOOINE

DIALOGUE:

ROTO:

The "title crawl" and opening sequence of *Star Wars*, with the Star Destroyer chasing the rebel blockade runner carrying the fugitive rebel commander, Daniels). Descending on top of the tiny rebel ship, the vast Star Destroyer, commanded by the menacing Darth Vader (David Prowse, with the voice

SHOT # 102B	BACKGROUND: STARS SLIGHTLY TRACKING	P.P. #	PAGE # 8
OPTICAL:			OPENING
		FRAME COUNT:	BOARD # 7

DESCRIPTION: BLOCKADE RUNNER GETS ZAPPED BY STAR DESTROYER. MAIN SOLAR FIN OF REBEL CRAFT DISINTEGRATES.

DIALOGUE:

ROTO:

SHOT # 106	BACKGROUND: STARS (slight track R to L)	P.P. #	PAGE # 10
OPTICAL:			**OPENING**
		FRAME COUNT:	BOARD # 10

DESCRIPTION: Black 6 frames/flash 15 frames include Nurnies blowing around/25 frames Pod going away (POV from pod docking port so back end of pod is visible.)

DIALOGUE:

ROTO:

SHOT # 107	BACKGROUND: STARS	P.P. #	PAGE # 11
OPTICAL:			**OPENING**
			FRAME COUNT: / BOARD # 11

DESCRIPTION: Life Pod to camera (ships in background). POD is moving slightly right to left. Rebel ship in Pod Bay.

DIALOGUE:

ROTO:

ABOVE AND RIGHT The pod emerges and is watched from the Star Destroyer as it makes its descent toward Tatooine.

SHOT # 108

OPTICAL:

DESCRIPTION:

DIALOGUE:

BACKGROUND:	P.P. #	PAGE # 12
STARS (slight move R to L)		**OPENING**
	FRAME COUNT:	BOARD #
		12

Life Pod drifting away on viewing screen

ROTO:

STAR WARS 93

SHOT # 109	BACKGROUND: STARS	P.P. #	PAGE # 13
OPTICAL:			**OPENING**
			FRAME COUNT:	BOARD #

DESCRIPTION: POD TO PLANET

DIALOGUE:

ROTO:

110 P	BACKGROUND: STARS POD	P.P. #	PAGE # 14 **OPENING**
OPTICAL:			FRAME COUNT:	BOARD #

DESCRIPTION: POV INTERIOR OF POD AWAY
DIALOGUE:

ROTO:

Apocalypse Now 1979

DIRECTOR Francis Ford Coppola
STORYBOARDS Alex Tavoularis and Thomas A. Wright

The revered production designer Dean Tavoularis (*The Godfather* trilogy) was one of the first on board the epic and revolutionary Vietnam War film *Apocalypse Now* and, as was his usual method, worked closely with his brother Alex to storyboard the film for director Francis Ford Coppola, alongside production illustrator Thomas A. Wright. ("It was especially Alex who worked on the storyboards," recalls Tavoularis, "although sometimes we worked on it together.")

Brought up in Hollywood around the old-style studios, the Greek-American Tavoularis brothers played a major part in the evolution of filmmaking as movies left the safety of those soundstages for a far more dangerous life of shooting on the road. They worked on *The Godfather* (1972) with Coppola and it was natural that they would move with him to *Apocalypse Now*, but in terms of road movies, they didn't come any more ambitious than the year-long Philippines shoot that followed an extensive pre-production process.

"I spent two years on that film," says Dean Tavoularis. "You'd get knocked off your feet at times, but you'd adapt to it, if you had time—and it seemed like we had more time than we should have had."

An adaptation of Joseph Conrad's novel *Heart of Darkness*, *Apocalypse Now* relates Captain Willard's (Martin Sheen) secret mission to follow the fictional Nung River from Saigon into the remote Cambodian jungle and terminate the life of American Colonel Kurtz (Marlon Brando), who has gone insane, building his own kingdom there. The horror intensifies as they draw closer.

ABOVE AND OPPOSITE Drawn by Alex Tavoularis and Thomas A. Wright in a wide-screen format (the film was shot on a 2:35 frame), the storyboards on these and the ensuing pages depict the famous Huey helicopter attack sequence where Lieutenant Colonel Kilgore (Robert Duvall) orders a napalm strike on a Viet Cong village at the mouth of the Nung delta.

96 FRESH FORCES IN AMERICAN FILMMAKING

montage. 34 s. Page 51.

Firing.

to Cam.
Past

APOCALYPSE NOW 97

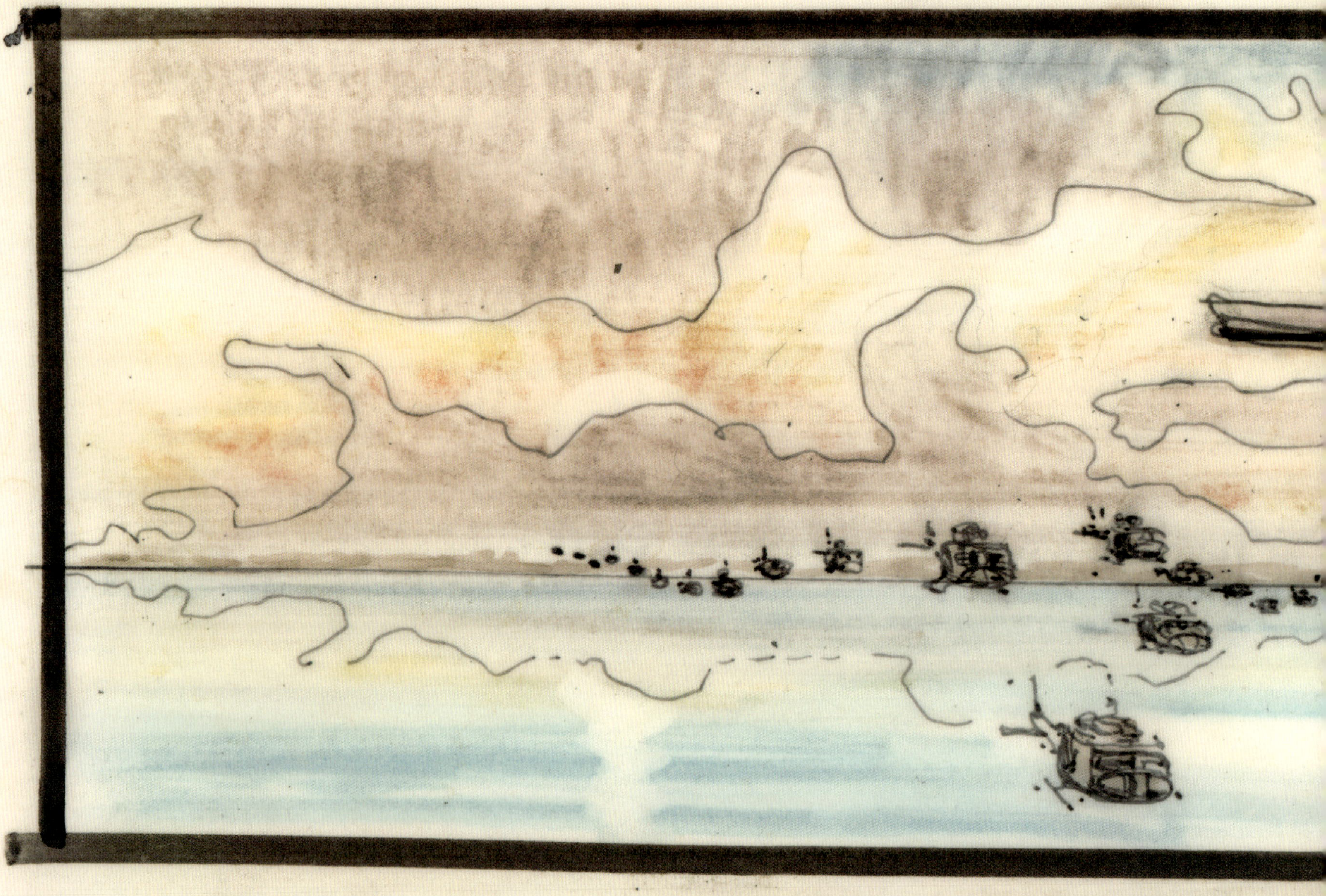

(15)

LEFT To the accompaniment of Wagner's "Ride of the Valkyries" blasting from his cockpit, Lieutenant Colonel Kilgore commands his fleet of Huey helicopters as they sweep across the delta.

100 FRESH FORCES IN AMERICAN FILMMAKING

LEFT Kilgore is tempted into the plan by the prospect of the surfer-friendly terrain below—although in the extended *Apocalypse Now Redux* (2001), Willard (Martin Sheen) is shown stealing Kilgore's surfboard.

APOCALYPSE NOW 101

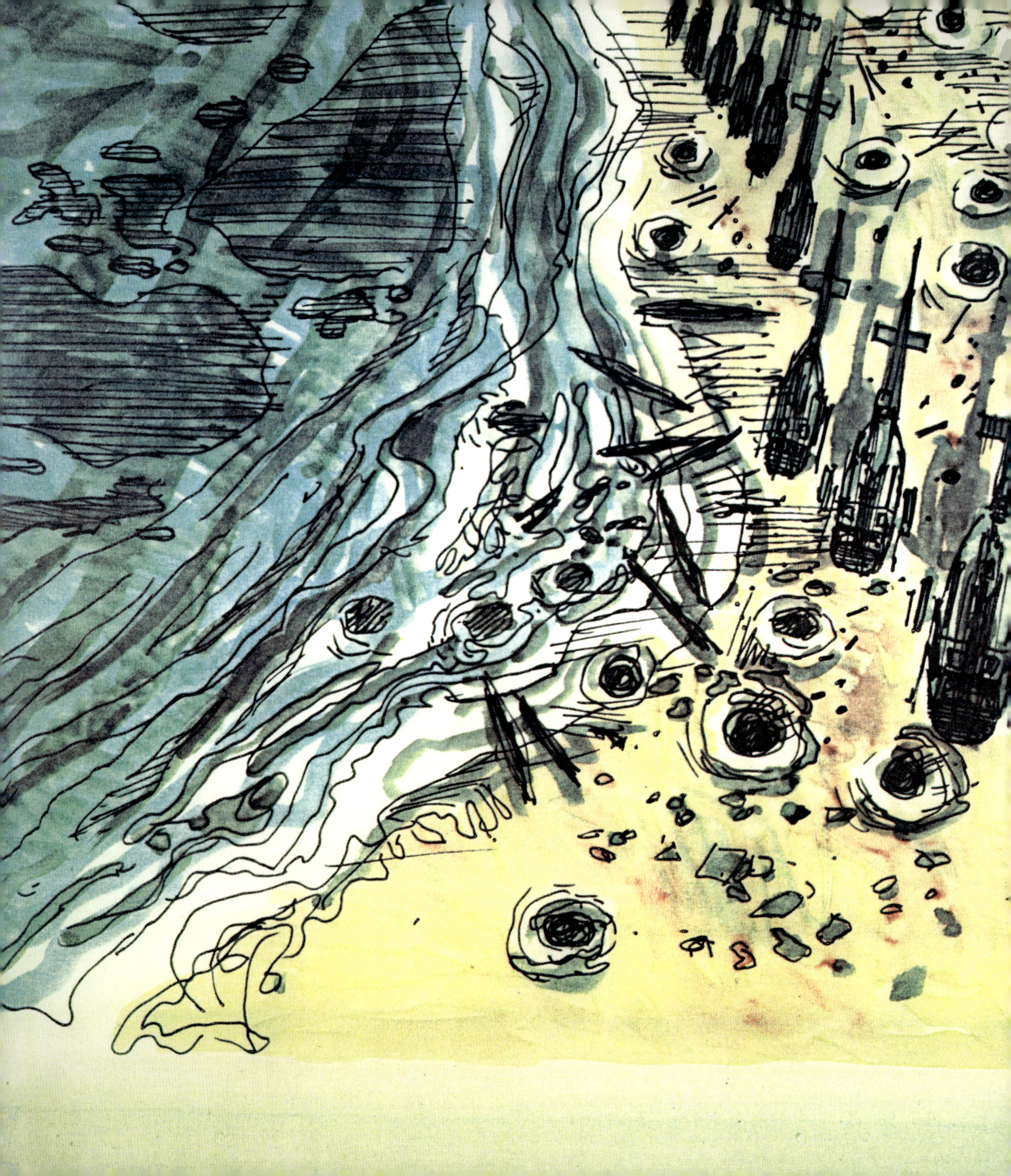

SC 46 Cont. As Copters Lift off
47.

Raging Bull 1980

DIRECTOR Martin Scorsese
STORYBOARDS Martin Scorsese

Martin Scorsese meticulously storyboards all of his films, viewing them as an essential part of visualizing the finished picture and also a crucial communication tool with his crew, particularly his cinematographer. While all his work is clearly carefully conceived, the black-and-white fight sequences in *Raging Bull*—considered by many to be Scorsese's "perfect film"—are a furious blend of physicality and raw emotion, a ballet of fists and fury that plays out against a confined ring, with the camera—and the viewer—often inside with the pugilists, at other times swooping down.

The eight painstakingly-staged fight sequences in *Raging Bull* occupy no more than nine or ten minutes of the film's running time, yet they took over ten weeks to film and were a complex editing challenge that gained Thelma Schoonmaker her first Academy Award.

At the beginning of Scorsese's storyboarding process for *Raging Bull*, he referred to videotaped practice sessions of fights choreographed by Jimmy Nickerson and Jake LaMotta—the fighter on whose life story the film is based. The actor Robert De Niro, who won an Academy Award for

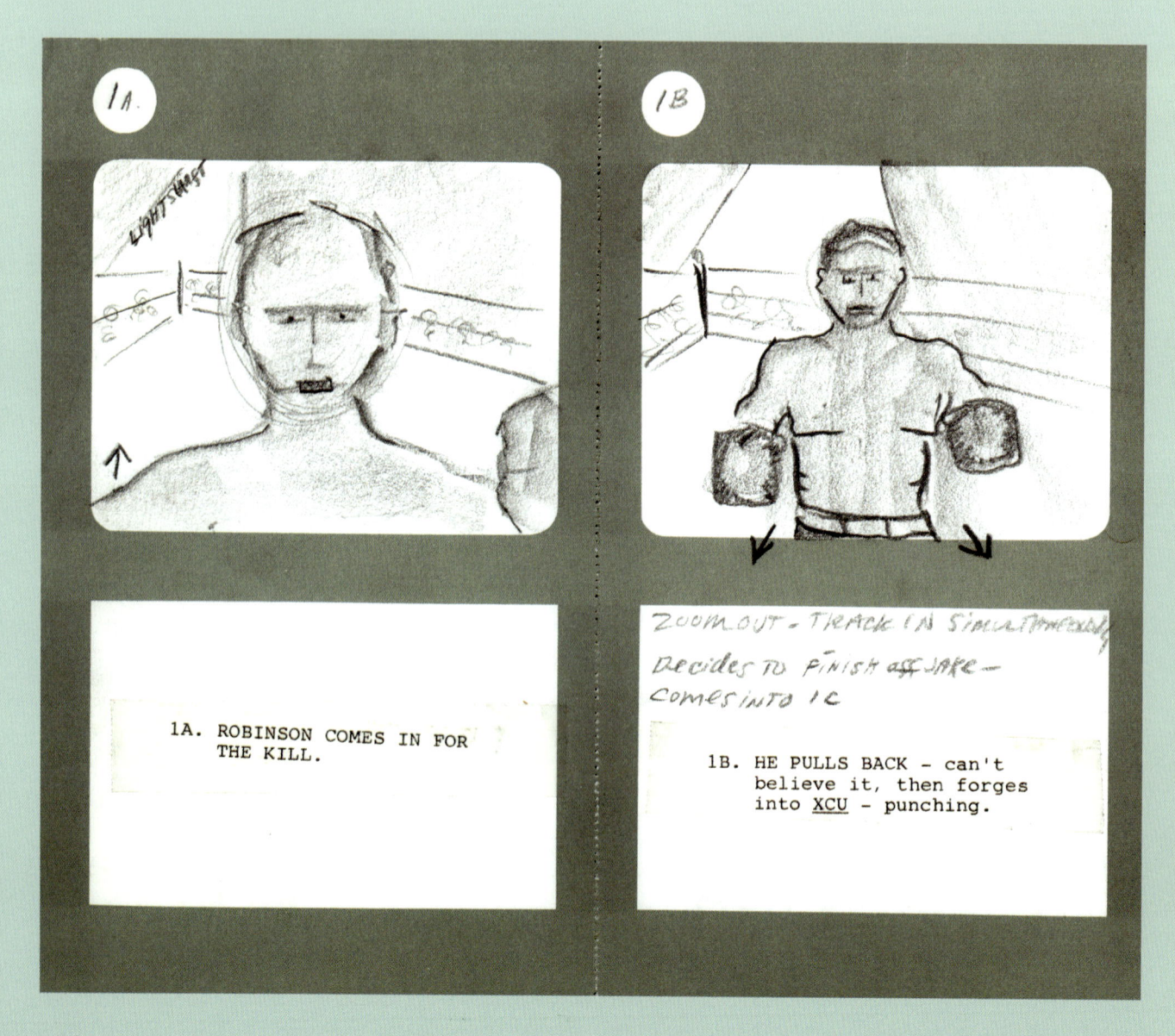

1A. ROBINSON COMES IN FOR THE KILL.

ZOOM OUT - TRACK IN SIMULTANEOUSLY
Decides to finish off Jake —
comes into 1C

1B. HE PULLS BACK - can't believe it, then forges into XCU - punching.

104 FRESH FORCES IN AMERICAN FILMMAKING

his portrayal of LaMotta, was then videotaped practicing these fights with another boxer. After making overhead diagrams of the bouts' choreography, Scorsese designed the shots in his boards, each frame a clear and specific composition.

Scorsese often checks into a hotel near his office to draw his storyboards; undisturbed, he focuses on composition, the movement of characters and objects within the frame, which lens to use, and how one shot will cut to the next, a process which he says is sometimes instinctual, sometimes harder-come-by.

Jake LaMotta takes on Sugar Ray Robinson three times in *Raging Bull*, and their final match is also the film's last, almost unbearably bruising fight sequence. It closely follows another fight, LaMotta's exhausting defense of his world middleweight championship title against Laurent Dauthuille over fifteen rounds. "Sugar Ray 3" is the longest fight sequence in the film, and the bloodiest, although Scorsese's use of red ink here is to indicate make-up effects shots, as well as being a dramatic underscore for himself and his cinematographer (Michael Chapman).

The director took a different approach to each fight depending on its function within the narrative, and this last match shows LaMotta as he loses, although he never goes down. His demeanor appears defeated between bouts but his determination to remain on his feet is raw and visceral. Blood covers his face and body as flashbulbs explode and the pounding continues; the camera rolls with the punches, LaMotta's legs buckle, and a climactic punch splatters the spectators with his blood (panel #39). With Sugar Ray Robinson now the new world middleweight boxing champion, a battered LaMotta, clinging to the ropes, still cries, "Hey Ray, I never went down, man!"

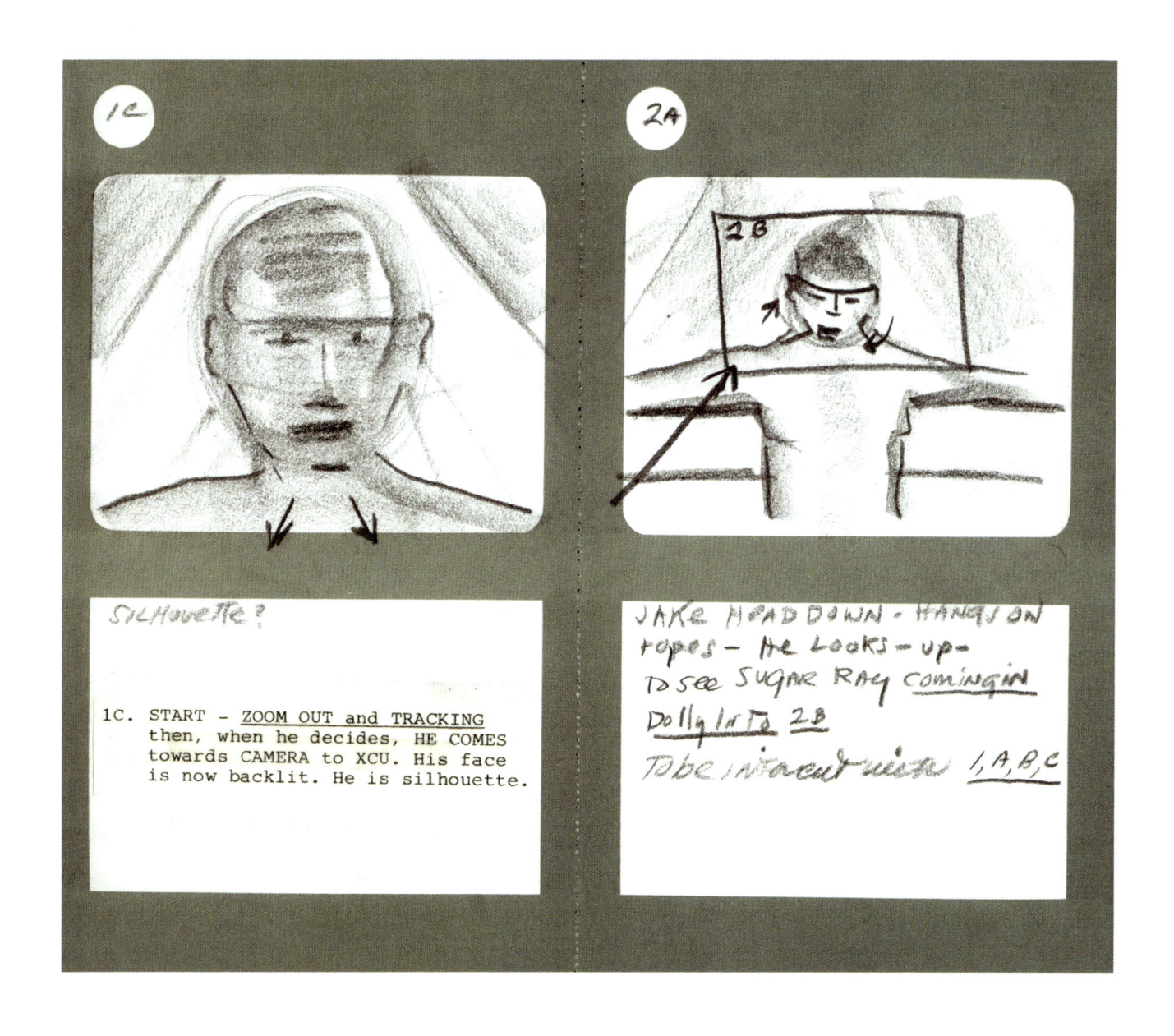

3. JAKE GETS HIT - MCU

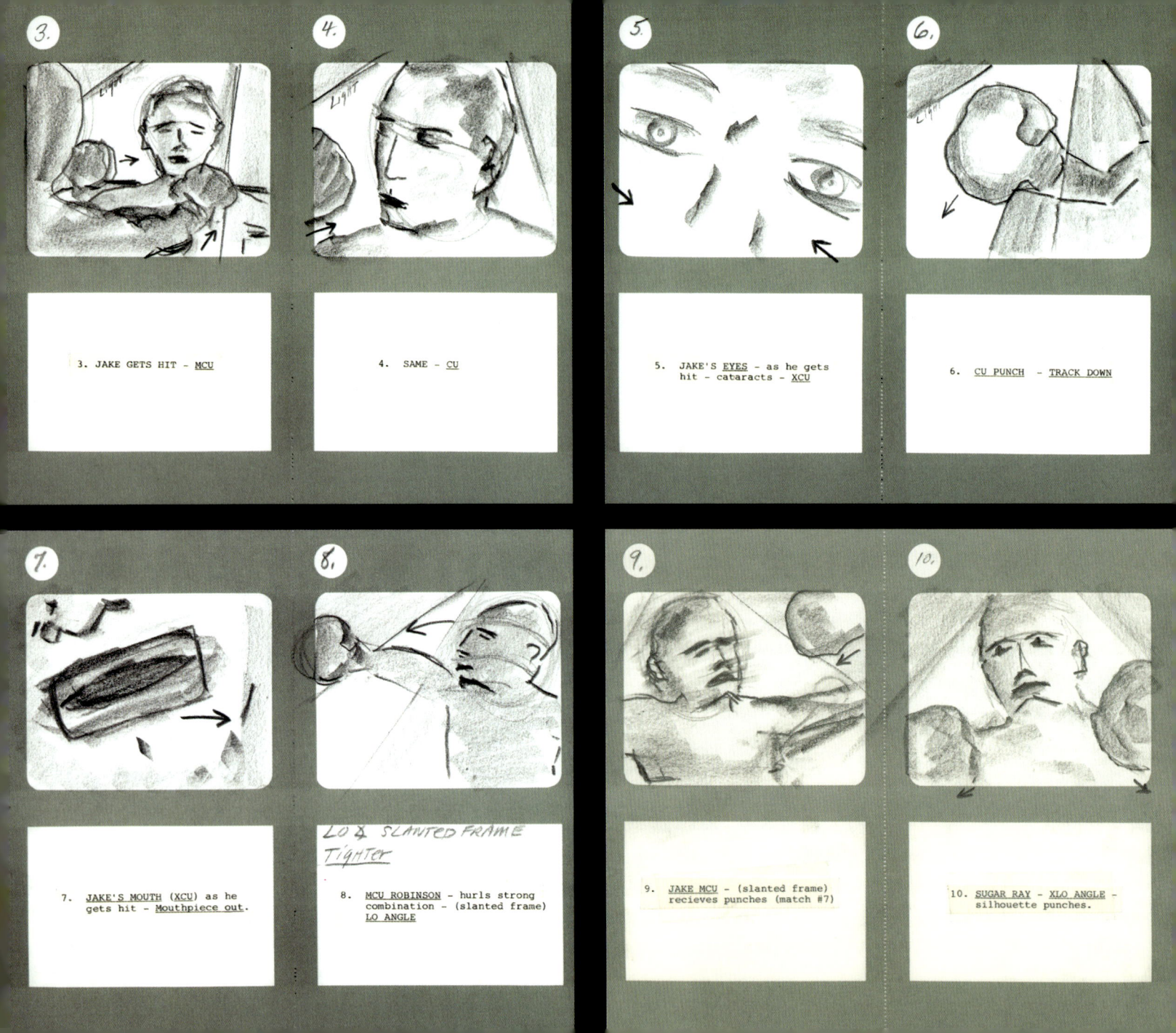

4. SAME - CU

5. JAKE'S EYES - as he gets hit - cataracts - XCU

6. CU PUNCH - TRACK DOWN

7. JAKE'S MOUTH (XCU) as he gets hit - Mouthpiece out.

LO & SLANTED FRAME TIGHTER

8. MCU ROBINSON - hurls strong combination - (slanted frame) LO ANGLE

9. JAKE MCU - (slanted frame) recieves punches (match #7)

10. SUGAR RAY - XLO ANGLE - silhouette punches.

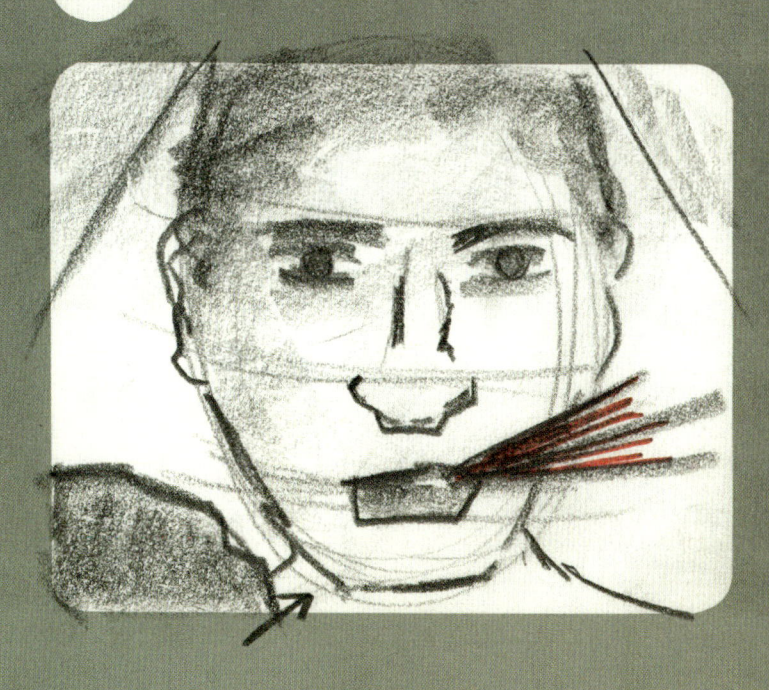

11. <u>HI ANGLE DOWN</u> - shock effect angle.

12. <u>XCU JAKE'S FACE</u> - first special effect - <u>BLOOD</u> shoots from MOUTH

13. HI ANGLE DOWN - TIGHTER

14. XCU FACE - PROFILE - second special effect BLOOD shoots from NOSE.

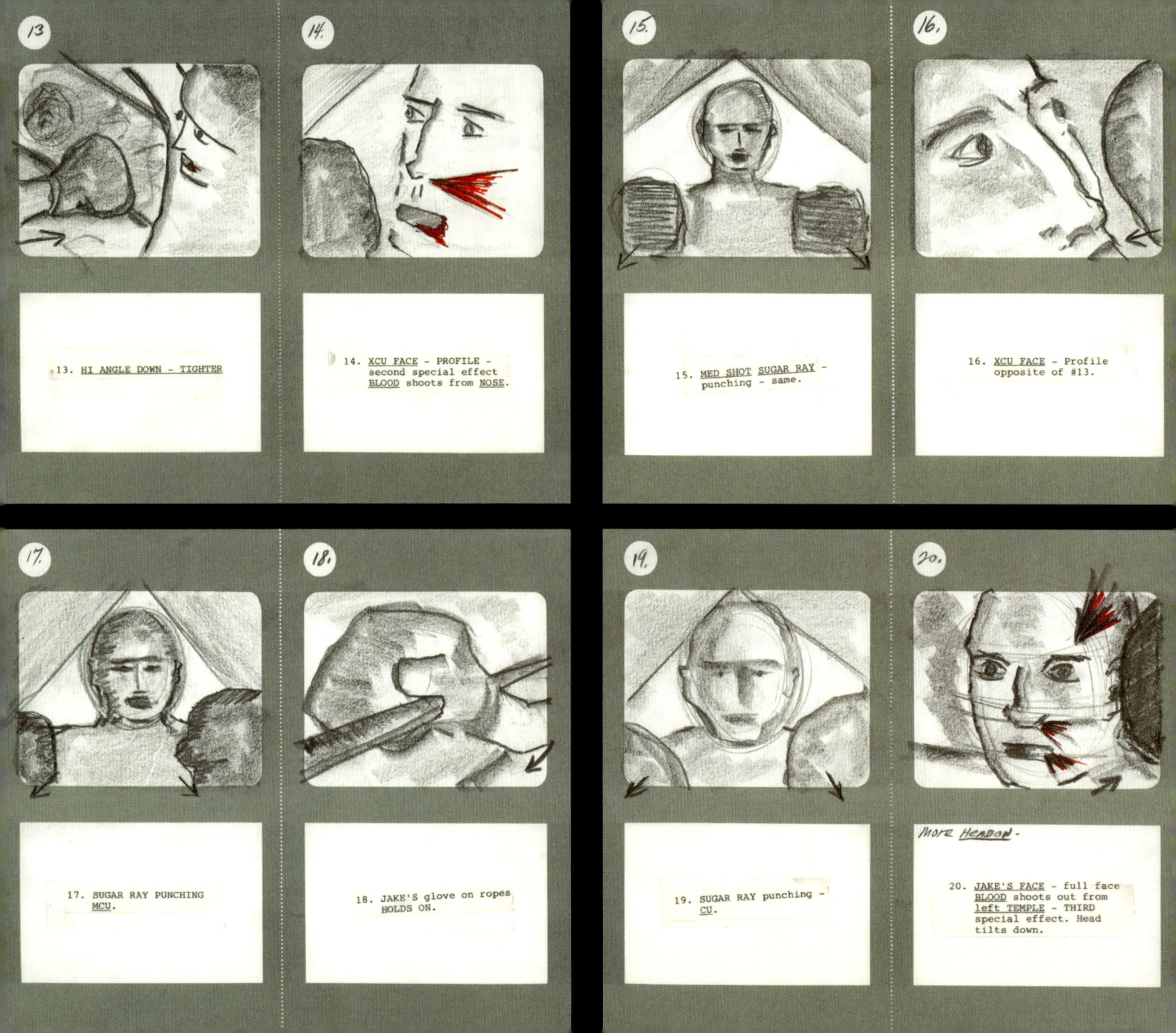

15. MED SHOT SUGAR RAY - punching - same.

16. XCU FACE - Profile opposite of #13.

17. SUGAR RAY PUNCHING MCU.

18. JAKE'S glove on ropes HOLDS ON.

19. SUGAR RAY punching - CU.

MORE HEADON -

20. JAKE'S FACE - full face BLOOD shoots out from left TEMPLE - THIRD special effect. Head tilts down.

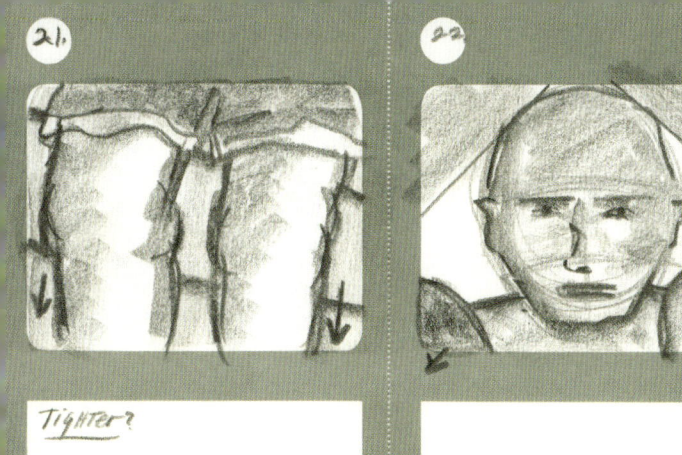

TIGHTER?

21. JAKE'S knees buckle.

22. SUGAR RAY punches - CU.

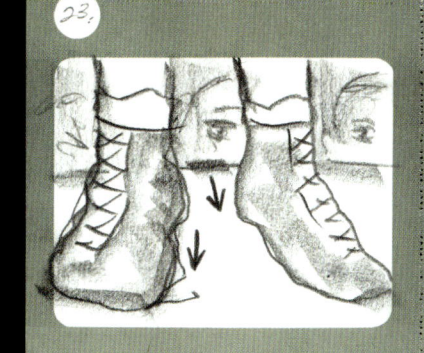

23. JAKE'S FEET - He's about to fall.

24. JAKE'S FACE MCU - wakes himself up - holds himself up.

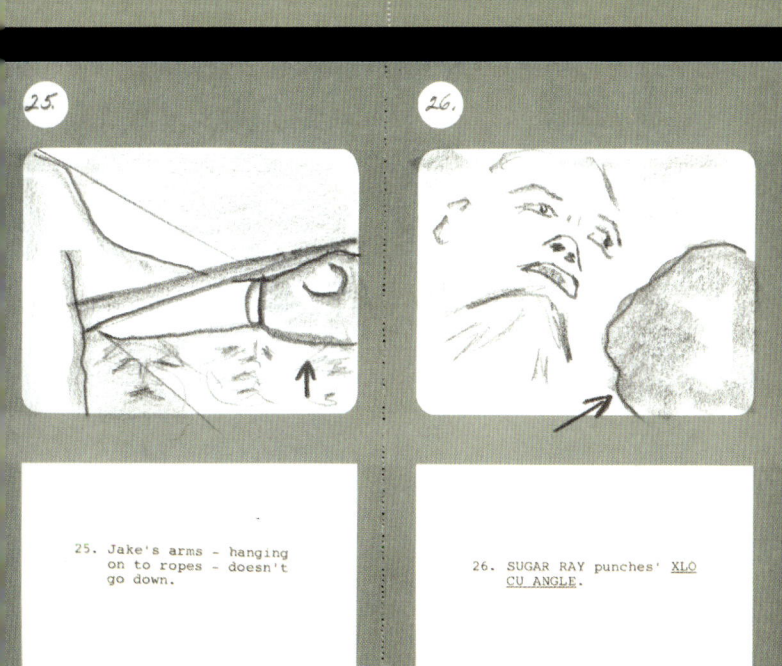

25. Jake's arms - hanging on to ropes - doesn't go down.

26. SUGAR RAY punches' XLO CU ANGLE.

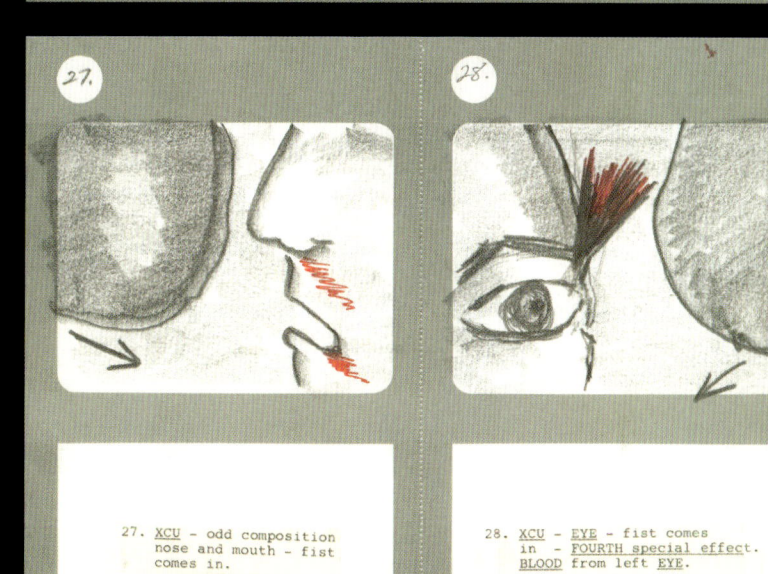

27. XCU - odd composition nose and mouth - fist comes in.

28. XCU - EYE - fist comes in - FOURTH special effect. BLOOD from left EYE.

29. SUGAR RAY – PUNCHING XCU HI ANGLE DOWN.

HI × DOWN – more extreme CU

30. JAKE's FEET – TILT UP to KNEES BUCKLING.

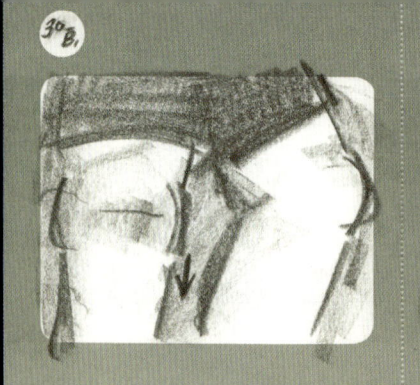

31. SUGAR RAY HITTING – HIGH ANGLE DOWN and REVERSE. Fist comes in.

32. XCU of right TEMPLE – as fist from #31 hits. BLOOD SHOOTS OUT – FIFTH special effect.

33. SUGAR RAY RAISES FIST – TILT UP and DOLLY IN to fist – swings out of frame.

Light moves with it

34. FIST from #33 lands powerfully on JAKE'S right EAR. BLOOD shoots out – SIXTH special effect.

EAR

35.

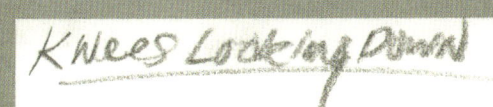

Knees Looking Down

35. KNEES BUCKLE - CU.

36.

36. JAKE'S FACE - HI ANGLE DOWN CU - gets punched.

37.

38.

Light →

↓

37. <u>SUGAR RAY</u> - <u>XCU</u> punches (LEFT HOOK).

38. Punch lands - sweat and blood <u>spray</u> - <u>LO ANGLE</u> UP on JAKE - P.O.V. of cameramen on canvas.

39. CAMERAMEN GET SPRAYED WITH BLOOD.

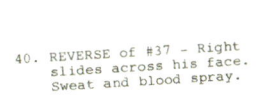

40. REVERSE of #37 - Right slides across his face. Sweat and blood spray.

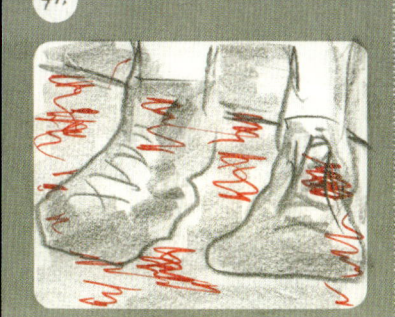

41. BLOOD splattered on canvas over JAKE'S FEET. Buckling but holding on.

42. ROBINSON hauls off a combination of punches. MCU - HEAD ON SHOT.

43. JAKE XCU - His right temple opens - BLOOD spurts - SEVENTH special effect - TIGHTER ?

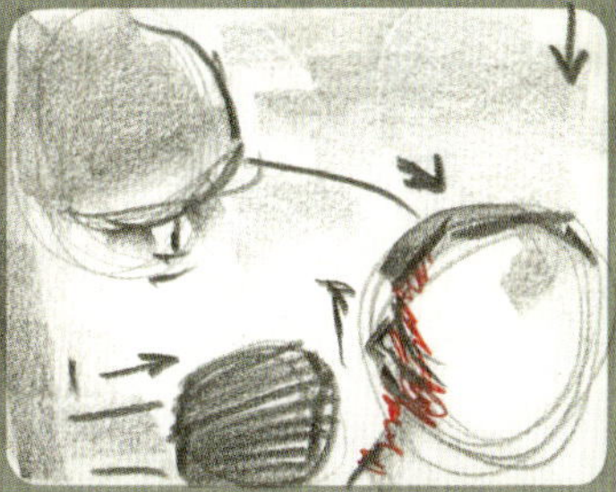

44. SUGAR RAY PUNCHING JAKE HI ANGLE DOWN - TRACK DOWN as REFEREE comes in to stop it.

44B. JAKE STAYS on the ROPES - one arm over.

44C. CAMERA goes with SUGAR RAY to his corner - WIDE distorted.

Raiders of the Lost Ark 1981

DIRECTOR Steven Spielberg
STORYBOARDS Ed Verreaux

In *Raiders of the Lost Ark*, adventuring archaeologist Indiana Jones (Harrison Ford) is charged with finding the long-lost Ark of the Covenant before the Nazis get their hands on it and assume its untold powers. After a chase halfway across the globe with his rival, the French archeologist Belloq (Paul Freeman), "Indy" finally lands on a secret island in the Mediterranean where Belloq and the Nazis plan to test the Ark's powers.

An attempt to recapture the spirit of the "serials" of the 1940s and 1950s, *Raiders of the Lost Ark* was a huge success on release, and this sequence, drawn by Ed Verreaux, depicts the film's satisfyingly explosive climax.

Although already an experienced illustrator by this point, *Raiders* marked Verreaux's first major feature film as a storyboard artist. He was hired after Steven Spielberg gave him three scenes to board over the course of a weekend as a trial. Says Verreaux: "At that time Steven was using the boards purely as a communication device—he would show the boards to the crew and they would be put up on a big board on set so everyone on set knew what was happening that day; when the shot was done, an X would be marked through it."

With the numerous effects shots and stunts contained in the film, storyboards were a necessity and used for nearly fifty percent of the movie's scenes. Verreaux would work closely with Spielberg from the director's flat line sketches, going through the script page by page. "Steven really knew what he wanted," recalls Verreaux, and corrections would be minimal—Indy looking right, as opposed to left.

An art school graduate who learned his craft at Hollywood's animation houses and pioneering effects house Abel and Associates in the late 1970s, Verreaux is now a respected production designer (*Looper*, 2012, being a recent credit). That's a natural progression, he feels, for a storyboard artist—who needs to hold the whole film in his head and must be able to visualize it technically as well as artistically.

Ed Verreaux's eerily evocative boards depict the final showdown between the Nazis and their allies and the unearthly powers that must not be disturbed in *Raiders of the Lost Ark*. Like the audience, Indiana Jones is by now a mere spectator—except one who is tied to a post with his love interest Marion Ravenwood (Karen Allen).

The first frames show Belloq performing a ceremonial opening of the Ark, which initially appears to contain only sand. Wraiths, resembling Seraphim, then emerge and pass through the assembled troops. Indy is aware of the dangers of looking into the opened Ark, however. ("Keep your eyes closed!" he exclaims overleaf.)

114 FRESH FORCES IN AMERICAN FILMMAKING

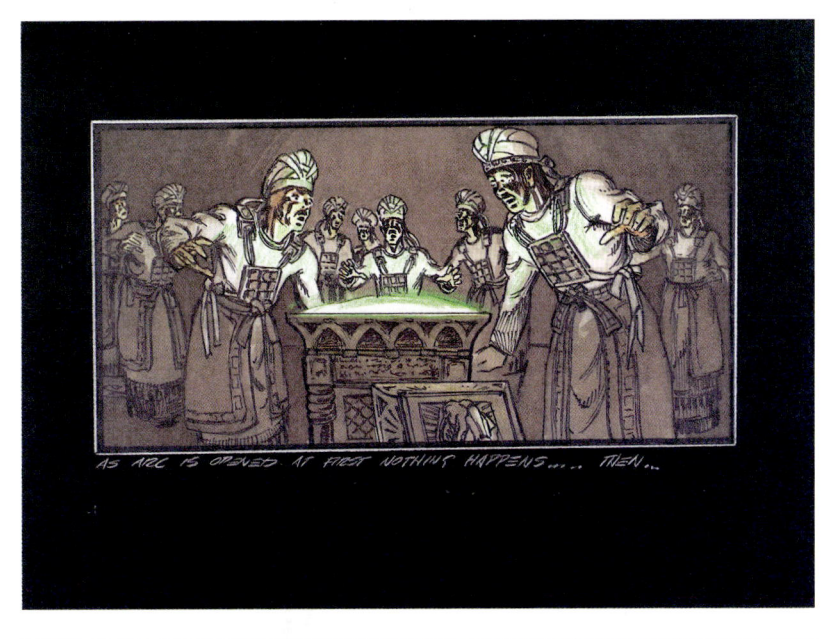

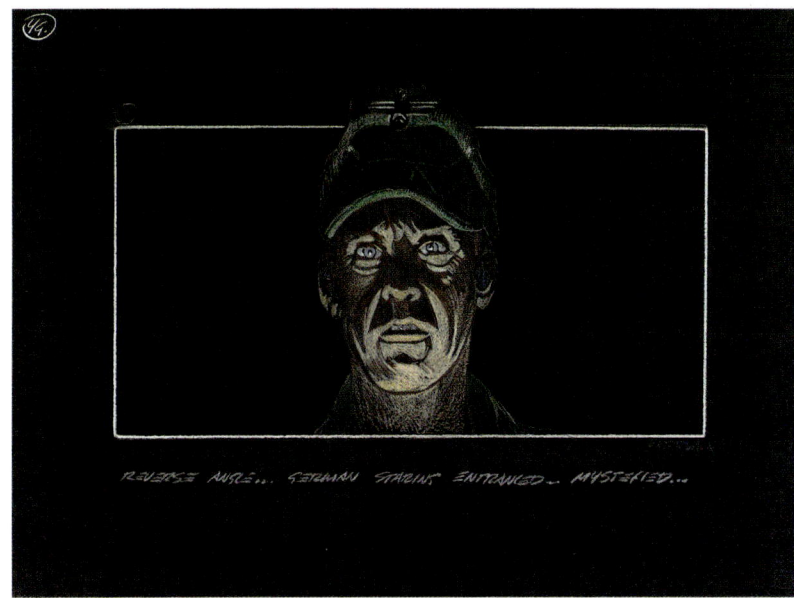

RAIDERS OF THE LOST ARK 115

116 FRESH FORCES IN AMERICAN FILMMAKING

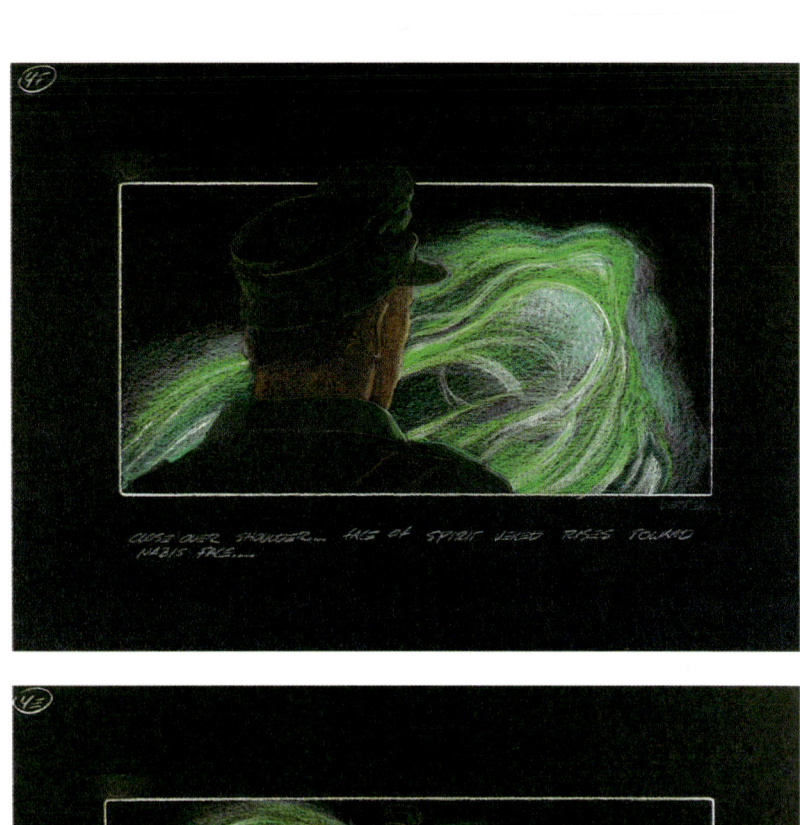

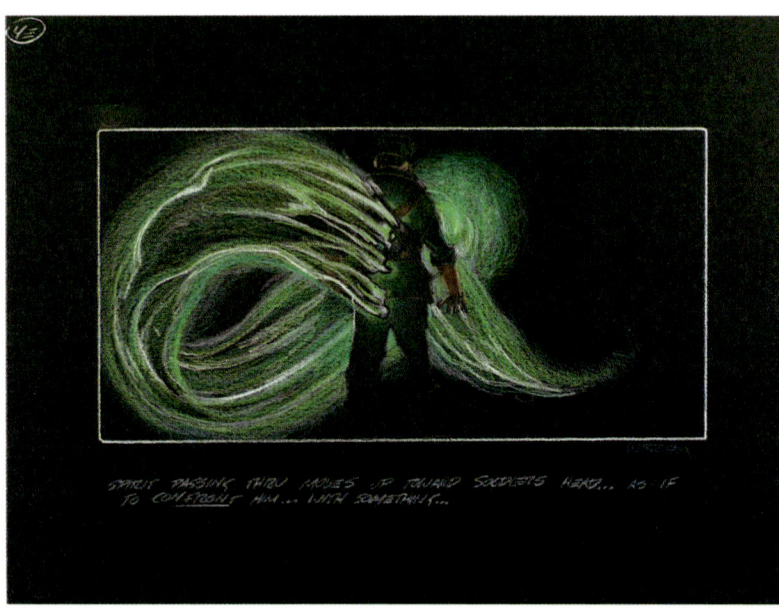

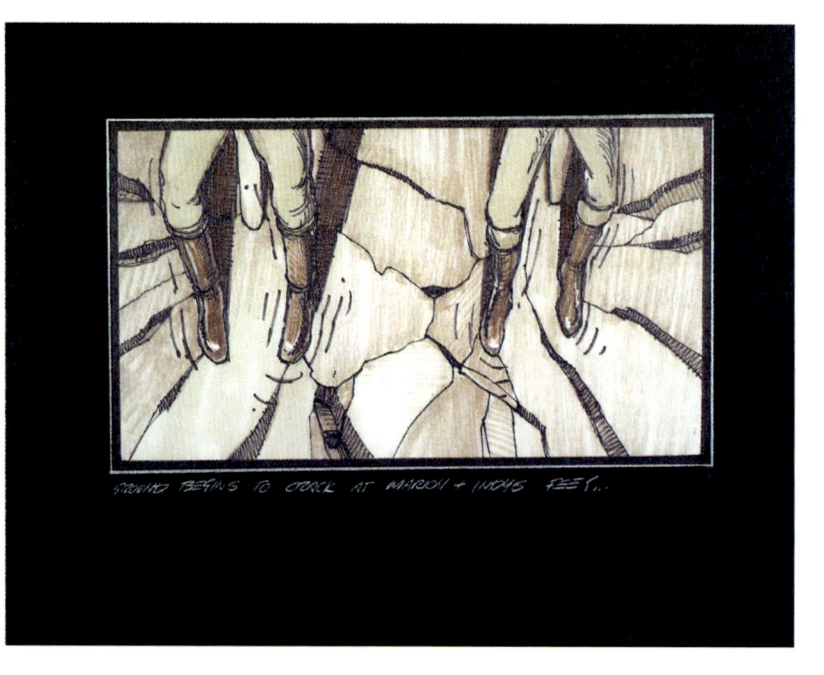

INDY... "KEEP YOUR EYES CLOSED!!"
SPIRITS TAUNT INDY AND MARION

COSMIC CONCUSSION BURSTS FORTH FROM THE ARC...

MARION SLOWLY OPENS HER EYES — LOOKS AT O.S. ARC...

RAIDERS OF THE LOST ARK 117

The apparitions suddenly turn into angels of death and bolts of lightning expand and explode out of the Ark, dealing the Nazis a grisly death. The angels rise to the sky in a vast fireball before falling back down into the Ark, which closes with a crash of thunder. As Verreaux's boards note, Indy then looks at Marion, "tears in his eyes."

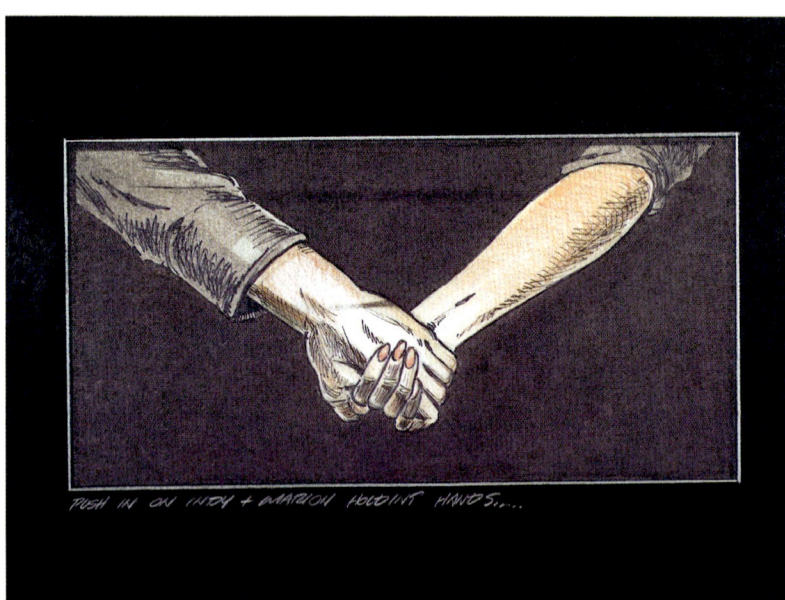

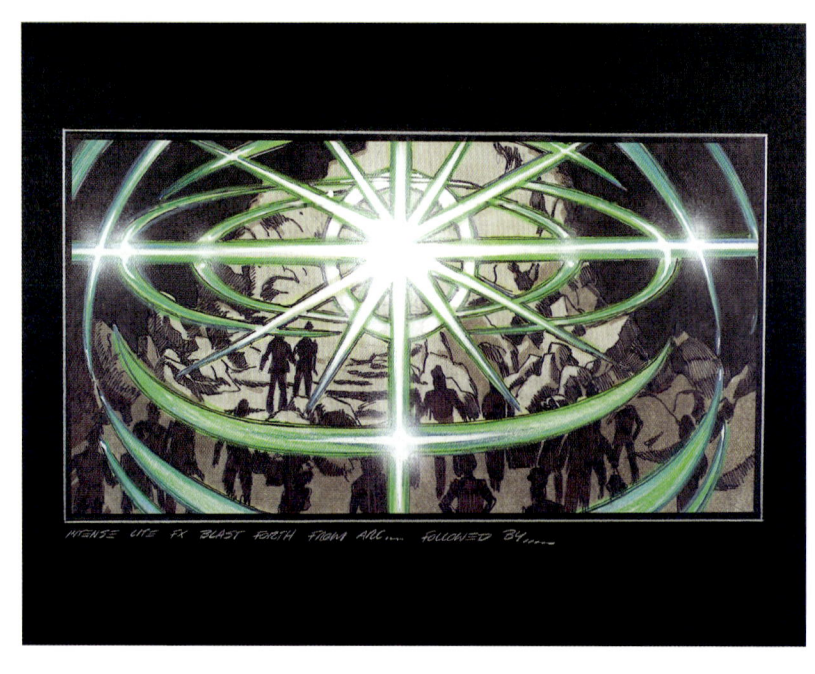

118 FRESH FORCES IN AMERICAN FILMMAKING

RAIDERS OF THE LOST ARK

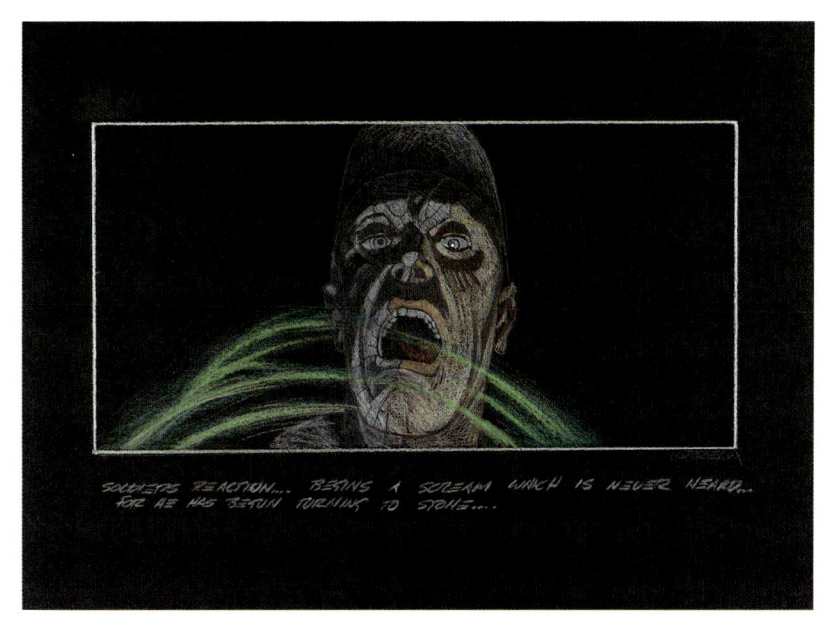

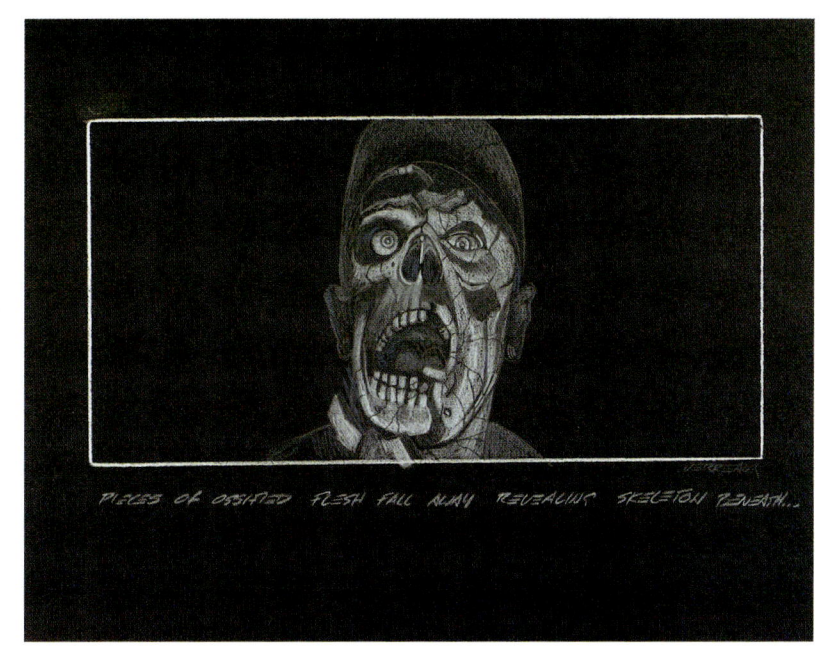

120 FRESH FORCES IN AMERICAN FILMMAKING

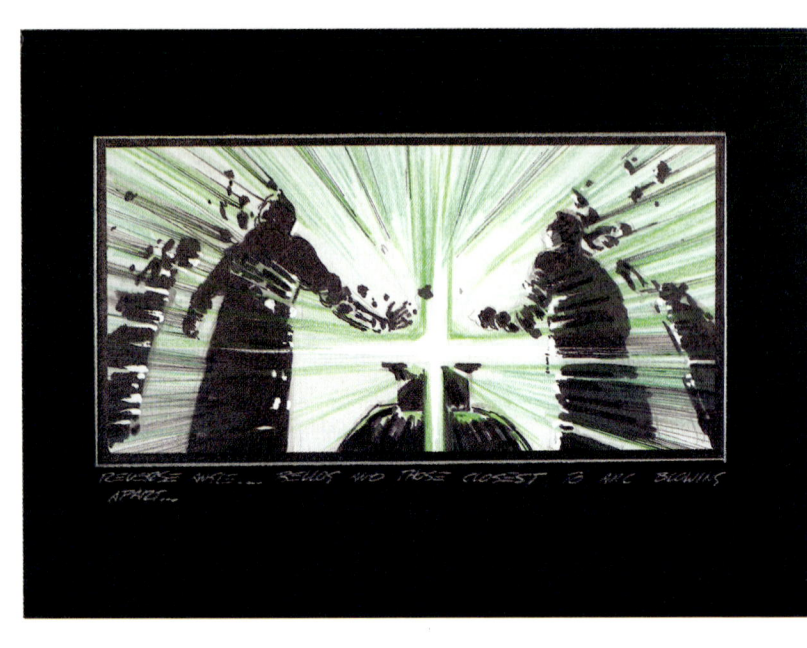

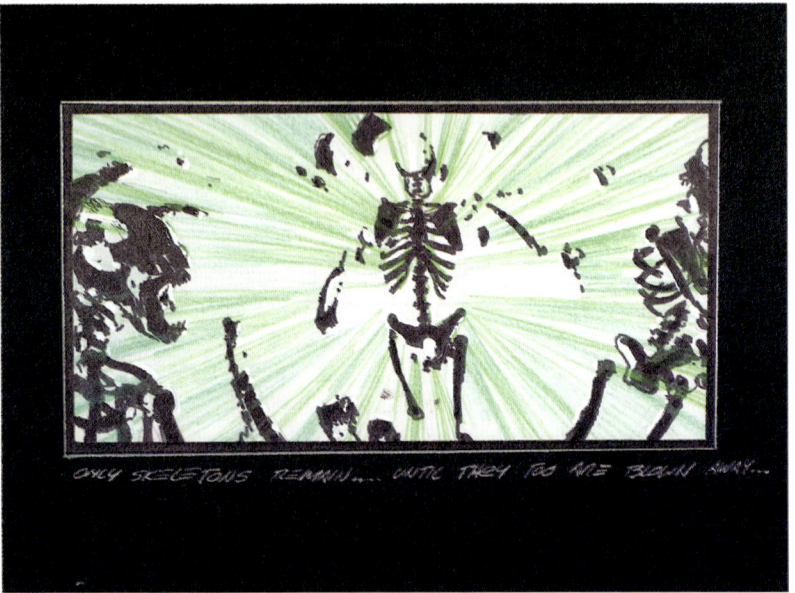

RAIDERS OF THE LOST ARK 121

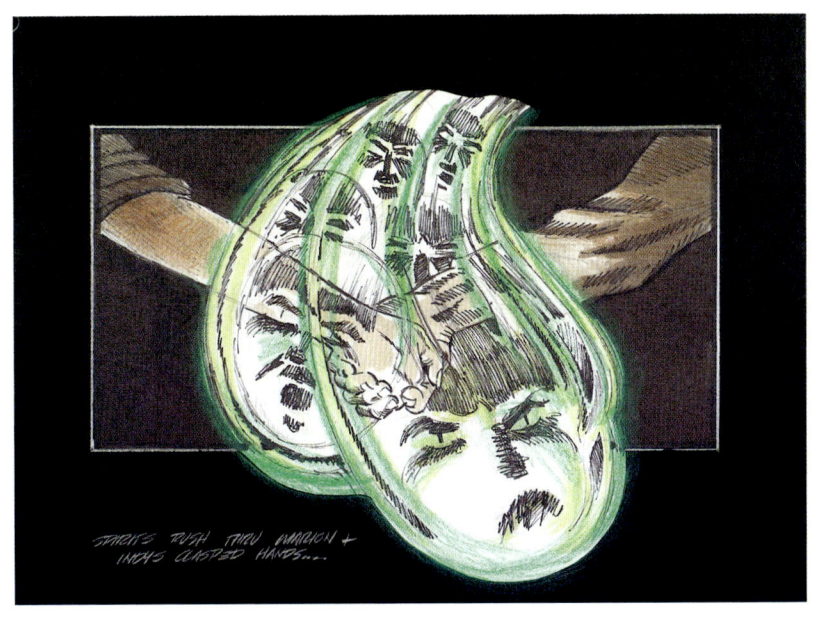

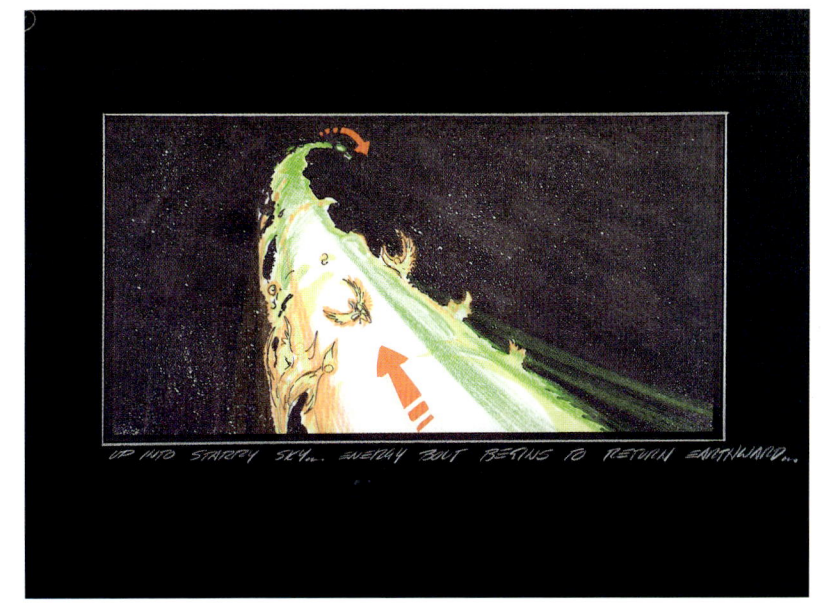

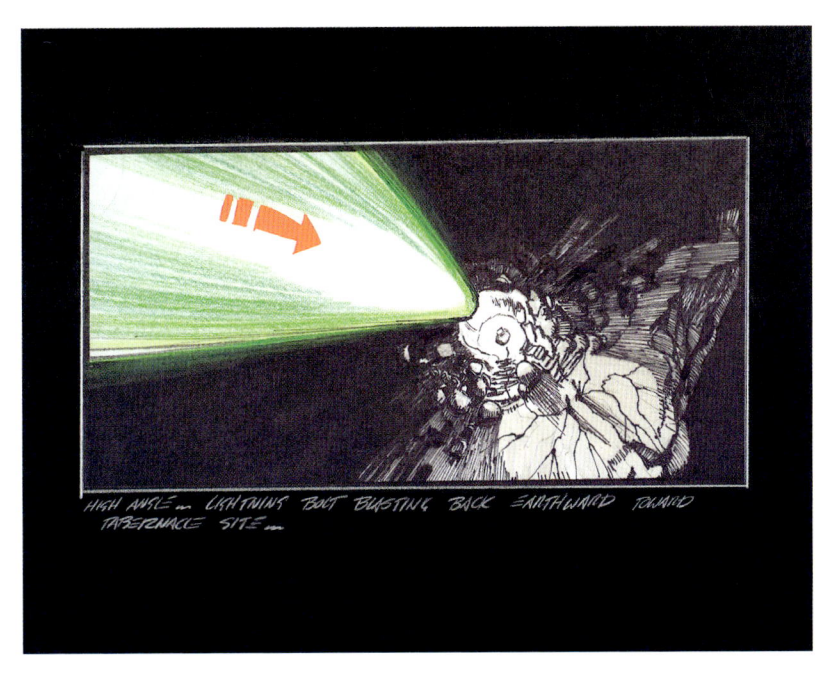

BOLT BLAST DIRECTLY BACK INTO ARC...

MIST FLOATS BACK INTO ARC...

CLOSE ON THE ARC... TOP IN PLACE... ALMOST ASLEEP...

(COSMIC CONCUSSION)

REVERSE ANGLE... MARION LOOKS AT INDY... TEARS IN HER EYES...

122 FRESH FORCES IN AMERICAN FILMMAKING

THRU A RING OF ANGELS...

(R.L.A.)

Verreaux worked on several more films with Spielberg, including *E.T.: The Extra-Terrestrial*, *Poltergeist* (both 1982), and *Empire of the Sun* (1987), as well on as the last two *Back to the Future* films (1989, 1990). By then, however, he was ready to expand his vision into the field of production design. As Verreaux says: "I'd imagine what the set would look like when I drew boards, and then it would look like that. Eventually I started saying, 'I can do that myself.'"

RAIDERS OF THE LOST ARK 123

Rain Man 1988

DIRECTOR Barry Levinson
STORYBOARDS unattributed

BELOW AND OPPOSITE In these unattributed storyboards for the "Who's on First" sequence, the text refers not to the scene's exact dialogue, but to the central instructions.

The "Who's on First" sequence from *Rain Man* is a pivotal one in the film's story arc, yet it is a talky shot sequence set in the Walbrook mental hospital featuring rapid-fire dialogue between Raymond Babbitt (Dustin Hoffman) and his brother Charlie (Tom Cruise), as Charlie's girlfriend Susanna (Valeria Golino) looks on and social worker Vern (Michael D. Roberts) tries to help out.

Raymond, described as a "high-functioning" autistic, has an ability to memorize complex sequences, and repeats the quick-fire Abbott and Costello routine whenever he gets nervous. It's not until the end of the film, however, and after several repetitions, that Raymond begins to understand that the skit is funny—and why, marking a breakthrough in his relationship with Charlie.

The sequence storyboarded here describes the first time Charlie meets Raymond (that Charlie remembers); he has talked his way into the hospital after being cut out of his father's $3m will in favor of the brother he never knew he had. His motives, at this stage of the film, are not entirely pure. Raymond reacts in panic after Charlie touches his books by embarking on the routine.

Barry Levinson shot *Rain Man* after the success of *Good Morning, Vietnam* (1987); it was a more intimate affair, its careful planning and tour-de-force performances winning four Academy Awards (including Best Film, Best Director, and Best Actor for Hoffman).

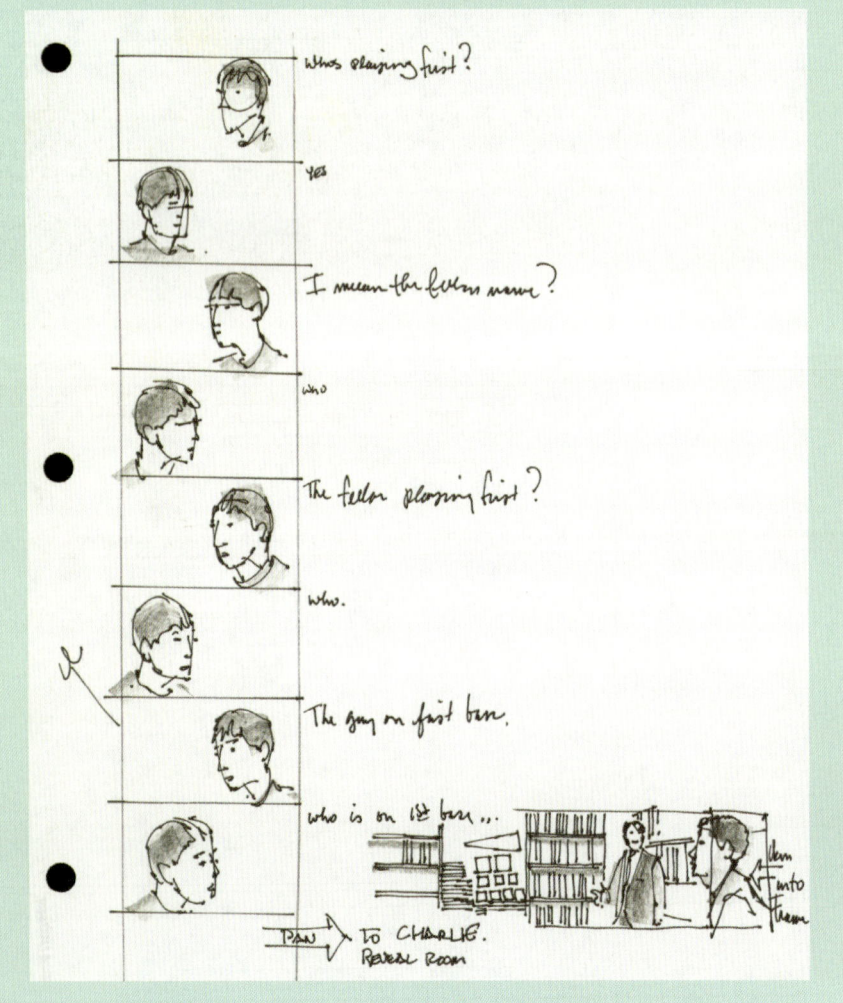

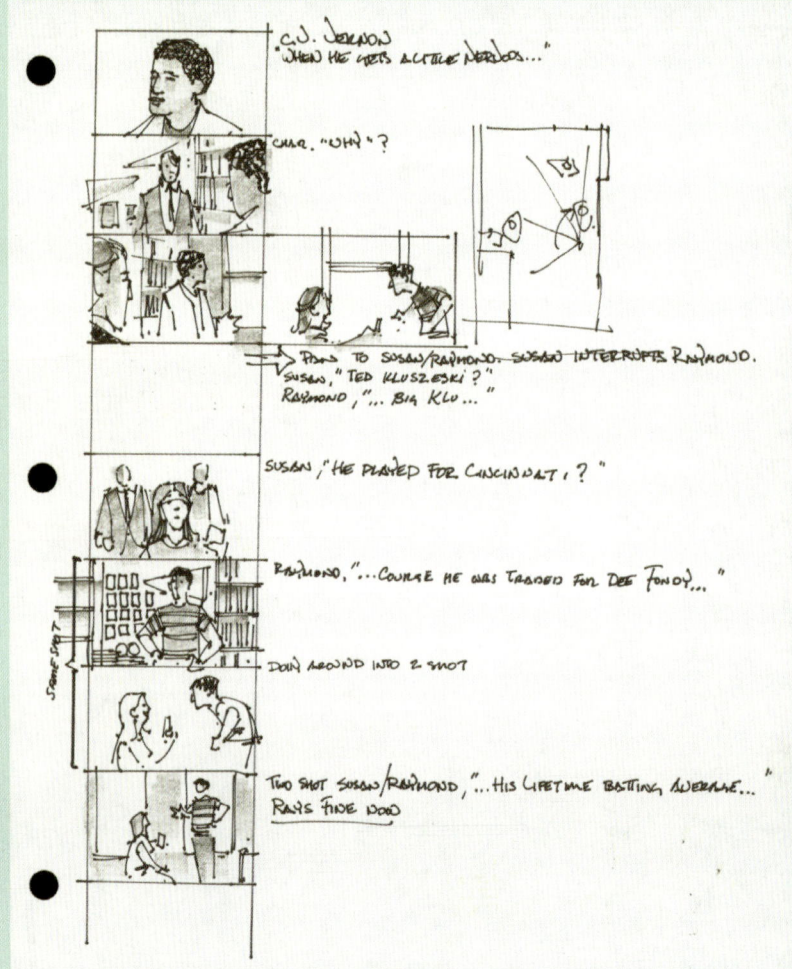

124 FRESH FORCES IN AMERICAN FILMMAKING

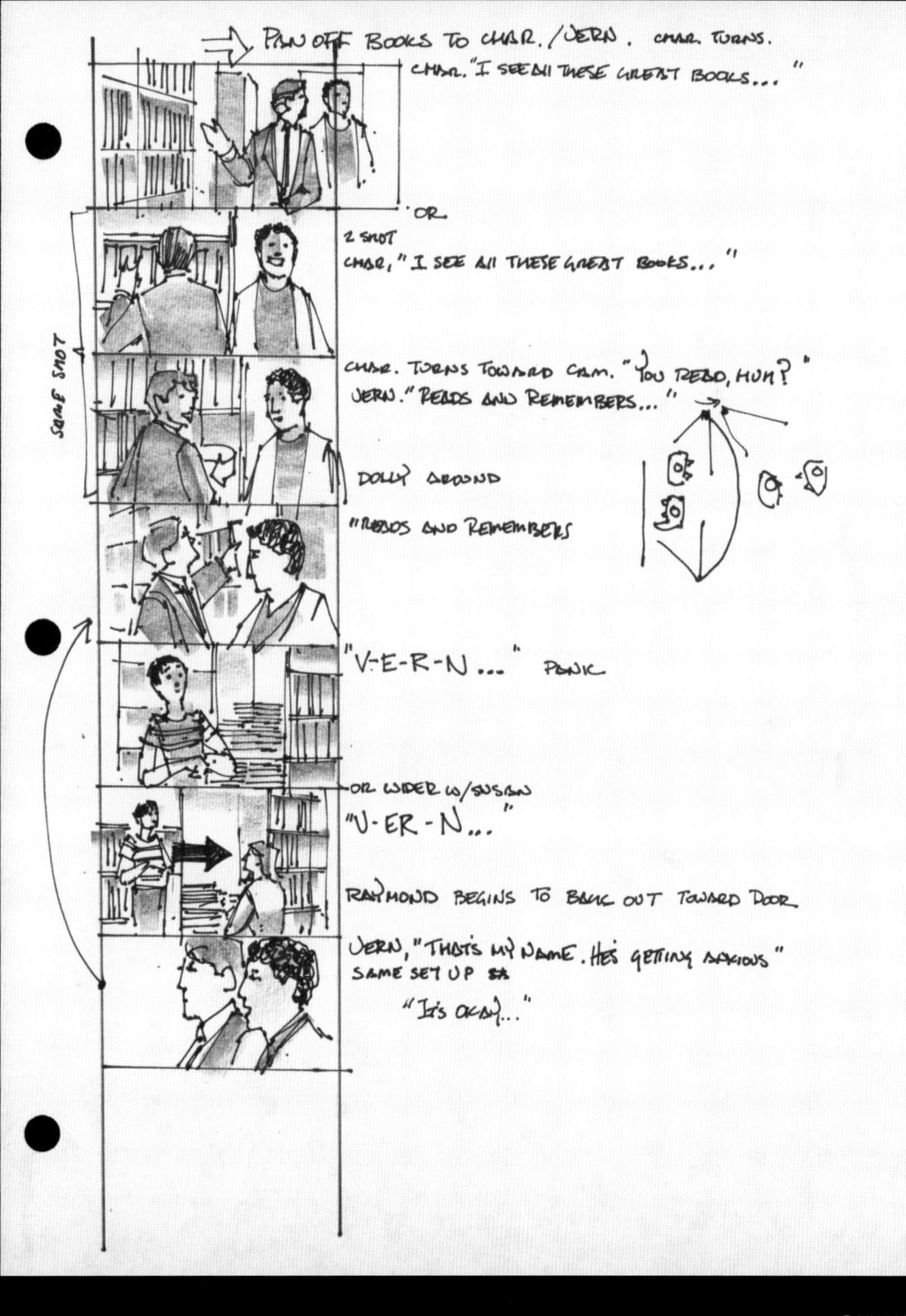

PAN OFF BOOKS TO CHAR./VERN. CHAR. TURNS.
CHAR. "I SEE ALL THESE GREAT BOOKS..."

OR
2 SHOT
CHAR. "I SEE ALL THESE GREAT BOOKS..."

SAME SHOT

CHAR. TURNS TOWARD CAM. "YOU READ, HUH?"
VERN. "READS AND REMEMBERS..."

DOLLY AROUND
"READS AND REMEMBERS"

"V-E-R-N..." PANIC

OR WIDER W/ SUSAN
"V-ER-N..."

RAYMOND BEGINS TO BACK OUT TOWARD DOOR

VERN, "THAT'S MY NAME. HE'S GETTING ANXIOUS"
SAME SET UP SA
"It's okay..."

RAIN MAN 125

The Crow 1994

DIRECTOR Alex Proyas
STORYBOARDS unattributed (possibly Hanna Strauss); production design by Alex McDowell

A dark, supernatural film—a reinvention of a comic book tale—*The Crow* tells the story of a rock musician called Eric Draven (Brandon Lee), who is murdered on Devil's Night and comes back to life a year later to avenge his own death and that of his fiancée. They were due to marry the day after their deaths, on Halloween.

The Crow was the first major film to be directed by the Australian Alex Proyas, who became known for his stylish, dark-edged visual esthetic in this and later films, including *Dark City* (1998) and *I, Robot* (2004). Gothic to its core, Draven's posthumous look includes Joker-like harlequin face paint and black clothing. To match the mood, the soundtrack for this cult supernatural horror fantasy, which also topped the charts, is studded by tracks from The Cure and the The Jesus and Mary Chain.

The film was very successful for the genre (grossing over $50m in the U.S.) and prompted a sequel (not directed by Proyas), *The Crow: City of Angels*, two years later. The original movie became significant in film history because of the death of its star, Brandon Lee (the son of Hong Kong kung fu legend Bruce), on the Wilmington, North Carolina set due to a shooting accident. Although *The Crow*'s shoot was not yet completed, Proyas and the producers decided to go ahead and finish it, and Lee's death certainly infuses a dark film with an extra layer of sadness and poignancy.

The storyboards shown here are unique in their comic-book styling and thumbnail sizing. The sixty black-and-white illustrations are read from top to bottom, left to right; it is possible that they have been cut up and reordered and are more suggestive than instructional.

126 FRESH FORCES IN AMERICAN FILMMAKING

THE CROW - © EDWARD R. PRESSMAN FILM CORPORATION

1A. MOVE IN ON DOOR
1B. POLICE TAPE RIPPED AWAY 
2. REVEAL ERIC 
3. C.U. ERIC 
4. ERIC ENTERS 
5. CAT MEOWS - ERIC LOOKS DOWN 
6. CAT WATCHES 
7. HAND REACHES OUT - TOUCHES CAT 
8. OPTICAL FLASH 
9. FLASH CUT - HAND STRUMS GUITAR STRINGS 
10. FLASH CUT - MOVE IN ON ERIC 
11. FLASH CUT - GUN FIRES

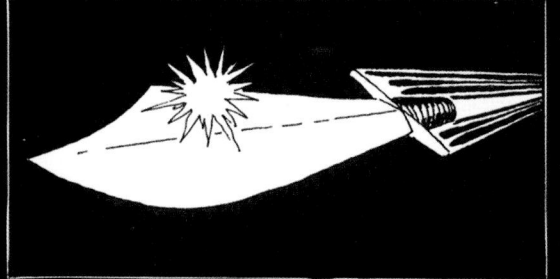

Panel	Caption
12	ERIC RECOVERS FROM MEMORY FLASH - PICKS UP CAT
13	HOLDS CAT - SUDDEN JOLT
14	MOVE IN ON EMPTY DOOR
15	OPTICAL FLASH
16	SHELLY & ERIC MAKE LOVE - SAME DOOR
17	FLASH CUT - GUITAR STRUMS
18	FLASH CUT - KNIFE THROWN
19	FLASH CUT - P.O.V. FALLS OUT OF WINDOW
20A	ERIC DROPS CAT...
20B	...CAT LANDS
22	E.C.U. BLOOD DROPS ON FLOOR
23	FLASH CUT - ERIC DEAD IN RAIN
24	FLASH BULB
25A	ERIC PINNED TO WALL
25B	MOVE IN - HE PULLS KNIFE
26	MEMORIES TOO STRONG
27	LOOKS UP

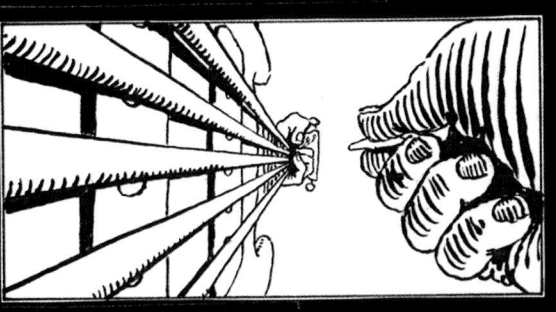

	33. ERIC RAISES ARMS	39. ERIC SHOT
28. E.C.U. FLASH BULB	34. HAND GRABBED	40. MOVE IN - WINDOW BREAKS
29. SHELLY SLAPPED	35. ERIC ALONE - ARMS RAISED	41. SLO MO - PAN WITH ERIC FALLING
30. SHELLY RAPED	36. ARM GRABBED	42A. ERIC FALLS...
31. GUN RISES INTO FRAME	37. TRIGGER SQUEEZED	42B. ...AWAY FROM CAM
32. MOVE INTO BARREL	38. SHOTS LIGHT UP FIGURES	43. FLASH BULB

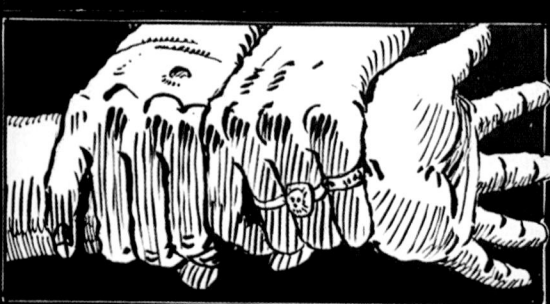

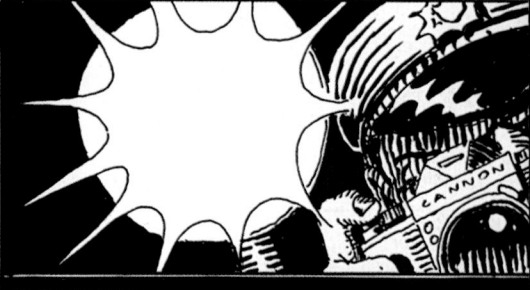

44. ROACH PAST ERIC ON FLOOR 
50. COWBOY HOLDS KNIFE
45. FLUTTERING WINGS O.S. 
51. ERIC - DIALOGUE
46. BLACK SHAPE GRABS ROACH 
52. COWBOY - DIALOGUE
47. CROW EATS ROACH 
53. COWBOY THROWS
48. ERIC LOOKS UP 
54. SEVERS STRING
49. SHADOWY SKULL-COWBOY
55. MASK FALLS

The visuals and vision of the film, from comic book to screen, are intense, and the storyboards, in pen and ink, reflect the darkness of the project. *The Crow* started life as a 1989 underground comic book series, written and drawn by the artist James O'Barr as a way of coping with his own girlfriend's death.

THE CROW 129

Great Eccentrics

Throughout the 1970s and particularly in the 1980s, as Thatcherism—the small state/free market/privatization policies pursued by the British Conservative Government under Margaret Thatcher—set in and punk took off, British filmmakers seemed to move in two distinct directions. There was the growing social realism of films from directors such as Ken Loach (*Kes*, 1969), Stephen Frears (*My Beautiful Laundrette*, 1985), and Mike Leigh (*High Hopes*, 1988), counterbalanced by the escapism of craft-laden Merchant-Ivory productions (*A Room with a View*, 1985) and the Oscar-winning geographical ambitions of *Gandhi* (1982) and *The Mission* (1986).

But, as time has only served to underscore, there's nothing quite like an English eccentric to start a bonfire of the vanities. The directors Ken Russell, Derek Jarman, and Terry Gilliam (who became a naturalized British citizen in 1968) were all outspoken iconoclasts who fought hard to realize their visions.

Ken Russell's outrageous X-rated 1971 film *The Devils*, in which deranged nun Vanessa Redgrave does some indecent things with a crucifix (and a scorched shinbone) whilst entertaining naughty notions about priapic priest Oliver Reed in seventeenth century France, actually gave the young artist and Slade School of Fine Art graduate Derek Jarman his start in the art department. Cut and slashed, X-rated and denounced from the pulpit, the fate of *The Devils* didn't deter Russell, known for going wild when unleashed, from making further hay with films including *The Boy Friend* (also 1971) and *Tommy* and *Lisztomania* (both 1975). The outspoken director continued to battle on until his last big studio film *Altered States* (1980) marked a downsizing in his budgets.

Sebastiane (1976), originally conceived as gay porn but turned by Derek Jarman into something entirely different, was the first feature from a unique voice that grew throughout the seven years it took to make *Caravaggio* (1986) and

Edward II (1991), by which time Jarman had become very ill (he died in 1994). But Jarman's art—he was a contemporary of David Hockney's at the Slade—was about more than politics or sexuality (although it had a lot to say on both fronts) and he had a resounding effect on how film is perceived as an art form today.

Terry Gilliam moved to the UK from his native America (he eventually renounced his American passport in 2003). An artist and animator, he started working with Monty Python, and after learning his filmmaking craft on the sets of the Python movies (*Monty Python and the Holy Grail*, 1975; *Life of Brian*, 1979), he set forth with his vastly imaginative, fantastical trilogy of *Time Bandits* (1981), *Brazil* (1985), and *The Adventures of Baron Munchausen*

ABOVE Derek Jarman photographed at his home on Charing Cross Road, London, circa 1986.

The Boy Friend 1971

DIRECTOR Ken Russell
STORYBOARDS Shirley Russell

After the outcry over his sex-and-Satan romp *The Devils* (also semi-released in 1971), the eccentric British director Ken Russell abruptly changed tack for his next film. As if to confound expectations, his light-as-air adaptation of Sandy Wilson's stage musical *The Boy Friend* saw Russell give the model Twiggy her big acting break in a lavish 1920s-set confection of elaborately-costumed song and dance numbers.

Russell's *The Boy Friend* wraps Wilson's play—which is about schoolgirls at "La Caprice" villa getting ready for a party—inside a story about a rundown theater in Portsmouth, which is staging the show in front of big-cheese Hollywood producer Mr. Cecil B. De Thrill. Twiggy plays understudy Polly Browne, in love with delivery boy Tony (Christopher Gable). In typically exuberant Ken Russell fashion, the film's Busby Berkeley-style dance sequences explode into money-is-no-object fantasy riffs that jump off the stage with the most extraordinary costumes designed by Ken's wife, Shirley.

Despite its sumptuous, over-the-top visuals, *The Boy Friend* was regarded as a commercial disappointment on release, and Russell's 136-minute cut was pared back by the studio. It certainly didn't dent his career, however, and Russell's star continued in the ascendant with the rock opera *Tommy* in 1975.

Shirley Russell, generally acknowledged to be one of Britain's costume design greats, produced the costume-focused storyboards reproduced on these pages, working directly from Ken Russell's screenplay. The sequence is probably the film's most elaborate, although there are many to choose from.

Ken and Shirley had first met at art school and married in 1956. While bringing up five children, Shirley worked with Ken on everything from his first, televised "biographies" of the great composers to his most ambitious productions, from *Women in Love* (1969) to *The Devils*, *The Boy Friend*, and onto *Tommy*. They divorced in 1978 and Shirley died in 2002; Ken Russell passed away in 2011.

OPPOSITE Ken Russell's dance sequences don't just unspool on the stage of the Theatre Royal in Portsmouth; they also take place in Cecil B. De Thrill's head as he plans his own lavish film extravaganza.

LEFT British director Ken Russell examines strips of film.

132 GREAT ECCENTRICS

RIVIERA

1) **CLAPPER BOARD**.

CLAPS!

[clapper board showing: 1 | 1, RIVIERA, DR. DE THRILL]

2)

REHEARSAL IN PROGRESS.

LARGE EMPTY STUDIO.

CUT TO 24 GIRLS DOING HIGH KICKS IN V FORMATION IN SILVER & BLUE COSTUMES.

3) OBECTS PASS BY IN FRONT OF KICKING GIRLS.

FAN'S ETC. PUSHED BY STAGE HANDS.

4) BLINDED BY LIGHTS WE GRADUALLY MAKE OUT DE THRILL & ENTOURAGE – SHIRLEY TEMPLE & AL JILSIN REHEARSING NEAR BY.

BABY TAKE A BOW.

MAMMY

5) TAP TA

GIRLS IN TRAIN ROUTINE AGAINST SMOKE

CUT IN SHOTS OF TRAINS.

6). CAR GOES BY WITH ALL THE CAST IN CARNIVAL COSTUMES

COMES IN THROUGH OPEN STUDIO DOOR.

CHUG   CHUG.

7) DE THRILL ON CRANE. SWOOPING TOWARD CAMERA.

8) CAMERA SWOOPS TOWARD PLANE.
24 GIRLS ON PLANE DRESSED IN BLACK AND SILVER.

OPPOSITE AND LEFT Here, in a tribute to the Fred Astaire/Ginger Rogers sequence "Flying Down to Rio," the showgirls ride the wings of a giant biplane in a spirited recreation/homage.

9/ ANOTHER ANGLE OF DE THRILL ON CRANE

10/ ANOTHER ANGLE OF PLANE

TOMMY e MAISIE ON TAIL-PLANE?

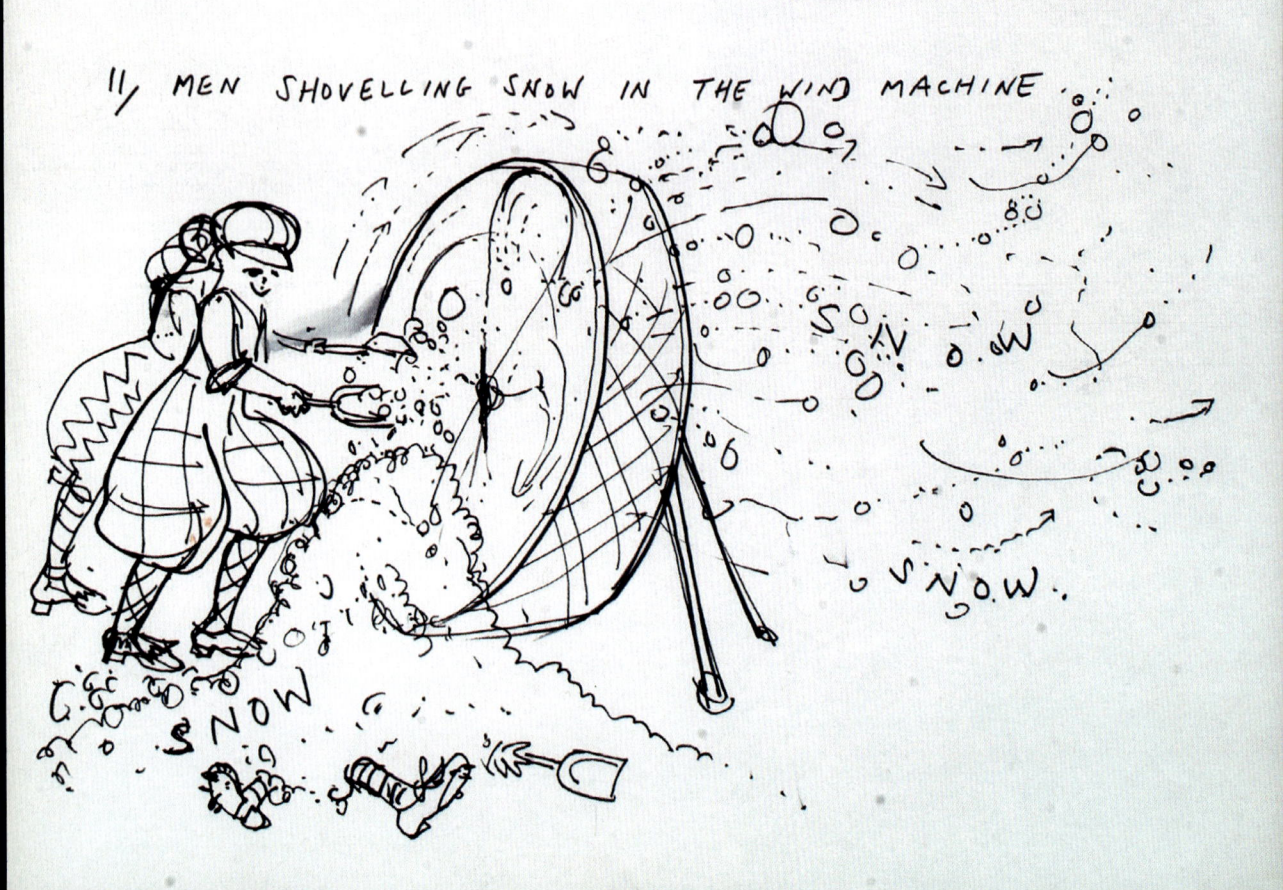

11/ MEN SHOVELLING SNOW IN THE WIND MACHINE

SNOW

SNOW

12) DE THRILL AND CREW IN BLIZZARD ON END OF CRANE.

13 3rd shot of Plane in Snow – Zoom in to Polly and Tony in Silver Flying Gear

THE END

OPPOSITE AND LEFT Shirley Russell's storyboards would appear to be the original plans for this over-the-top sequence (one of many), in which the main players take flight in De Thrill's imagination and come off the stage into his film scenarios—in which he himself appears.

Brazil 1985

DIRECTOR Terry Gilliam
STORYBOARDS Terry Gilliam

BELOW Surrounded by scattered papers, Terry Gilliam works on storyboards.

The renowned American-born director Terry Gilliam started out as an illustrator and animator, later (after his move to Britain) providing the distinctive animation sequences for *Monty Python's Flying Circus* and co-directing *Monty Python and the Holy Grail* (1975). Naturally, therefore, his imagination is also very closely linked with his pen, and he storyboards to help realize the complicated visions expressed in his films—a remarkable body of work that now includes *Time Bandits* (1981), *Brazil* (1985), *The Adventures of Baron Munchausen* (1988), *The Fisher King* (1991), *The Imaginarium of Doctor Parnassus* (2009), and *The Zero Theorum* (2013).

"When I start writing, when I start to imagine a film, I begin to draw it," says Gilliam, explaining his process. "And a lot of new ideas happen when I'm drawing. They change the story. Then, when I start to shoot the film, those boards I've produced are the thing I can hang onto as chaos descends around me. With them, I know what I have to do in the shot. I can see through the disorder."

Not, stresses Gilliam, that his storyboards are cast in stone (or rather, drawn with pen and pencil on paper): "There's a danger that you can be trapped by the boards," he says. "If you can see the scene would be better another way, okay, change it. But it's astonishing how much they help the production team. I can see the film before I shoot it and the storyboard is the image I have in my head. It's the best way to communicate your ideas and give your team ideas too. The people I work with need to know they have space to create."

Set in a dystopian retro-future, *Brazil* is an at-times savage satire of visual and creative brilliance. Writer-director Terry Gilliam remembers the film being born of a growing frustration and anger at the way the world was. It's a story of bureaucracy gone mad, as clerk Sam (Jonathan Pryce) tries to correct an administrative error and himself becomes an enemy of the state.

In a way, Gilliam's vision is even more apt today than it was on release in 1985. Or rather, partial-release: *Brazil* is also known for its complicated post-production life, when the director was forced to defend his vision after the studio refused to release it in the U.S. and eventually attempted its own edit.

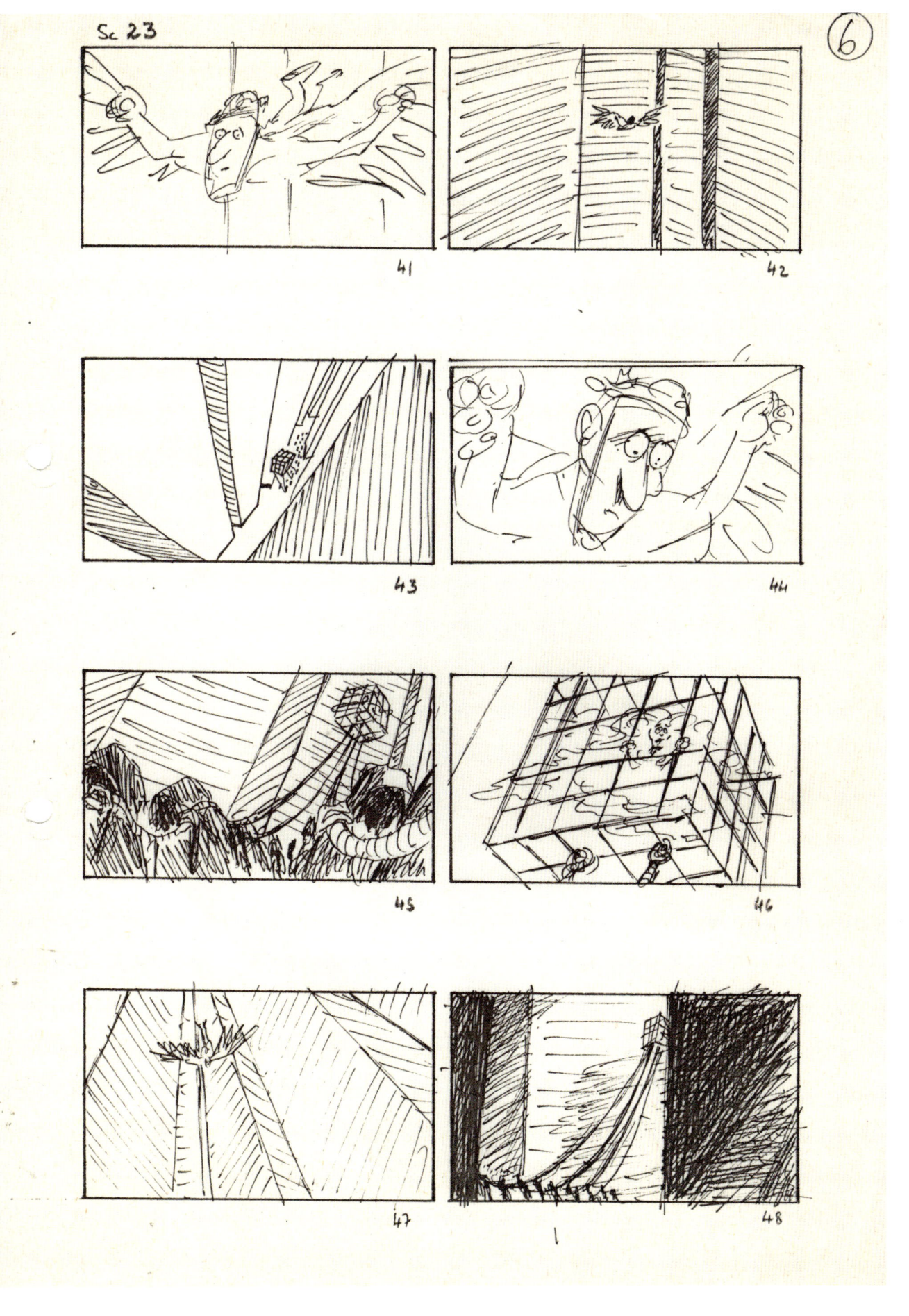

LEFT One of the film's key visual sequences is Sam's dream world, which starts out wide and expansive and free in the clouds, unlike the real world in which he lives. However, this dream world is soon interrupted by dark monoliths. Says Gilliam: "It becomes a labyrinth of corridors and streets that seem to go nowhere and everywhere. In the labyrinth are what we call the Forces of Darkness, Sam's nightmare images, including baby-face creatures, which are the real force of darkness."

BRAZIL 139

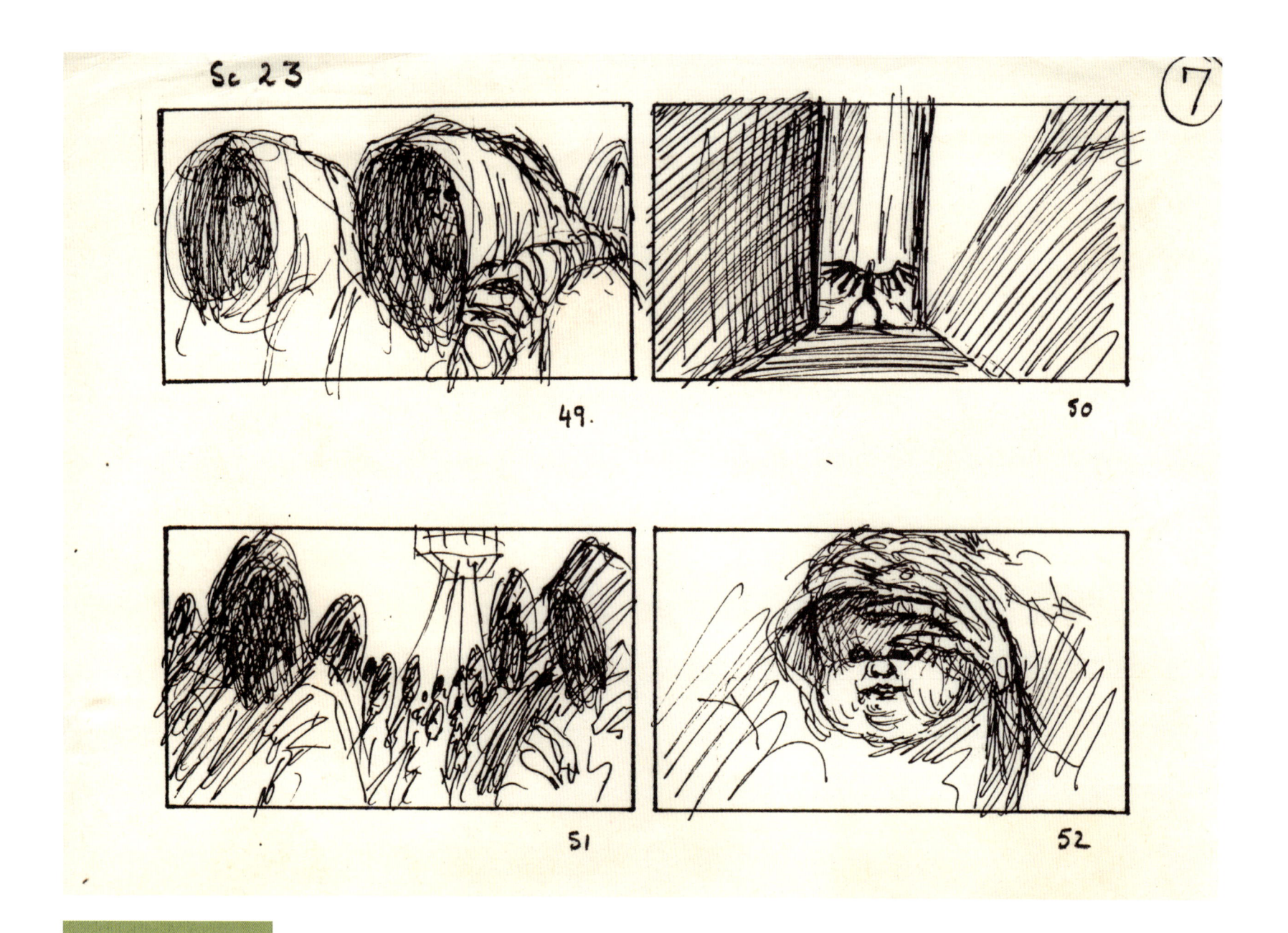

ABOVE AND OPPOSITE Gilliam was inspired to create his "Buddha-faced babies" by a memory he had of seeing a rotting doll's head in his parents' back yard. He modeled the baby faces on this, blending the doll's head with a Buddha face. "You had this mixture of something that was almost benign, combined with something that's evil and rotting at the same time."

140 GREAT ECCENTRICS

BRAZIL 141

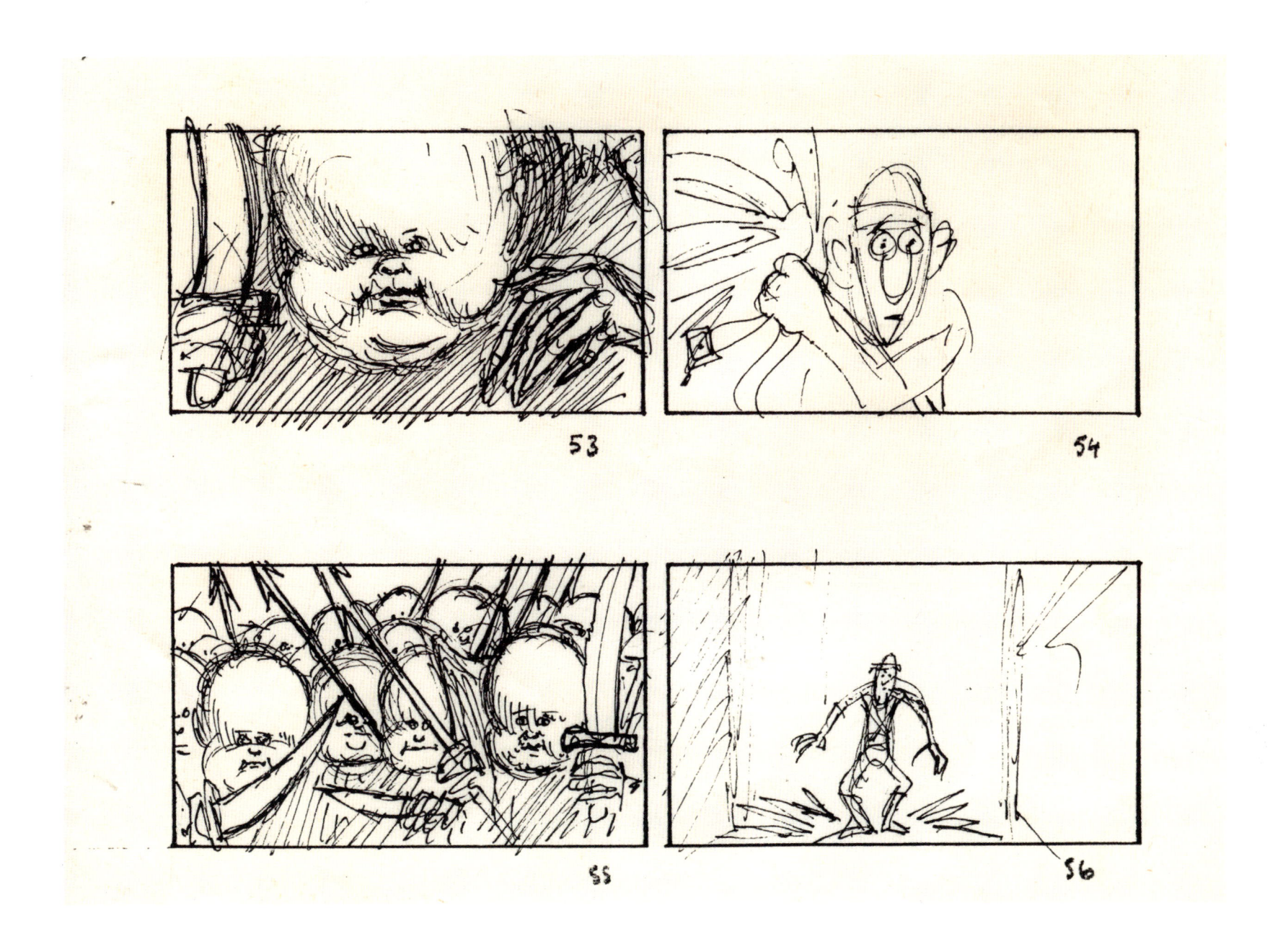

Caravaggio 1986

DIRECTOR Derek Jarman
STORYBOARDS Christopher Hobbs

BELOW Scene 1: The proposed opening shot in storyboards drawn by Christopher Hobbs in 1978 shows St. Peter's Basilica as a distant view on the horizon; the camera moves down through the arches to a craning shot of Valentino's studio-factory where Caravaggio worked as a boy, making paintings for tourists. The interior shot was to "be made entirely out of drawings with no individual architecture, that was my conceit," says Hobbs. These boards were also used to raise money for the project.

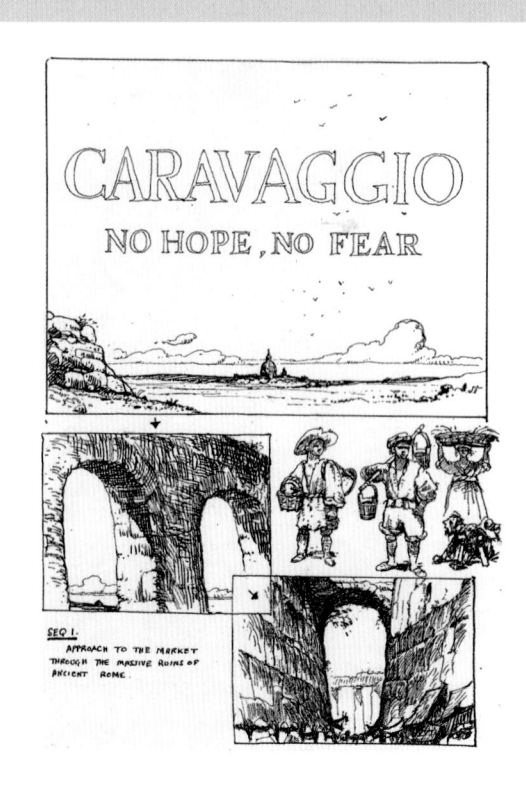

The artist and production designer Christopher Hobbs enjoyed a lengthy collaboration with Derek Jarman, from the director's first full-fledged film, *Sebastiane*, in 1976 until his death in 1994 (they had previously worked together on two Ken Russell films). *Caravaggio*, released a decade on from their first film, was the most enduring of their projects, with a seven-year gestation period as they, alongside producer Nicholas Ward-Jackson, looked for ways to finance it. The storyboards on these pages date from different periods during that process, which started in 1978.

A recreation/reimagining of the Baroque artist's life, starring Nigel Terry, Sean Bean, and a young Tilda Swinton, the look of *Caravaggio* was deeply informed by the painter's work (particularly with regard to lighting). The first storyboards shown on these pages date from Hobbs's initial, more elaborate vision of the film, drawn as he sat on top of a hill in Tuscany, imagining an expensive production set in the great palaces of Rome.

As time, and script drafts, went by, the vision changed, and the film was finally shot for under £1m (roughly $1.5m) in a leaky warehouse with a corrugated iron roof in London's Isle of Dogs, where Canary Wharf now stands. Shot just as the developers were moving in, the entire film had to be redubbed because of the persistent ambient noise. Still, today, Hobbs feels that despite—or perhaps because of—the constrictions (his art department ended up with a month of preparation on a £35,000 budget), *Caravaggio* is still one of the strongest evocations of Rome as it must have been like at that time; Hobbs, a self-taught artist, drew the Caravaggio paintings displayed in the film himself (they needed to be freshly-colored, and sometimes half-drawn).

The early boards shown here were also used to try to raise money for *Caravaggio*, while "the last boards [drawn in 1985] may be more simple, but I believe they are better drawn," says Hobbs now. "And none are done like 'proper' storyboards at all, which tend to follow the action very closely. I was giving an overall view. I could show Derek what he was going to get; at the end of it, we had a very clear idea of what it was going to look like."

The lighting was crucial in *Caravaggio*. Jarman, says Hobbs, "was never very strong on story, to be honest. Funding was always a problem for us and while most directors make more and more expensive films, Derek's just got cheaper and cheaper. He didn't think of them as films, though. He thought of them as paintings and light."

142 GREAT ECCENTRICS

LEFT Scene 10 from the 1978 storyboards shows the interior of Cardinal del Monte's office, where Caravaggio threatens the prelate who takes his knife in exchange for a painting (this scene appears in the final film). Del Monte was Caravaggio's patron, but he also had a sexually ambiguous relationship with the young artist. The walls of his study are covered with objects and statues for which Hobbs eventually lacked the money in the 1986 finished film: "We couldn't afford casts of ancient objects by then. So I disguised our problem by making giant covered 'statues' that were eighty percent wrapping," recalls Hobbs. "Much more stylish than the first version!"

10 (b) DEL MONTE HANDS BACK CARAVAGGIO'S DAGGER.

CARAVAGGIO 143

LEFT A later drawing of Cardinal del Monte's office, "Lit as if by a tall window."

LEFT AND OPPOSITE *Caravaggio* features several, very deliberate anachronisms, including in Scene 27 (left) and Scenes 31 and 35 (opposite). In the former, two people sit at a table with waiters in modern dinner jackets behind them. One is Cardinal del Monte (Michael Gough) and the other is Giustiniani (Nigel Davenport) the banker; they are discussing the price of paintings using a gold calculator. In the latter, the critic Baglione (Jonathan Hyde) is shown typing his invective in the bath. Says Hobbs: "Derek wanted him writing with a quill pen, but I suggested an old-fashioned typewriter would clack in a very 'vicious' way. It's also a visual joke on the famous painting of Marat in his bath, which has nothing to do with the story whatsoever! Baglione is also shown here dressing for the party, for which I created a mirror set."

144 GREAT ECCENTRICS

LEFT Scene 6: This depicts Caravaggio's room in Rome— "little more than a squat really, where a tourist is about to buy one of his paintings."

Straw mattresses piled on top of one another. DIRTY!

Floor painted, or possibly with real planks. (scaffold planks?)

The Squat. This has discoloured green distemper walls. The woodwork is natural grey.

Baglione's mirrored Boudoir. Shot through 2-way mirror on wall behind 5 linked mirrors.

Baglione's Bathroom.

CARAVAGGIO 145

Long Vatican Corridor
/ drapes lit through hanging
muslin 'windows'.
Doorcase flats.

White draped Apse

Black Drapes

White draped Table

Vatican Interior.

146 GREAT ECCENTRICS

huge
chandeliers
Hung very low.

Del Monte's
Bed.
(all drapery).
Blackout Behind.

LEFT "This shows the main Vatican interior which we lit using two huge chandeliers which we found in the Isle of Dogs warehouse when we moved in [to shoot]," recalls Hobbs. "The floor was supposed to be shiny marble but we only had an uneven concrete surface, so I flooded it with water and it worked, as long as the actors didn't move. They thought it was quite fun—they really hadn't seen such cheap things before, although we just used it for the high shots looking down." There is, notes Hobbs, almost no architecture at all in this sequence, and the actors were lit as they walked in and out of the light source.

ABOVE Scene 44: Cardinal del Monte's bedroom, with its "rather grand" bed. This is direction for a sequence in which the Cardinal has been woken up after Elena, "Caravaggio's girl," played by Tilda Swinton, has been found drowned in the river, presumably by Caravaggio's jealous lover Ranuccio (Sean Bean).

CARAVAGGIO 147

The Adventures of Baron Munchausen 1988

DIRECTOR Terry Gilliam
STORYBOARDS Terry Gilliam

Set in an unnamed war-torn European city in the late eighteenth century, *The Adventures of Baron Munchausen* opens in a theater where the real-life Baron interrupts a fanciful rendition of his life story. With the Turkish guns pounding, he eventually escapes to the Moon in a hot-air balloon ship, with the ultimate ambition of saving the city.

"My storyboards are less and less definite as time goes by and I don't want to be too precise," says Gilliam. "I do little arrow movements to indicate the camera movement, but I normally put that in later."

Here, for example, Gilliam has suggested rather than prescribed certain elements—indicating that the ship will "knock over brick chimney stack—possibly crash through exposed rafters." "Could pull back from tighter shot of balloon" is another direction, noting it will be a blue-screen shot.

"We always put the storyboards up for what we're going to shoot that day so people can see what we're doing," Gilliam explains. "I tend to talk less when I'm directing, so they're there as a guidance."

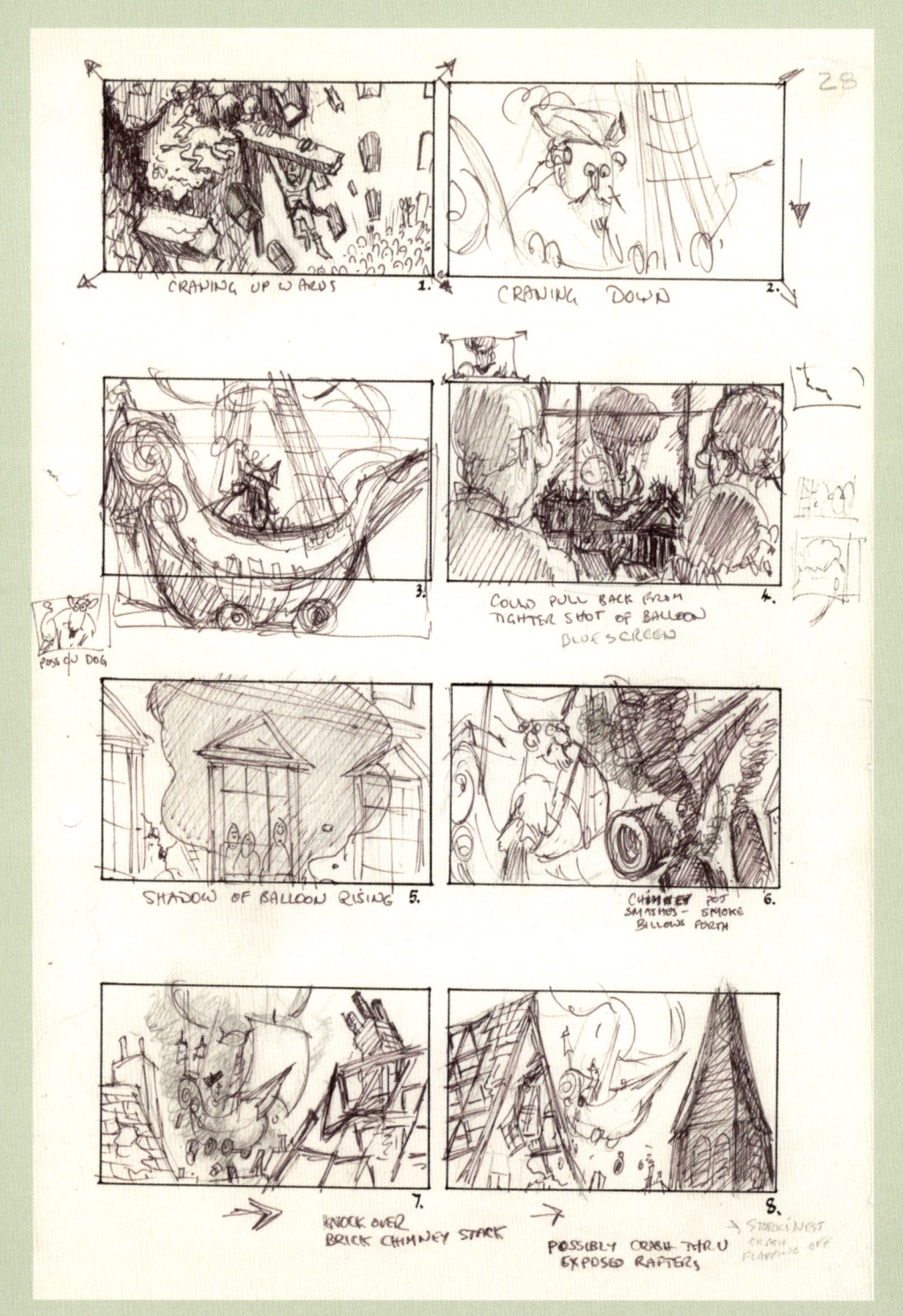

148 GREAT ECCENTRICS

LEFT AND OPPOSITE
The "Escape to the Moon" sequence, in *The Adventures of Baron Munchausen*.

The art of storyboarding started with animation and it is still extensively used on all forms of animation today—unlike, say, action films, where storyboarding is often confined to the development of tricky shots or effects work. Animated features, whether they be 3D, cel, or stop-motion (or claymation), are storyboarded from first frame to last, using teams of artists devoted to the development of story and character. The storyboard artist is crucial to the animated feature, working to create character and develop the story without the set-in-stone scripts of the live action world.

The rebirth of the modern animated feature—mostly associated with the live-action/animated hybrid *Who Framed Roger Rabbit* (1988), closely followed by *The Little Mermaid* (1989)—signified giant leaps for the animated film industry in terms of characterization and story, before even the CGI animation pioneered by Pixar came into play. Today, some of the highest-grossing, biggest-ticket films are animated features; the *Ice Age* series (2002–) alone accounts for over $3bn in worldwide revenues. Just as elastic animated characters can out-perform humans, the truly great animated features have no geographical or demographic limitations. As *Wall-E* (2008) demonstrated,

Creatively, animation has been a trailblazer in times when live action has faltered. Those clear lines of story and character are the result of an intense process whereby the head of story at a large studio initially works with up to ten storyboard artists to create a film—from characters to gags to cliffhangers—before it goes to the animation team. In the case of a "story crunch," up to thirty storyboard artists can brainstorm a sequence or a section of a film until it has been laid to rest.

Storyboard artists provide an engine room for the animated feature in which boards come and go quickly and entire sequences can be lost. The important thing, say the artists, is to focus on the end result and not how pretty the boards in hand are (although they are, as the ensuing pages illustrate, invariably remarkable). Despite the array of computer programs available to them, storyboard artists generally prefer to start their roughs in pencil on good old-fashioned paper, and that goes for animation as well as live-action. The result can be scanned, if necessary, and form part of a story-reel in which the film is fully devised before it is "locked down" and goes through to the animation department.

OPPOSITE Aardman's Nick Park pictured with his most famous creations, Wallace and Gromit, in 1995.

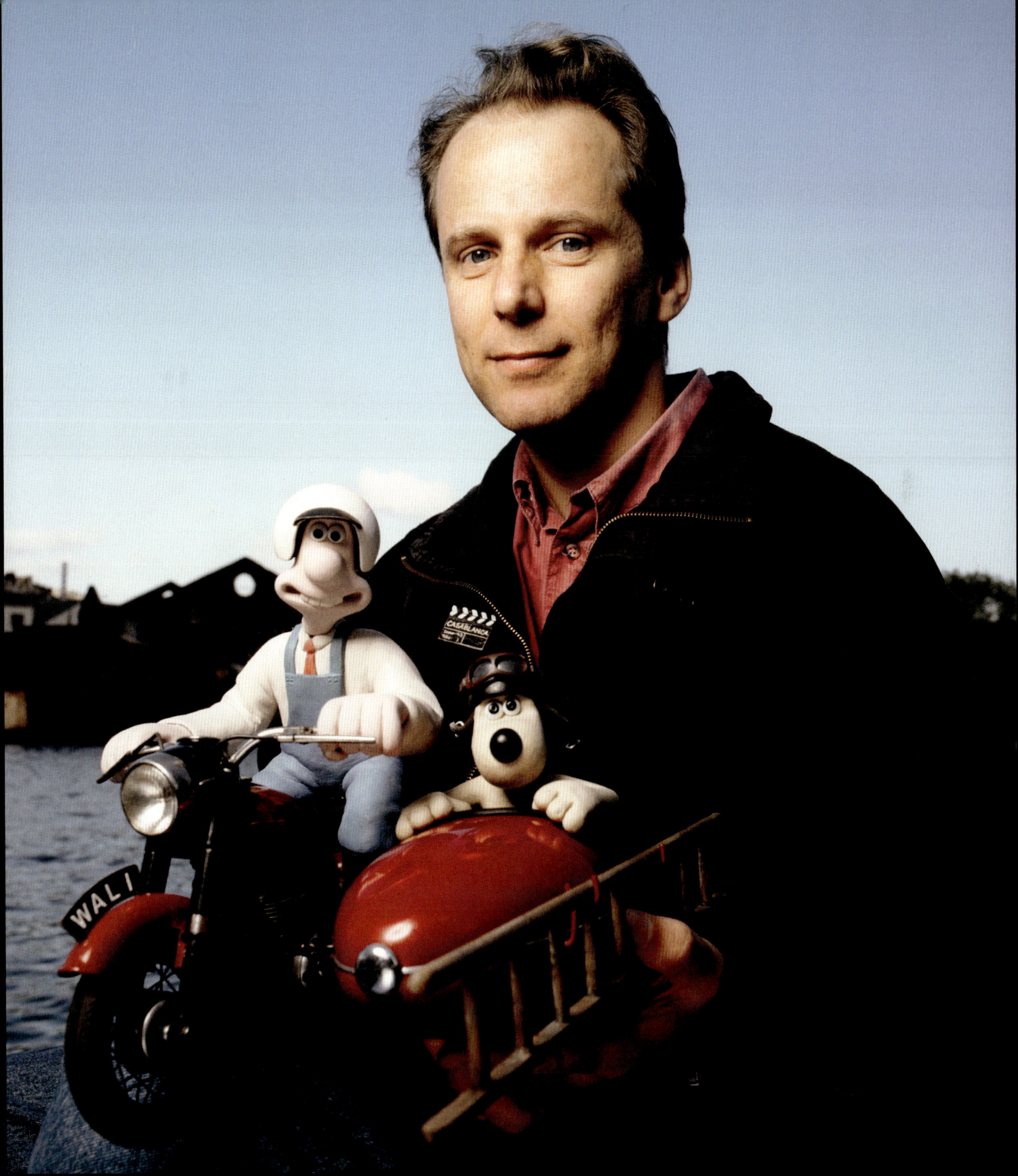
CASABLANCA
WALI

Animal Farm 1954

DIRECTORS John Halas & Joy Batchelor
STORYBOARDS Philip Stapp

The first British animated full-length feature to be released theatrically in the UK, *Animal Farm* also boasted the unusual distinction of being secretly part-funded by the CIA: the agency covertly bought the rights to George Orwell's 1945 novel through producer Louis de Rochemont, who secured the services of British animation company Halas & Batchelor, who were unaware of the ultimate source of much of their funding (Louis de Rochemont also put in some of his own money).

Formed in 1940 by Hungarian émigré John Halas and his wife, Joy Batchelor, Halas & Batchelor initially produced animated propaganda shorts during World War II, and continued to make government information films—along with commercials and sponsored films—after the war and into the 1950s. The company swiftly became the UK's largest animation studio, later taking on commissions from other studios, including the animated *Popeye* (1960) and *Lone Ranger* (1966) TV series.

Production on *Animal Farm* began in 1951, and the film would eventually employ around 100 animators, among them Philip Stapp, who created the storyboards seen on these pages. Generally acclaimed on release, some criticism was leveled at *Animal Farm* at the time due to its more upbeat ending, although it seems likely that that was less a product of the CIA's influence than of a desire by John Halas to give audiences a glimmer of hope for the future.

Philip Stapp was an American artist, animator, and writer who worked in the information division for the Marshall Plan Organization. With Joy Batchelor he wrote the script for *The Shoemaker and the Hatter* (1949), and was key in introducing Louis de Rochemont to Halas & Batchelor and in the studio being chosen to animate *Animal Farm*.

ABOVE AND OPPOSITE Philip Stapp's storyboards for *Animal Farm* are presented here alongside segments of the original script, affording an insight into how Stapp interpreted the dialogue and descriptions.

22. "As for you young porkers, every one of you will scream your lives out at the block before you are a year old."

23. The pigs react in horror to this.

24. They visualise the butcher's shop that awaits them while Major goes on: "Is this land of ours so poor it cannot afford a decent life to those who live on it? No Comrades! A thousand times no!"

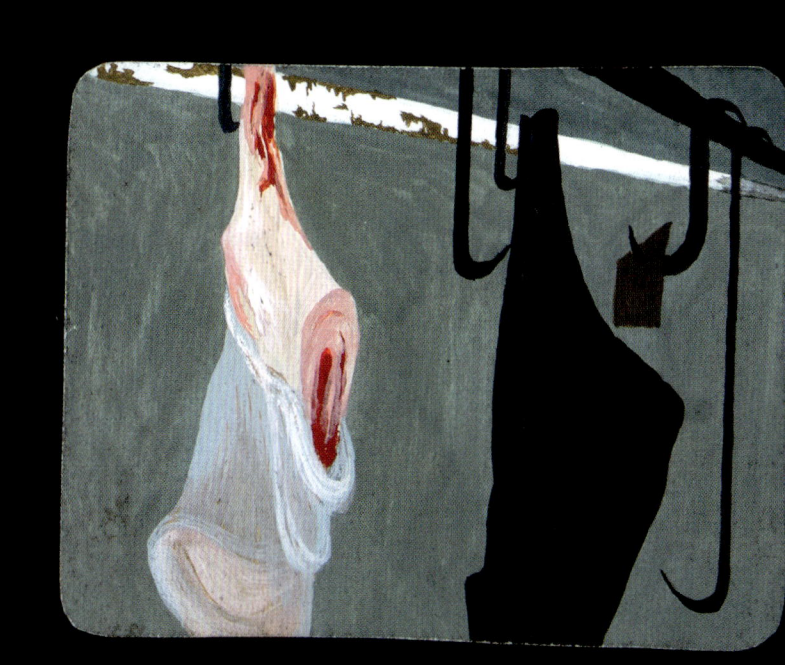

Who Framed Roger Rabbit 1988

DIRECTOR Robert Zemeckis
STORYBOARDS David Russell

David Russell's career encompasses many creative milestones in modern cinema, starting with his feature work on *Return of the Jedi* (1983) through to *The Wolverine* (2013). He has collaborated with the world's great directors (Steven Spielberg, George Lucas, Martin Campbell, and Peter Weir, among others) on some of their most memorable works. In a career that also includes films such as *A River Runs Through It* (1992), *Moulin Rouge!* (2001), and two films in *The Chronicles of Narnia* series—*The Lion, the Witch and the Wardrobe* (2005) and *The Voyage of the Dawn Treader* (2010)—Russell has been a tireless innovator and collaborator in award-winning art departments in San Francisco—where he started out as a post-production storyboard artist on *Jedi*—Los Angeles, and Australia, where he now lives. (Russell's storyboards for *The Voyage of the Dawn Treader* appear on pages 218–221.)

Russell remembers *Who Framed Roger Rabbit* (1988) as a "remarkable production in so many ways." He says he was "swept up in the magic of the show, producing some of my best work to date.... The film's key players—Steven Spielberg, Kathleen Kennedy, [director of animation] Richard Williams, and Robert Zemeckis—were reaching the pinnacle of their creative power. This focused energy was poured into the making of *Who Framed Roger Rabbit*. The film likewise stands as a testament to the advantages of cooperation; competitive studios such as Disney and Warner's agreed to pool resources, a decision which greatly enriched the production."

Russell worked on *Who Framed Roger Rabbit* for about six months with fellow illustrator Marty Kline. "On a strictly technical level, the Toon characters were treated as interactive VFX elements—but they were also actors, and much effort went into staging shots and actions that would blend smoothly with the live players," he recalls. "Jessica Rabbit posed a particular challenge, although this classic femme fatale was the most human-like of the animated retinue. I created some of the initial designs of this memorable character.

"*Who Framed Roger Rabbit* was a revolutionary melding of two divergent mediums. Richard Williams must ultimately be credited with the success of the film; his animation direction, which deftly encompassed multiple styles, was truly a work of genius."

Despite the twenty-five years of technological developments that have taken place since *Who Framed Roger Rabbit* was made, the film's artistic achievement is still remarkable, its characters and gags remaining fresh and funny—and seamless—to new generations of viewers.

154 STORYBOARDING ANIMATION

The exciting and crucial sequence shown on these pages takes place when the private eye Eddie Valiant (played by Bob Hoskins) and (the animated) Jessica Rabbit try to escape back to Los Angeles through the Toontown Tunnel, using the cartoon car Benny.

156 STORYBOARDING ANIMATION

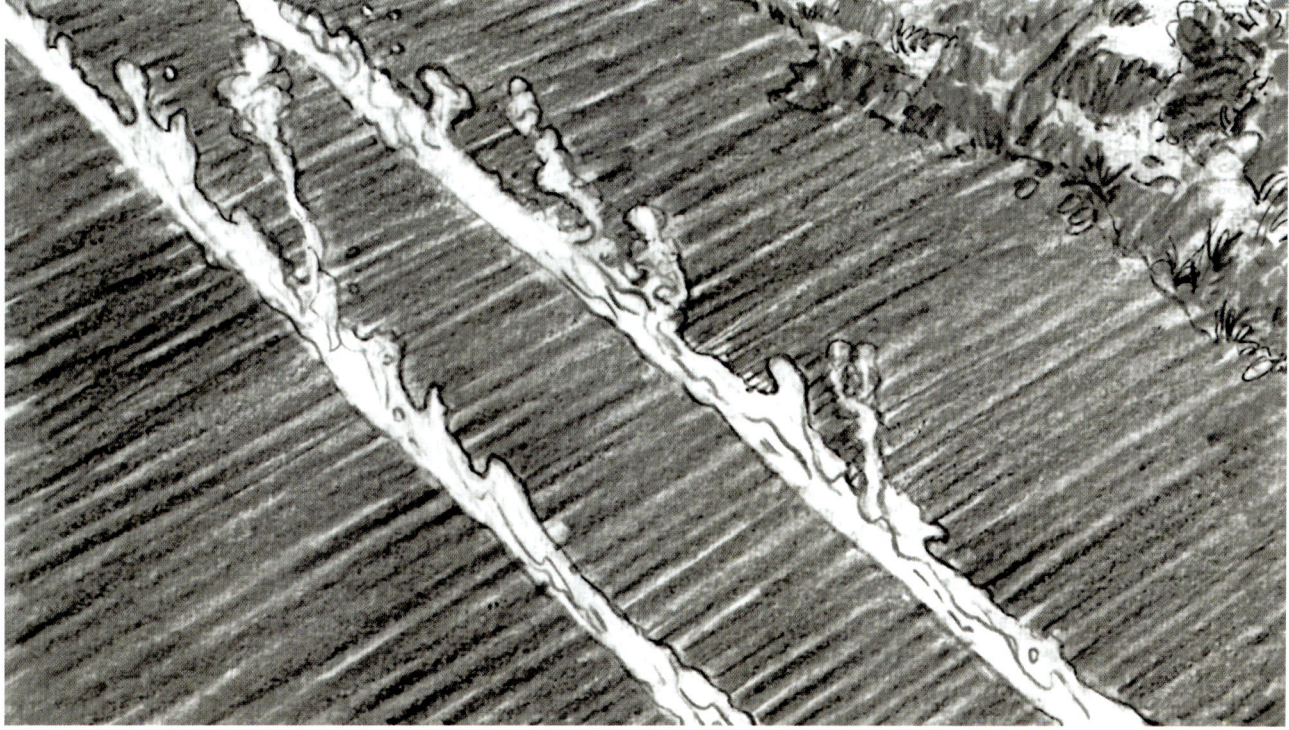

The action ramps up at this point in the film as the implied pace in the boards indicates: the climax is approaching. The sinister Judge Doom (Christopher Lloyd) and his gang of weasels are waiting on the other side of the tunnel with the Toon-killing "Dip" ("Solution Final"), which flattens Benny the Cab's tires, causing him to crash. The Toon car's "face," as the Dip approaches, conveys his panic. Doom is waiting to take them to the Acme Factory and explain his master plan . . .

WHO FRAMED ROGER RABBIT 157

The final image demonstrates the direction of the action as the Dip takes effect and Benny turns and skids to a halt. "Most film storyboards are still created by hand, in pencil, pen, markers, etc.," says David Russell. "I use a Staedtler mechanical pencil for my work, alternating between 2 and 4B leads."

158 STORYBOARDING ANIMATION

WHO FRAMED ROGER RABBIT 159

The Wrong Trousers 1993

DIRECTOR Nick Park
STORYBOARDS Nick Park

The much-loved characters of Wallace, an absent-minded cheese-loving inventor who lives in Wigan in the north of England, and Gromit, his intelligent, mutely-expressive dog, first appeared in Nick Park's animated short *A Grand Day Out* in 1989. (Park had already produced the animation *Creature Comforts* that same year.)

Park joined Bristol-based animated studio Aardman in 1985 as an animator. Wallace and Gromit's adventures continued with *The Wrong Trousers* in 1993 and *A Close Shave* in 1995, both of which won Academy Awards. Painstakingly constructed using the stop-motion technique of "claymation," these classic comedies are still beloved bestsellers today.

Aardman has also gone from strength to strength, turning almost into a mini animation studio through production deals with DreamWorks (*Chicken Run*, 2000) and later Sony (their most recent film being *The Pirates! In an Adventure with Scientists!*, 2012; U.S. title *The Pirates! Band of Misfits*). Senior storyboard artist Michael Salter has been at Aardman since *The Wrong Trousers*, and recalls Nick Park drawing the storyboards himself. "It was extraordinary really, he sat down and drew it all out himself, page after page, like a comic strip."

Things have changed a lot since the early 1990s. "We used to storyboard on paper, photocopy it to make it darker, and stick it up on a board," says Salter. "The animators would time it out, working with a stopwatch. Starting with *Chicken Run*, it was scaled up. An animatic was created of our boards, to feed into what we now call a 'story reel,' which is created prior to full animation. Now it is all done digitally, although I'll still go for my pencil."

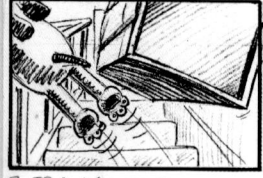

160 STORYBOARDING ANIMATION

62

Sc 59. Shot 15. INT. HALLWAY. NIGHT.
PENGUIN CHECKS HIS ESCAPE ROUTE AGAIN.
TRACKING SHOT.

Sc 59. Shot 16. INT. HALLWAY. NIGHT.
PENGUINS P.O.V.   PENGUIN FLAP APPROACHING.
TRACKING SHOT.

Sc 59. Shot 17. INT. HALLWAY. NIGHT.
PENGUIN TAKES AIM AND A POT SHOT.
TRACKING SHOT.

Sc 59. Shot 18. INT. HALLWAY. NIGHT.
PENGUIN FLAP IS BLOWN OFF ITS HINGES.

Sc 59. Shot 19. INT. HALLWAY. NIGHT.
GROMIT REACHES FOR A BUTTON.
TRACKING SHOT.

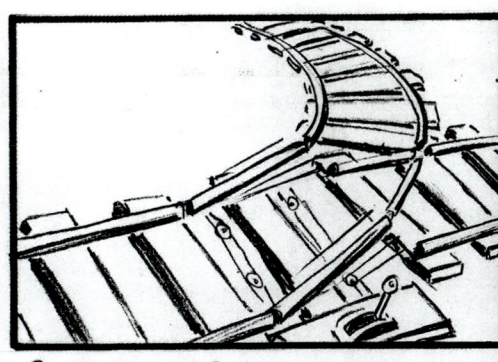

Sc 59. Shot 20. INT. HALLWAY. NIGHT.
GROMIT CHANGES THE POINTS.

In *The Wrong Trousers*, Gromit finds himself edged out of the house by a lodger—a diamond-thieving penguin who takes a sinister interest in Wallace's latest invention, the Techno Trousers.

Unambiguously hilarious (the criminal penguin has disguised himself wearing a yellow rubber glove on his head; a "Wanted" poster asks, "Have you seen this chicken?"), *The Wrong Trousers* still makes children—and adults—shriek with laughter.

Sc 59. Shot 21. INT. HALLWAY/DINING ROOM. NIGHT.
PENGUINS P.O.V. RACING DOWN THE TRACK
TRACKING SHOT.

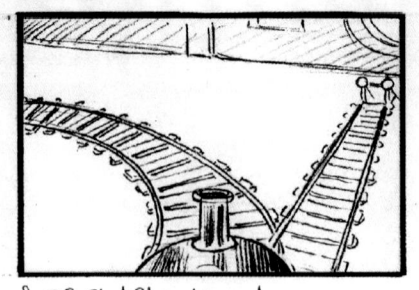

Sc 59. Shot 21 continued
PENGUINS P.O.V.
HE SUDDENLY SWITCHES DIRECTION AT THE POINTS
TRACKING SHOT.

Sc 59. Shot 21 continued.
PENGUIN P.O.V. THE TRAIN RACES INTO THE DINING ROOM.
TRACKING SHOT.

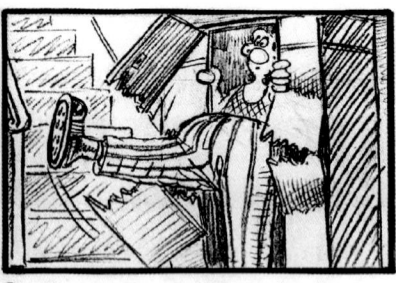

Sc 59. Shot 22. INT. HALLWAY. NIGHT.
WALLACE, STILL OUT OF CONTROL, KICKS HIS WAY OUT OF THE WARDROBE.

Sc 60. Shot 1. INT. DINING ROOM. NIGHT.
PENGUIN TAKES A COUPLE OF SHOTS AT GROMIT.
TRACKING SHOT.

Sc 60. Shot 2. INT. DINING ROOM. NIGHT.
GROMIT HEARS WALLACE SHOUTING BEHIND HIM.
"DON'T WORRY GROMIT,...."
TRACKING SHOT

Sc 60. Shot 3. INT. DINING ROOM. NIGHT.
WALLACE JUST KEEPS BALANCE.
"....I'M... WOAH.... RIGHT BEHIND YOU!"
TRACKING SHOT.

Sc 60. Shot 4. INT. DINING ROOM. NIGHT.
PENGUIN TAKES AIM AND ANOTHER POT SHOT.
TRACKING SHOT.

Sc 60. Shot 5. INT. DINING ROOM. NIGHT.
PENGUIN SHOOTS THE POINTS LEVER THAT WALLACE IS PASSING.
TRACKING SHOT ??

Sc 60. Shot 6. INT. DINING ROOM. NIGHT.
HEADING WALLACE OFF ON ANOTHER TRACK.
"WOAH!" TRACKING SHOT.

Sc 60. Shot 7. INT. DINING ROOM. NIGHT.
WALLACE OVER TAKES GROMIT.
"HANG IN THERE GROMIT. EVERYTHING'S UNDER CONTROL".
TRACK WITH WALLACE.

Sc 60. Shot 7 continued.
WALLACE CATCHES UP ON PENGUIN UNAWARE OF WALLACE. HE SNATCHES THE GUN OFF PENGUIN.
"I'LL HAVE THAT IF YOU DON'T MIND – EH"
WALLACE LOOKS AHEAD AS HE LEAVES SHOT LEFT.

162 Storyboarding Animation

The sequence seen here, created by Nick Park, is a heart-stopping chase at the climax of the action where the penguin—clutching his stolen diamond—is pursued down the stairs by Wallace (in a wardrobe) and Gromit. The dog and the penguin land in Wallace's train set before the boards track to the penguin's POV—a potential escape through the dog-flap. Tracking shots follow the dog and the penguin in the train as Wallace—wearing the Techno Trousers—breaks out of the wardrobe in (somewhat haphazard) pursuit. "Don't worry Gromit . . . I'm . . . whoah . . . right behind you!"

The trousers come off, of course; the penguin flies through the air; and a crushed Gromit unexpectedly catches the diamond. ("Attaboy Gromit lad!") The instructions in this sequence from the creator and director are, unsurprisingly, very specific.

Sc 60. Shot 8. INT. DINING ROOM, NIGHT.
WALLACES P.O.V. OF END OF TRACK, BUFFERS AND BRICK WALL APPROACHING.
TRACKING SHOT.

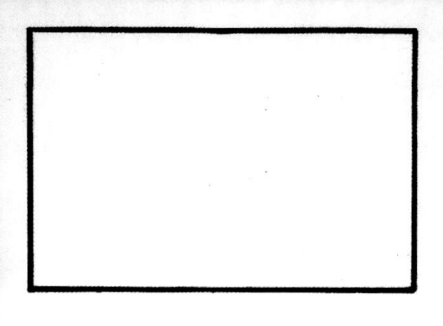

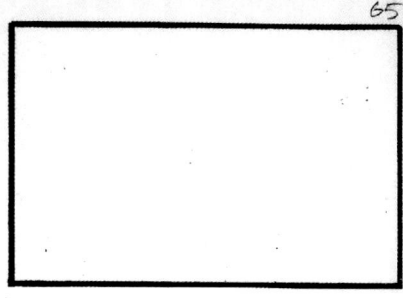

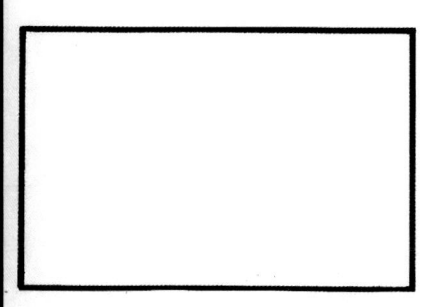

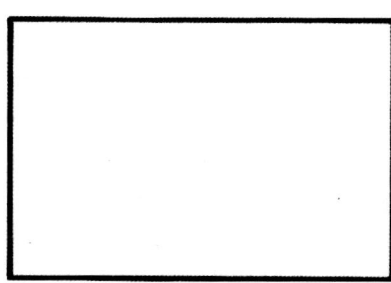

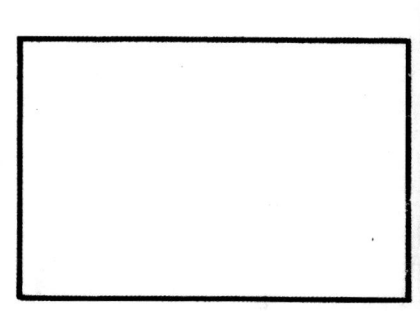

Sc 60. Shot 9. INT. DINING ROOM, NIGHT.
WALLACE REACTS HORRIFIED AT HIS APPROACHING FETE.

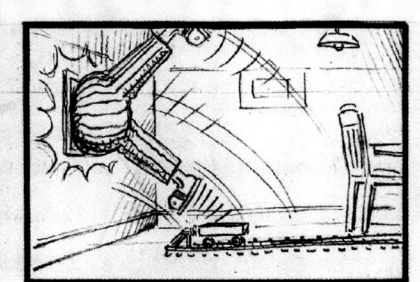

Sc 60. Shot 10. INT. DINING ROOM, NIGHT.
WALLACE HITS THE BUFFERS AND FLIES INTO THE FOOD SERVING HATCH.
TRACK AND STOP.

Sc 61. Shot 1. INT. KITCHEN, NIGHT.
WALLACE IS PLUCKED FROM THE 'TECHNO-TROUSERS'.

Sc 61. Shot 2. INT. KITCHEN. NIGHT.
AND LANDS ON A VEGETABLE TROLLEY.
PAN WITH WALLACE

Sc 61. Shot 2 Continued.
WALLACE ZOOMS THROUGH KITCHEN TURNING AS HE GRABS A DOOR JAM.

Sc 62. Shot 3. INT. DOORWAY/STUDY. NIGHT.
TRAIN ZOOMS TOWARD CAMERA.
ZIP PAN AS TRAIN APPROACHES

THE WRONG TROUSERS 163

Sc 62. Shot 3 continued.
PAN WITH TRAIN AS THEY SPEED INTO THE STUDY AND ROUND A CORNER.

Sc 62. Shot 4. INT. STUDY. NIGHT
GROMIT SHEDS HELMET AND ATTEMPTS TO CRAWL ALONG THE TRAIN.
TRACKING SHOT.

Sc 62. Shot 5. INT. STUDY. NIGHT
PENGUIN LOOKS BACK SURPRISED.
TRACKING SHOT.

Sc 62. Shot 6. INT. STUDY. NIGHT.
WALLACE OVERTAKES GROMIT WIELDING A FISHING NET.
"LEAVE HIM TO ME" –
TRACK WITH WALLACE

Sc 62. Shot 6. CONTINUED.
.."I'LL GET THE BOUNDER"
WALLACE RAISES HIS NET.

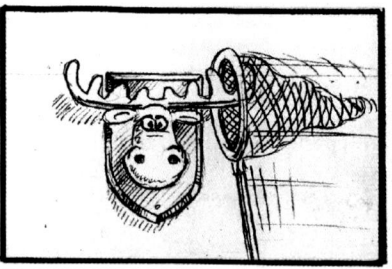

Sc 62. Shot 7. INT. STUDY. NIGHT
BUT... THE NET CATCHES THE MOOSES HEAD.

Sc 63. Shot 7. INT. LIVING ROOM. NIGHT.
EXTREMELY FAST GROMIT LAYS THE SPARE TRACKS.
TRACKING SHOT.

Sc 63. Shot 8. INT. LIVING ROOM. NIGHT.
GROMIT STEERS THE TRAIN JUST AVOIDING A CRASH.
TRACKING SHOT.

Sc 63. Shot 9. INT. LIVING ROOM. NIGHT.
HE STEERS THE TRAIN AWAY FROM THE FRENCH WINDOWS.
PAN WITH TRAIN.

Sc 63. Shot 9 continued.
"MIND THE TABLE GROMIT".
PAN WITH TRAIN.

Sc 63. Shot 10. INT. LIVING ROOM. NIGHT.
TRACK IN TO TABLE AND CHAIR LEGS

Sc 63. Shot 11. INT. LIVING ROOM. NIGHT.
GROMIT HORRIFIED STILL LAYING TRACKS MANICALLY.

"We used square boards back then for TV," says senior storyboard artist at Aardman Michael Salter. "And it was quite remarkable to see Nick drawing it all out, page after page. He'd do one drawing with an arrow as you see here to indicate the penguin going down the banisters. But now, instead of one shot with an arrow, there'll be around three shots in black and white. That goes into making up a story reel, which is a virtual black-and-white animation using our boards. The film is refined this way until it goes to full animation."

69

Sc 63. Shot 1. INT. LIVING ROOM. NIGHT.
PENGUIN CHANGES POINTS AS HE PASSES.
TRACKING SHOT.

Sc 63. Shot 2. INT. LIVING ROOM. NIGHT.
SEND WALLACE AND GROMIT OFF ON ANOTHER TRACK.
TRACKING SHOT.

Sc 63. Shot 3. INT. LIVING ROOM. NIGHT.
GROMIT LOOKS AHEAD HORRIFIED.
TRACKING SHOT.

Sc 63. Shot 4. INT. LIVING ROOM. NIGHT.
THE END OF TRACK APPROACHES AND THE FRENCH WINDOWS.
TRACKING SHOT.

Sc 63. Shot 5. INT. LIVING ROOM. NIGHT.
GROMIT REACHES OUT...
TRACKING SHOT.

Sc 63. Shot 6. INT. LIVING ROOM. NIGHT.
...TO GRAB A BOX.

68

Sc 62. Shot 8. INT. STUDY. NIGHT.
WALLACE IS YANKED INTO THE AIR. "YAAAH!"
TRACKING SHOT.

Sc 62. Shot 9. INT. STUDY. NIGHT.
GROMIT RESUMES CREEPING UP ON PENGUIN.
TRACKING SHOT.

Sc 62. Shot 9 continued.
HE'S DISTRACTED BY THE SOUND OF WALLACE WAILING.

Sc 62. Shot 10. INT. STUDY. NIGHT.
WALLACE HAS LANDED ON THE BACK OF THE TRAIN. "YAAAGH!"
TRACKING SHOT.

Sc 62. Shot 11. INT. STUDY. NIGHT.
THIS GIVES PENGUIN THE CHANCE TO UNHITCH THE CARRIAGES.
WE ALSO PASS FROM STUDY TO LIVING ROOM.
TRACKING SHOT.

Sc 62. Shot 11. continued.
THE GAP WIDENS AS GROMIT MAKES A GRAB... BUT MISSES.

Sc 63. Shot 12. INT. LIVING ROOM. NIGHT.
GROMITS P.O.V. MEANDERING THROUGH THE TABLE LEGS.
TRACKING SHOT.

Sc 63 shot 12Ⓐ LIVING ROOM. NIGHT
GROMIT LOOKS BACK OVER HIS SHOULDER.
TRACKING SHOT

Sc 63. Shot 13. INT. LIVING ROOM. NIGHT.
WALLACE SNAKES THROUGH TABLE LEGS. "YAAAGH!"
TRACKING SHOT.

Sc 64 Shot 1. LIVING ROOM/HALLWAY. NIGHT
WALLACE P.O.V OF GROMIT ENTERING HALL TRAIN DISAPEARS AROUND WALL AND WALL PASSES CAMERA
TRACKING SHOT

Sc 65. Shot 1. INT. DINING ROOM. NIGHT.
GROMIT SPEEDS OUT FROM HALLWAY INTO THE DINING ROOM. LOOKS TO FRAME RIGHT.

Sc 65. Shot 2. INT. DINING ROOM. NIGHT.
PENGUIN COMES HURTLING ROUND THE BEND. TRIES TO BRAKE.
ALMOST GROMITS P.O.V.

Sc 65. Shot 3. INT. DINING ROOM. NIGHT.
GROMIT CROSSES PENGUINS TRACK, PENGUIN ABOUT TO COLLIDE WITH TRAIN.

Sc 65. Shot 3 continued.
WALLACE TRIES TO GRAB PENGUIN...

Sc 65. Shot 3 continued.
...BUT PENGUIN TRUNDLES ON ENGINELESS.

Sc 65. Shot 4. INT. DINING ROOM. NIGHT.
WALLACE HAS GRABBED THE ENGINE
TRACKING SHOT.

Sc 65. Shot 5. INT. DINING ROOM. NIGHT.
GROMITS TRAIN CURVES AROUND TO COME UP PARALLEL TO PENGUINS TRACK. GROMIT RUNS OUT OF TRACK AND DISCARDS THE BOX. TRACK WITH PENGUIN.

Sc 65. Shot 6. INT. DINING ROOM. NIGHT.
PENGUINS P.O.V. TROUSERS STEP ON HIS TRACK. (WE'RE HEADING FOR KITCHEN)
TRACKING SHOT.

Sc.65. Shot 7. INT. DINING ROOM. NIGHT.
PANICKED PENGUIN TRIES TO BRAKE AND WALLACE AND GROMIT OVERTAKE.
TRACKING SHOT.

Sc.65. Shot 7. CONTINUED.
TROUSER FOOT COMES DOWN ON THE TRACK. PENGUIN GOES FLYING.

Sc.66. Shot 1. INT. KITCHEN. NIGHT.
WALLACE REACHES UP TO GRAB PENGUIN.
TRACKING SHOT

Sc.66. Shot 2. INT. KITCHEN. NIGHT.
GROMIT ANTICIPATES A CATCH.
TRACKING SHOT.

Sc.66. Shot 3. INT. KITCHEN. NIGHT.
PENGUIN SALES THROUGH THE AIR.
TRACKING SHOT.

Sc.66. Shot 4. INT. KITCHEN. NIGHT.
GROMIT SMASHES INTO KITCHEN UNIT CUPBOARD
TRACK THEN STOP.

Sc.66. Shot 5. INT. KITCHEN. NIGHT.
THE CRASH CAUSES A BOTTLE TO TOPPLE OFF THE COUNTER.

Sc.66. Shot 6. INT. KITCHEN. NIGHT.
PENGUIN DESCENDS TRY TO FLAP ONE WING.

Sc.66. Shot 7. INT. KITCHEN. NIGHT.
BOTTLE LANDS IN GROMIT LAP....

Sc.66. Shot 7 Continued.
...PERFECTLY POSITIONED TO CATCH THE PENGUIN AND THE DIAMOND.
"ATTABOY GROMIT LAD!"

Sc.66. Shot 8. INT. KITCHEN. NIGHT.
WALLACE SLIDES INTO FRAME:
"WELL DONE! WE DID IT!"

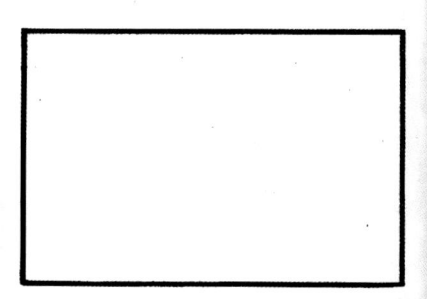

While Britain tends to mirror America in its filmmaking practices, the international marketplace did not immediately adopt storyboarding as an industry standard. With budgets low in many domestic industries—such as the high volume of Bollywood or the kung fu/action spectaculars of Hong Kong—production tended to be faster and "on the hoof" until relatively recently.

There were exceptions, of course. The first films to veer close to storyboarding were those to emerge in the "art house" marketplace—where the director as an artist would draw what was in his mind's eye as a personal expression not intended for a production crew. Italy's Federico Fellini sketched constantly throughout his career, for example, although he did not storyboard.

In India, the great Satyajit Ray came close to storyboarding for his debut, *Pather Panchali* (1955), which was derived entirely from his note-pads, which he would show to potential backers. That was also the case for the Japanese director Akira Kurosawa, who spent a decade painting "storyboards" for *Ran* (1985), which were used to raise money. These could be termed "concept storyboards" in today's terminology.

As the marketplace has become more international, budgets have risen across the board for foreign-language films that might previously have been made on micro financing. This has led to storyboarding being widely adopted at the high end of the international marketplace, particularly for effects shots and as a fundraising tool.

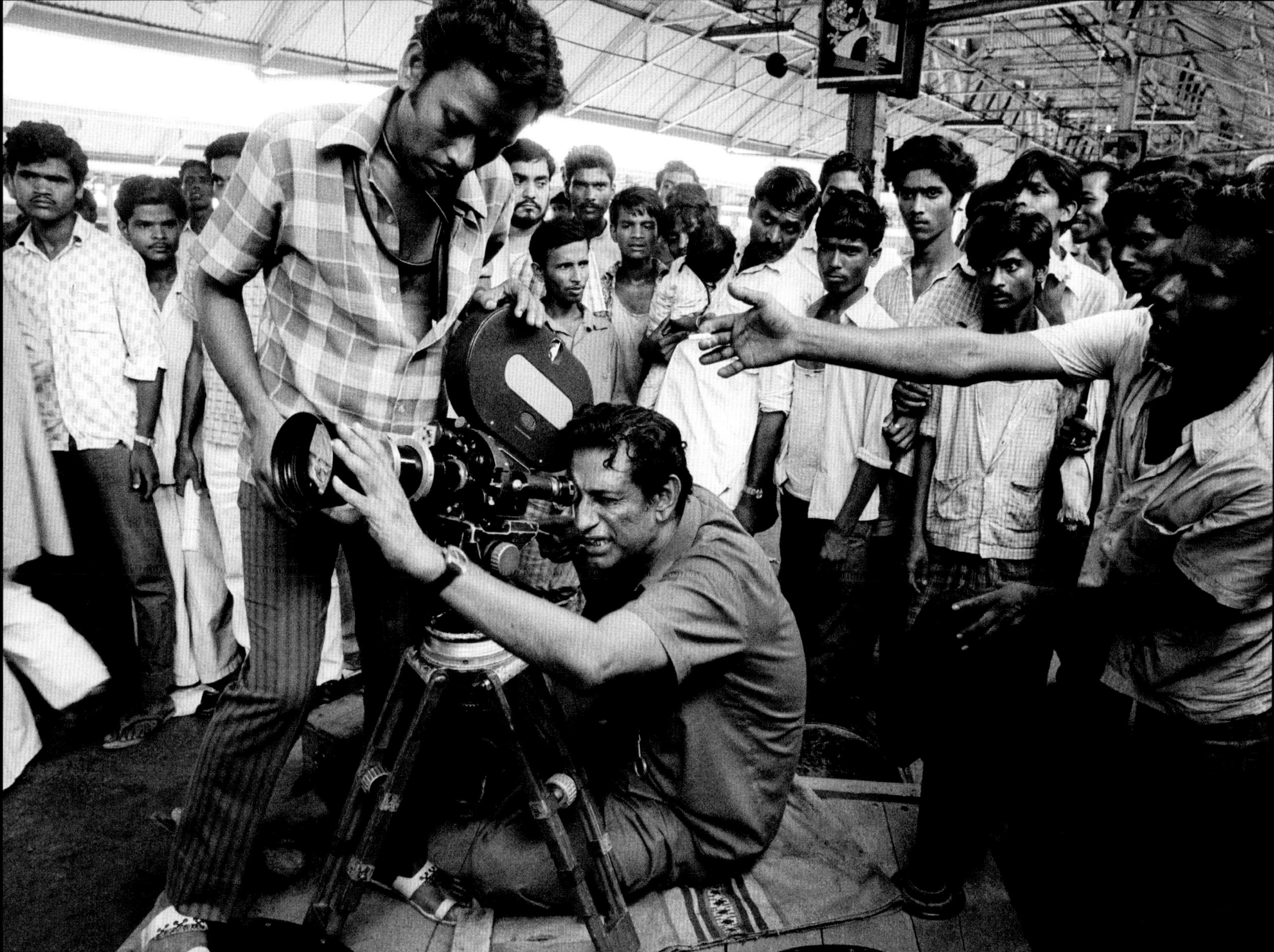

Pather Panchali 1955

DIRECTOR Satyajit Ray
STORYBOARDS Satyajit Ray

Pather Panchali (translated as "Song of the Little Road") was Satyajit Ray's first film, adapted by Ray from a 1928 Bengali novel of the same name. Previously, while working as a graphic artist at a Calcutta publishing house, Ray illustrated a children's version of the novel, and it remained dear to his heart as he moved closer to realizing his dream of becoming a filmmaker.

Filming on *Pather Panchali* started, financed by the director's own funds and any loans he could raise, in 1952, when Ray was thirty-one years old, and collapsed and re-started on various occasions, only finishing in 1955 thanks to a grant from the Museum of Modern Art in New York.

Throughout the three years of intermittent production, Ray searched for funding armed with two tools to show potential backers. One was a small notebook, filled with sketches, dialogue, and the treatment; the other was more of a sketchbook containing gouache illustrations of the film's key dramatic moments. Ray later donated these to the Cinémathèque Française in Paris.

With its extraordinary, naturalistic sequences—Ray was inspired by the Italian neorealist movement—*Pather Panchali* never had a complete script and was made entirely from these sketches and notes. The original drawings have sadly now been lost, but these black and white copies still reveal the beauty of his preparatory work.

Pather Panchali tells the story of a Brahmin family in Bengal at the beginning of the last century. The father is an impoverished priest, and the mother is left alone to look after impish older daughter Durga and young Apu. *Pather Panchali*'s neorealist take on the Bengal countryside (Ray was inspired by Vittorio De Sica's 1948 film *Bicycle Thieves*) is rightly hailed for the magnificent beauty and majesty of its black and white sequences, which detail the simple joys of life for a small boy. Perhaps the most famous of these depicts Apu and Durga running through kans grass to see a train; on their return, they find the dead body of their Aunt Indir. Music by Ravi Shankar heightened the intensity of emotion.

Pather Panchali was the first in Ray's *Apu* Trilogy, and was succeeded by *Aparajito* (1956) and *Apur Sansar* (1959).

INTERNATIONAL PERSPECTIVES

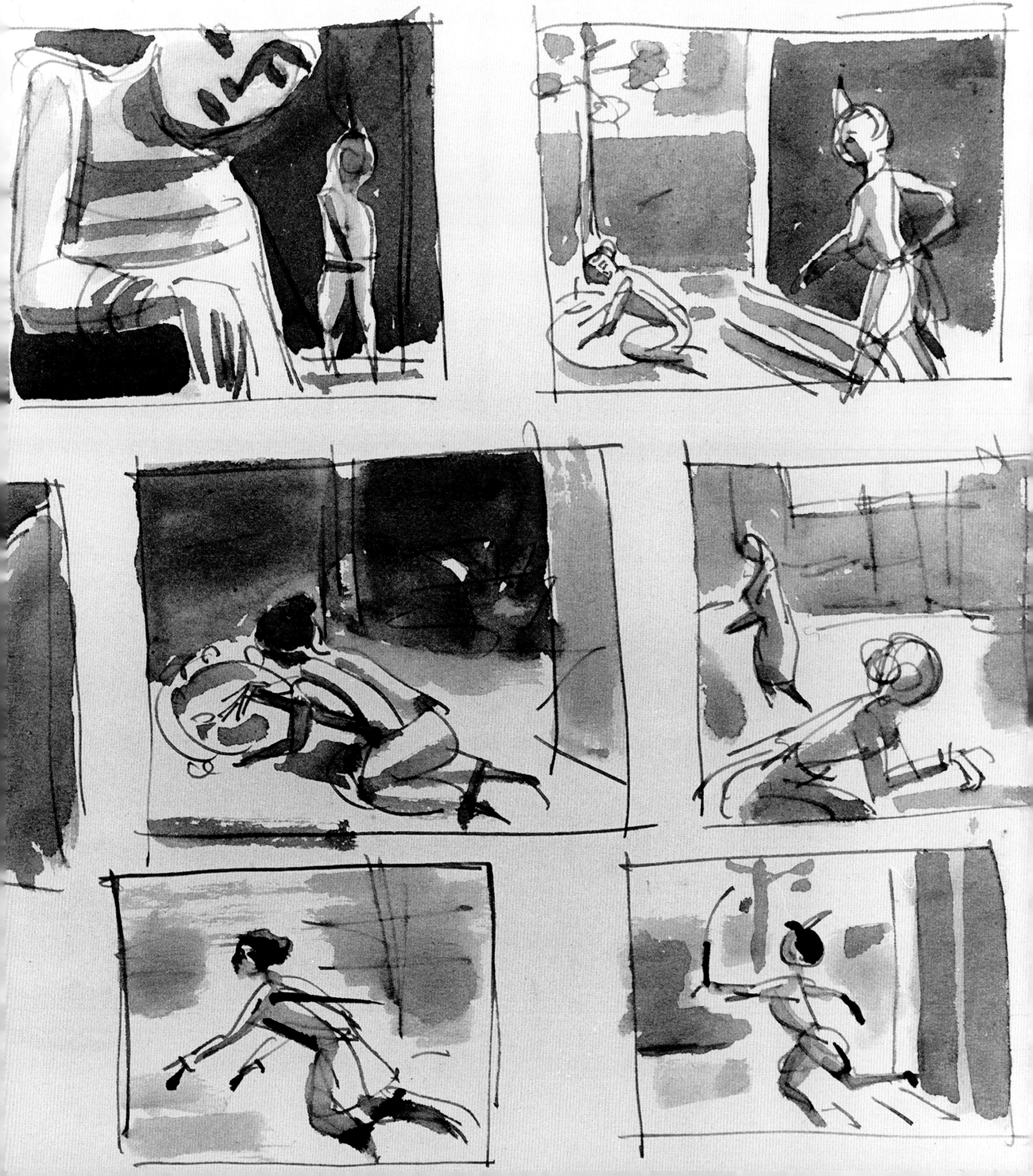

172 INTERNATIONAL PERSPECTIVES

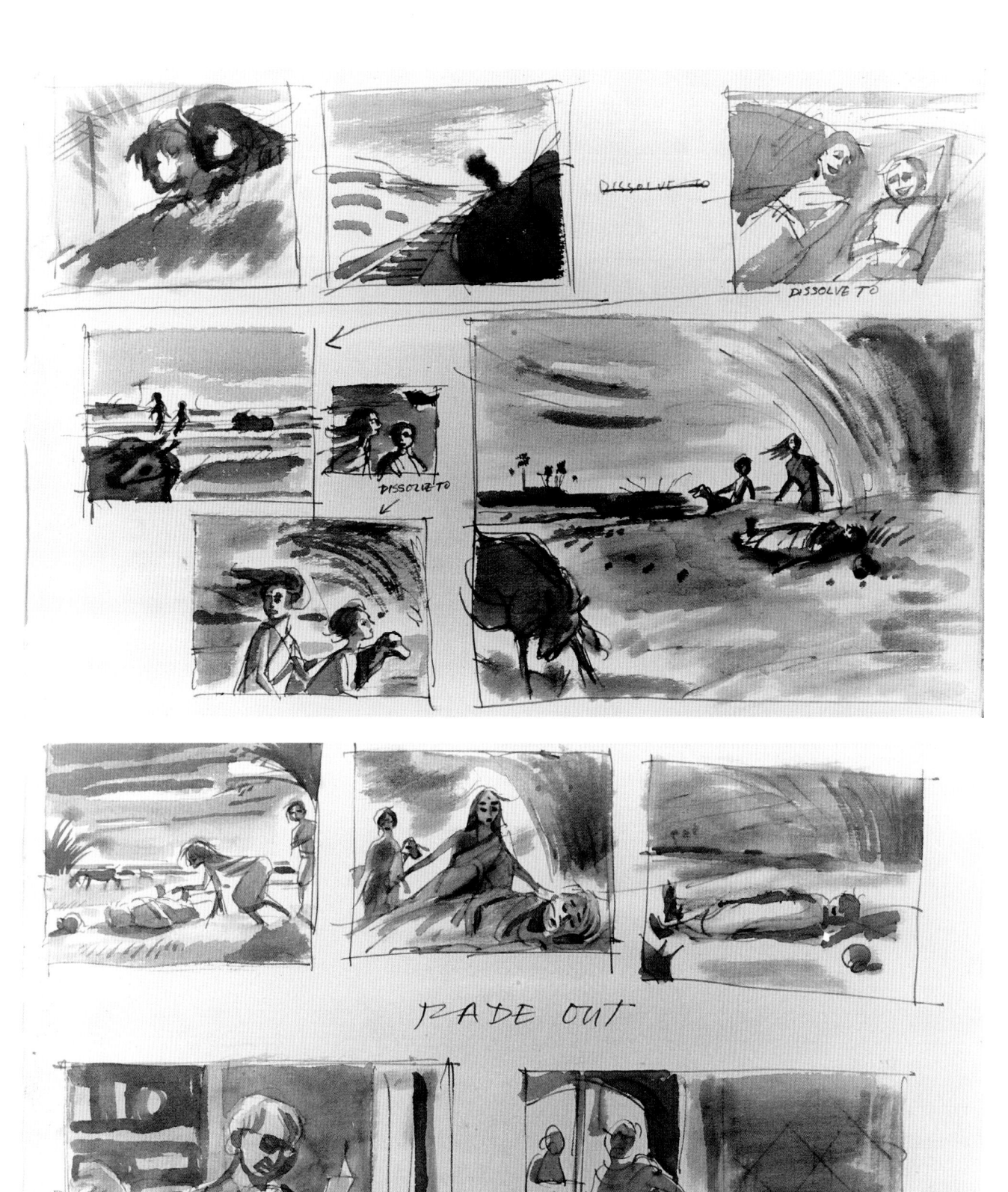

OPPOSITE AND LEFT Perhaps the most memorable sequence in *Pather Panchali* features Apu and Durga sprinting through kans grass in order to glimpse a passing steam train. On their way back to the village, they encounter the corpse of their Aunt Indir.

PATHER PANCHALI 173

Satyajit Ray later said of *Pather Panchali:* "The script had to retain some of the rambling quality of the novel because that in itself contained a clue to the feel of authenticity: life in a poor Bengali village does ramble."

DISSOLVE TO

174 INTERNATIONAL PERSPECTIVES

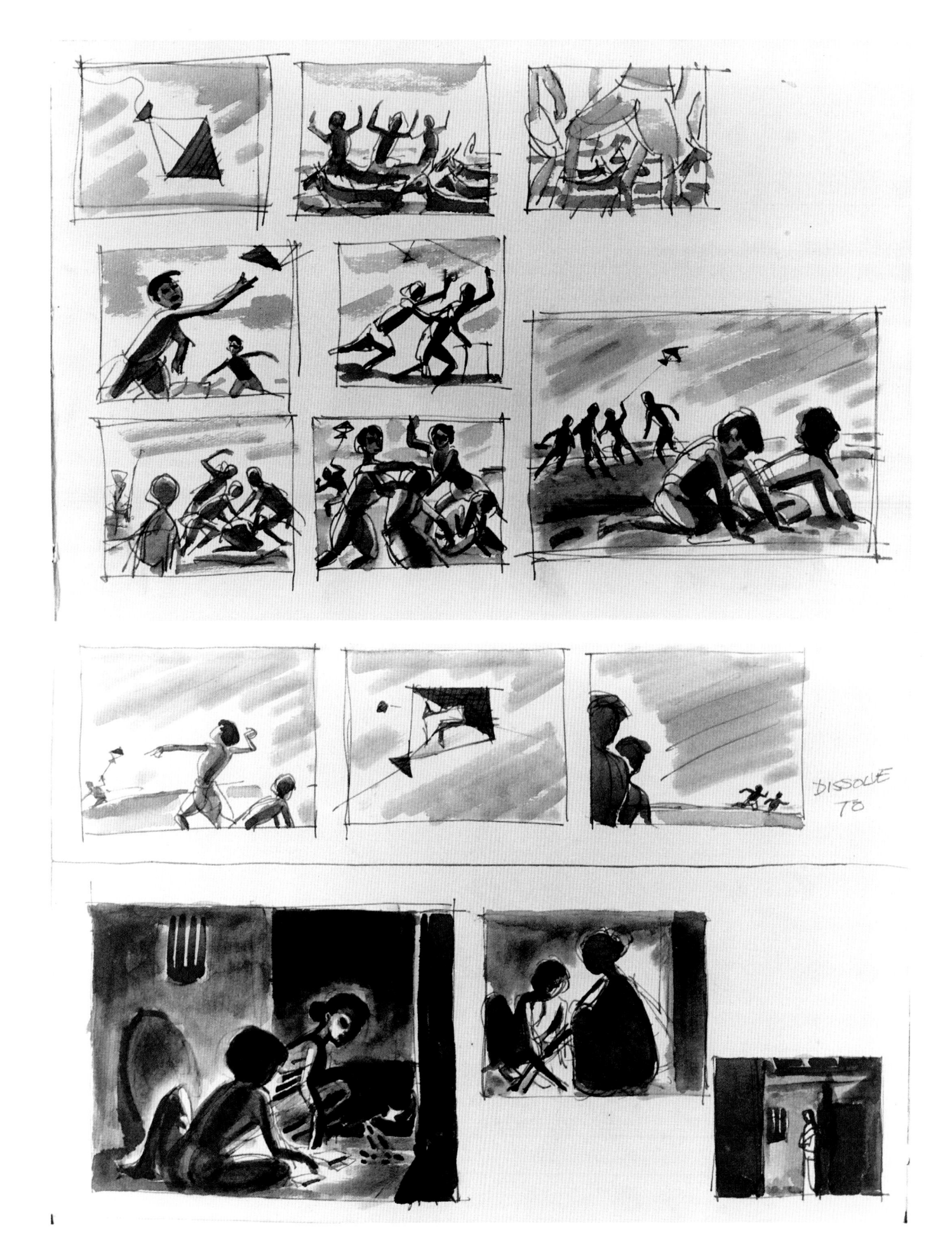

PATHER PANCHALI 175

Ran 1985

DIRECTOR Akira Kurosawa
STORYBOARDS Akira Kurosawa

The Japanese director Akira Kurosawa, universally acknowledged as one of the most influential voices in cinema history, originally conceived *Ran* in 1975 after reading an ancient Japanese parable, only later realizing its parallels with Shakespeare's *King Lear*. He wrote the script, and then let it lie for almost a decade while he created hand-painted storyboards, running to over 800 works of art, many individually signed.

At the time the most expensive Japanese film ever made (it was budgeted at $12m), *Ran* was framed—typically for Kurosawa—mostly in long-shot, with the director using three cameras to capture some exquisitely staged battle and pastoral sequences. His boards are crystal-clear representations of what he would shoot, from the colors to the tone and atmosphere, elaborate costuming (Emi Wada would win an Academy Award for her work), and intense color contrasts.

INTERNATIONAL PERSPECTIVES

Unsurprisingly, perhaps, when one looks at his art, Kurosawa nurtured ambitions to be a painter prior to moving into film at the behest of his older brother, but failed to make a living from his canvases. He was also greatly influenced by Vincent van Gogh.

There are no examples of storyboards of Kurosawa's work prior to *Kagemusha* (1980), which he found difficult to finance; he used his paintings to persuade the studio (Toho) to back his ideas. He was to experience the same problems with *Ran*. "A long time passed before production got underway . . . I used this time to draw pictures illustrating the images I had for the film," he said. When the paintings eventually emerged, they quickly found an international following.

"Are they worthy of being called art? My purpose was not to paint well," said the director after the storyboards were collated in a book in 1986. "I intended to be a painter before I became involved with film. When I changed careers, I burned all the pictures that I had painted up til then. As a well-known Japanese proverb says, 'If you chase two rabbits you may not even catch one.' I cannot help but be fascinated by the fact that when I tried to paint well, I could only produce mediocre pictures. But when I concentrated on delineating the ideas for my films, I unconsciously produced works that people find interesting."

Kurosawa's famous admirers in the U.S.—including Francis Ford Coppola, George Lucas, and Martin Scorsese—used some of this work to help get American financing and distribution for *Ran* (French-backed, it flopped at home even as it was nominated for four Academy Awards, including Best Director for Kurosawa). It was to be Kurosawa's last epic film; he died in Tokyo in 1998.

In the Sengoku period that preceded the Shogunate, the elderly warlord Hidetora decides to retire, splitting his estate between his three sons: Taro (married to the evil and conniving Lady Kaede), Jiro, and Saburo, the youngest (they are signified in the film by, respectively, the colors yellow, red, and blue). When Saburo is banished by Hidetora after a misunderstanding, Lady Kaede engineers Taro's dominance and the older brothers band together. Hidetora finds himself alone and an outcast.

LEFT The screenplay describes, and Kurosawa illustrates: "The Samurai in the lead, old but tough, draws his bow, aiming at the prey—the magnificent vision of a great warrior who has survived hundreds of battles." Thus Kurosawa introduces the Great Lord Hidetora Ichimonji, the tragic figure at the heart of *Ran*.

RIGHT Defeated in Saburo's abandoned castle by the combined forces of his older sons in a gruesome massacre, and surrounded by deceit and connivance, Hidetora goes insane, haunted by visions of the brutal murders he committed during the course of his rise to power. He is depicted here "[staggering] over the field scattered with autumn flowers in the moonlight, as if running from something fearful."

178 INTERNATIONAL PERSPECTIVES

LEFT Armies prepare for war in the film's climactic battle, which takes place on Hachiman Field. The soldiers depicted are Jiro's troops, signified by the color, red, and the two horizontal lines on their shields ("Jiro" means second son).

ABOVE Jiro's loyal general Kurogane draws his sword and kills Lady Kaede, the film's dark force, who has engineered the end of Hidetora's clan as revenge for his massacre of her family. "A stream of smoke comes hovering over [the] blood-drenched corpse," notes the screenplay.

RAN 179

Amélie 2001

DIRECTOR Jean-Pierre Jeunet
STORYBOARDS Luc Desportes

The whimsical romance *Amélie* (or *Le fabuleux destin d'Amélie Poutin*) marked a turning point in the director Jean-Pierre Jeunet's work. This was his first French-language solo project after previously working with the graphic artist Marc Caro on the dark dramas *Delicatessen* (1991) and *The City of Lost Children* (1995), which he followed up with his English-language debut for 20th Century Fox, the science fiction blockbuster *Alien: Resurrection* (1997; Caro also worked on the visuals for that film).

Back in France and working alone, Jeunet decided to embrace the light. "After *Alien* I realized I had never made a truly positive film," he said at the time. "Building, rather than destroying, presented me with a new, interesting challenge. I wanted to make a sweet film at this point in my career and life to see if I could make people dream and give them pleasure."

Amélie, written by Jeunet with Guillaume Laurant, is set in Paris's Montmartre district and centers on a shy waitress (Audrey Tautou) who changes the lives of those around her yet struggles to break through her own isolation. An international hit, *Amélie* was not a simple film for Jeunet to make, taking a year and eighteen drafts of the screenplay to complete. It was also entirely storyboarded by the French artist Luc Desportes (who worked again with Jeunet on his next film, *A Very Long Engagement*, 2004). A graduate of Paris's École Nationale Supérieure des Beaux Arts, Desportes got his break into filmmaking when he met the director Cédric Klapisch at college and worked on his first short film (they have collaborated together ever since).

Said Jeunet: "I hate to waste time on the set, you have to keep a good pace because the clock is your master. For that reason, I have to know exactly what I'm trying to do beforehand. I spend about two months doing the storyboards. I'm very slow, and I do everything myself." Those sketches were then turned over to Luc Desportes for more precise renderings. "Desportes knows me well enough to draw what I want, but that I cannot draw myself. My sketch and short explanatory note are enough for him to know what to do."

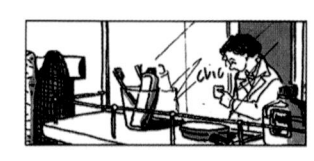

180 INTERNATIONAL PERSPECTIVES

OPPOSITE, ABOVE, AND RIGHT These are the original storyboards Desportes turned over to Jean-Pierre Jeunet for *Amélie*; stage directions and dialogue were added into later versions.

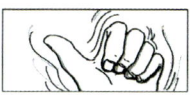

AMÉLIE 181

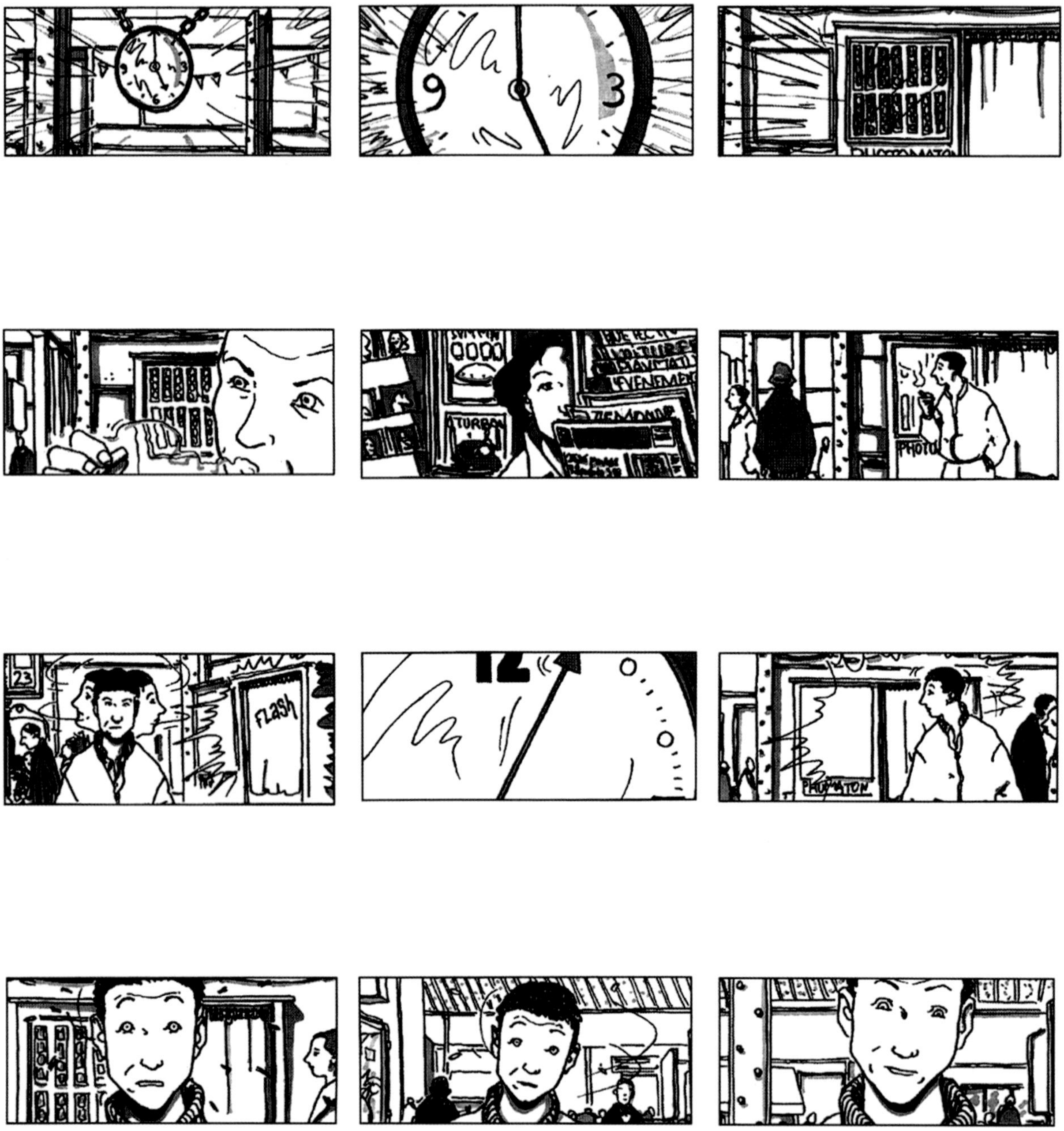
TURBAN
PHOTO
23
FLASH

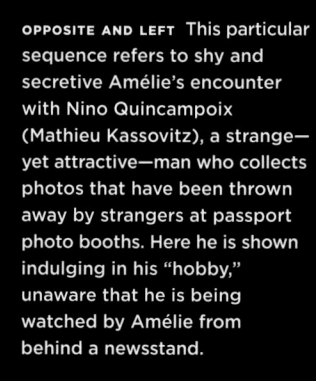

OPPOSITE AND LEFT This particular sequence refers to shy and secretive Amélie's encounter with Nino Quincampoix (Mathieu Kassovitz), a strange—yet attractive—man who collects photos that have been thrown away by strangers at passport photo booths. Here he is shown indulging in his "hobby," unaware that he is being watched by Amélie from behind a newsstand.

Oldboy 2003

DIRECTOR Park Chan-wook
STORYBOARDS Sang-yong Jung

The second installment in South Korean director Park Chan-wook's Vengeance Trilogy, *Oldboy* is a highly disturbing, visceral film with a cold and deliberate esthetic. It's also an ultra-violent piece of filmmaking, with the odd jarring comic note, which relies on calibrated imagery to produce a slow-burning effect.

Park Chan-wook obsessively storyboards all his films, telling an interviewer: "I shoot and edit almost exactly to the storyboard. There are minor changes depending on the production, but I have spent a lot of time imagining every shot in advance so there is really not that much to change."

Here, unusually, is a sequence that is not shot according to the meticulous boards shown on these pages. On the day of the shoot, Park Chan-wook decided to come up with something different—a stylized tableau that is an instantly recognizable feature of the finished film.

The sequence shown on these pages takes place when the lead character, Dae-su, or Oldboy, goes back to the private prison where he was incarcerated for fifteen years and is forced to fight his way out again.

"Originally [the sequence] was to be comprised of many hundreds of shots and I had in mind a multitude of unique shots, angles, movements, visual effects, and moments of violence," says Park. But, while he "thoroughly prepares storyboards" in an attempt to "control my production as much as I can, an actor's performance is the only element that cannot be calculated 100%. Amid all these things that I've predicted and prepared for and the plans, that is the variable. If it weren't for that, shooting film would be a boring process where everything is predictable and everything goes according to plan."

And it was, in fact, the performance of Choi Min-sik as Dae-su and the way he moved his body on the day that caused Park to throw out the storyboards. "It inspired me," he says, simply.

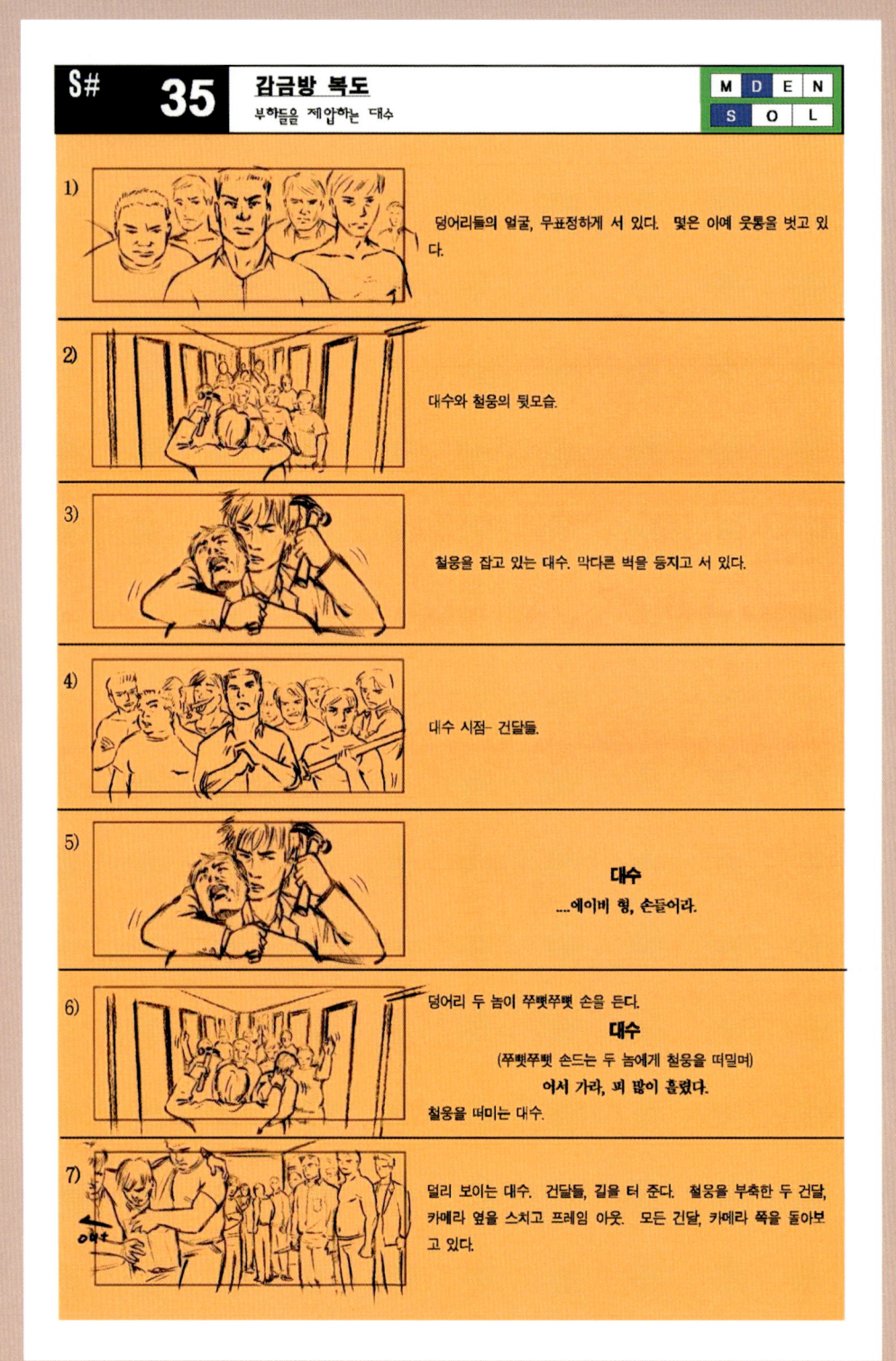

INTERNATIONAL PERSPECTIVES

In these carefully calibrated storyboarded sequences prepared by Park Chan-wook and drawn by Sang-yong Jung, the scene is set at "Corridor of the prison," as identified by the characters at the top of the pages. The characters in bold are dialogue, and those not highlighted are all instructions.

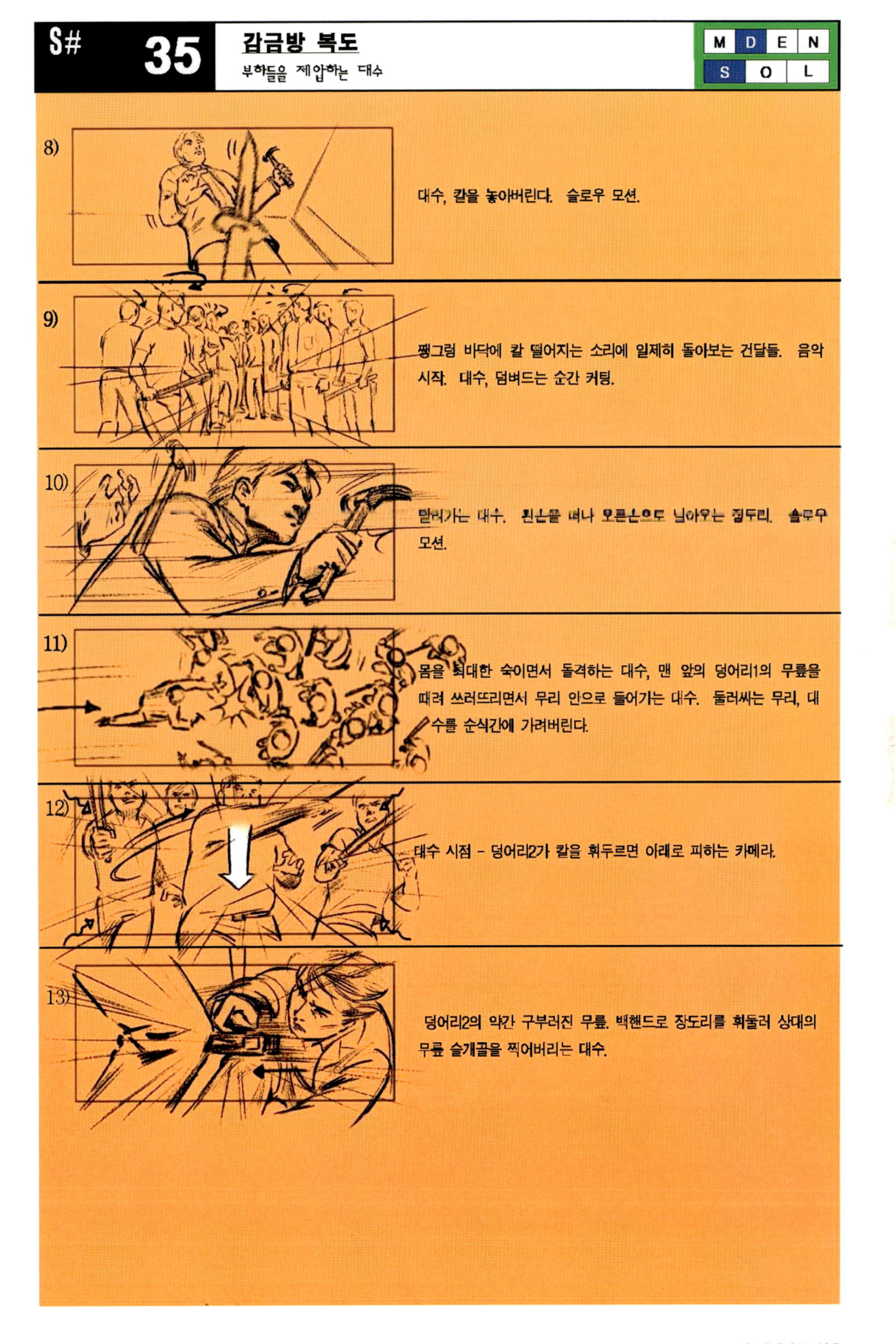

S# **35** 감금방 복도
부하들을 제압하는 대수

M	D	E	N
S	O	L	

8) 대수, 칼을 놓아버린다. 슬로우 모션.

9) 쨍그렁 바닥에 칼 떨어지는 소리에 일제히 돌아보는 건달들. 음악 시작. 대수, 덤벼드는 순간 커팅.

10) 달려가는 대수. 왼손들 떠나 오른손으로 날아오는 장도리. 슬로우 모션.

11) 몸을 최대한 숙이면서 돌격하는 대수, 맨 앞의 덩어리1의 무릎을 때려 쓰러뜨리면서 무리 안으로 들어가는 대수. 둘러싸는 무리, 대수를 순식간에 가려버린다.

12) 대수 시점 - 덩어리2가 칼을 휘두르면 아래로 피하는 카메라.

13) 덩어리2의 약간 구부러진 무릎. 백핸드로 장도리를 휘둘러 상대의 무릎 슬개골을 찍어버리는 대수.

OLDBOY 185

S# 35 감금방 복도
부하들을 제압하는 대수

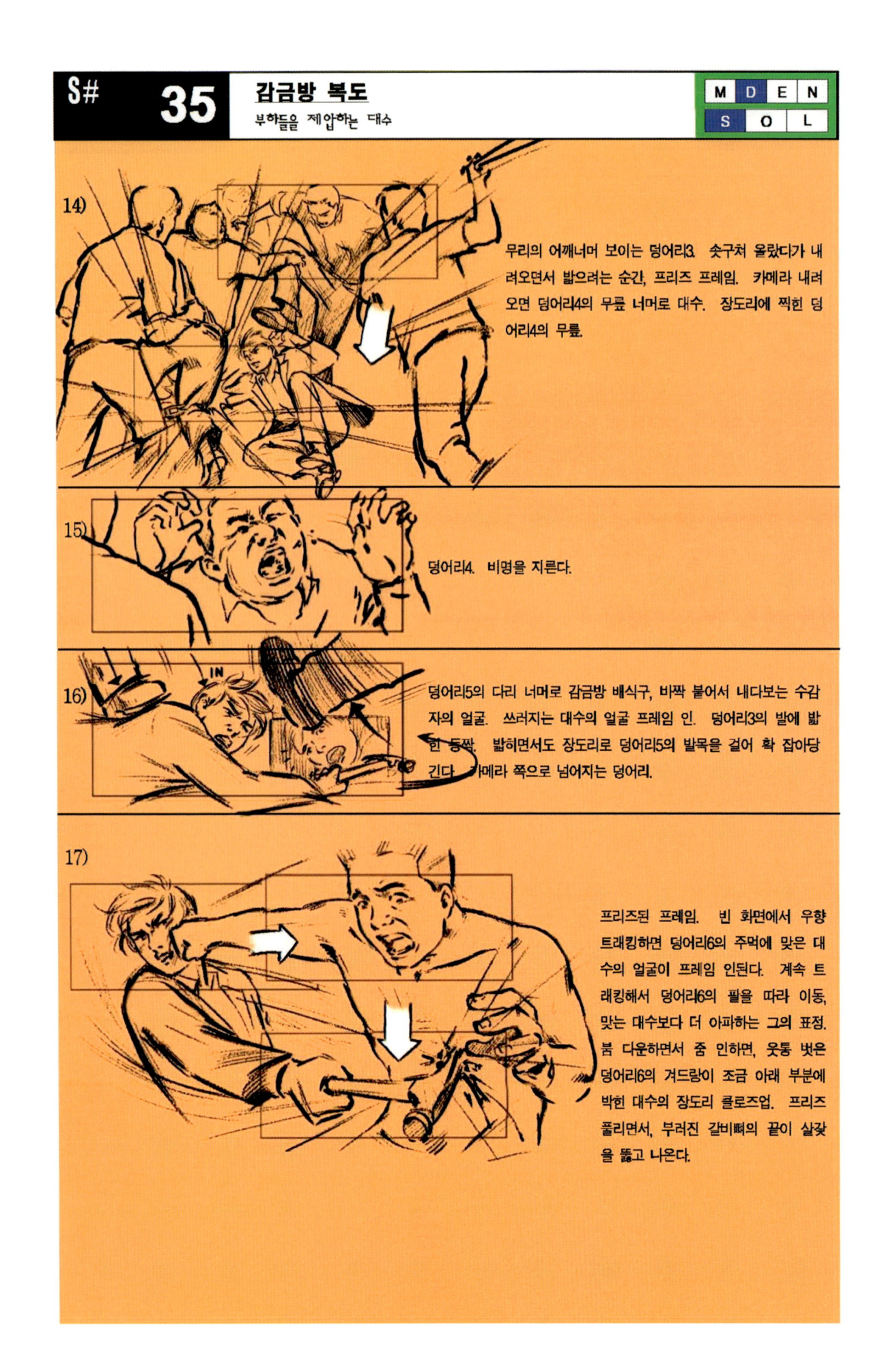

M D E N
S O L

14) 무리의 어깨너머 보이는 덩어리3. 솟구쳐 올랐다가 내려오면서 밟으려는 순간, 프리즈 프레임. 카메라 내려오면 덩어리4의 무릎 너머로 대수. 장도리에 찍힌 덩어리4의 무릎.

15) 덩어리4. 비명을 지른다.

16) 덩어리5의 다리 너머로 감금방 배식구, 바짝 붙어서 내다보는 수감자의 얼굴. 쓰러지는 대수의 얼굴 프레임 인. 덩어리3의 발에 밟힌 동싹. 밟히면서도 장도리로 덩어리5의 발목을 걸어 확 잡아당긴다. 카메라 쪽으로 넘어지는 덩어리.

17) 프리즈된 프레임. 빈 화면에서 우향 트래킹하면 덩어리6의 주먹에 맞은 대수의 얼굴이 프레임 인된다. 계속 트래킹해서 덩어리6의 팔을 따라 이동, 맞는 대수보다 더 아파하는 그의 표정. 붐 다운하면서 줌 인하면, 웃통 벗은 덩어리6의 겨드랑이 조금 아래 부분에 박힌 대수의 장도리 클로즈업. 프리즈 풀리면서, 부러진 갈비뼈의 끝이 살갗을 뚫고 나온다.

The scene shows Dae-su, or Oldboy, having to fight his way back out of the prison where he was incarcerated for fifteen years. Despite this careful planning, Park decided to abandon these storyboards on the day of shooting for a sequence that was shot in a single take and is a more stylized, instantly recognizable, tableau.

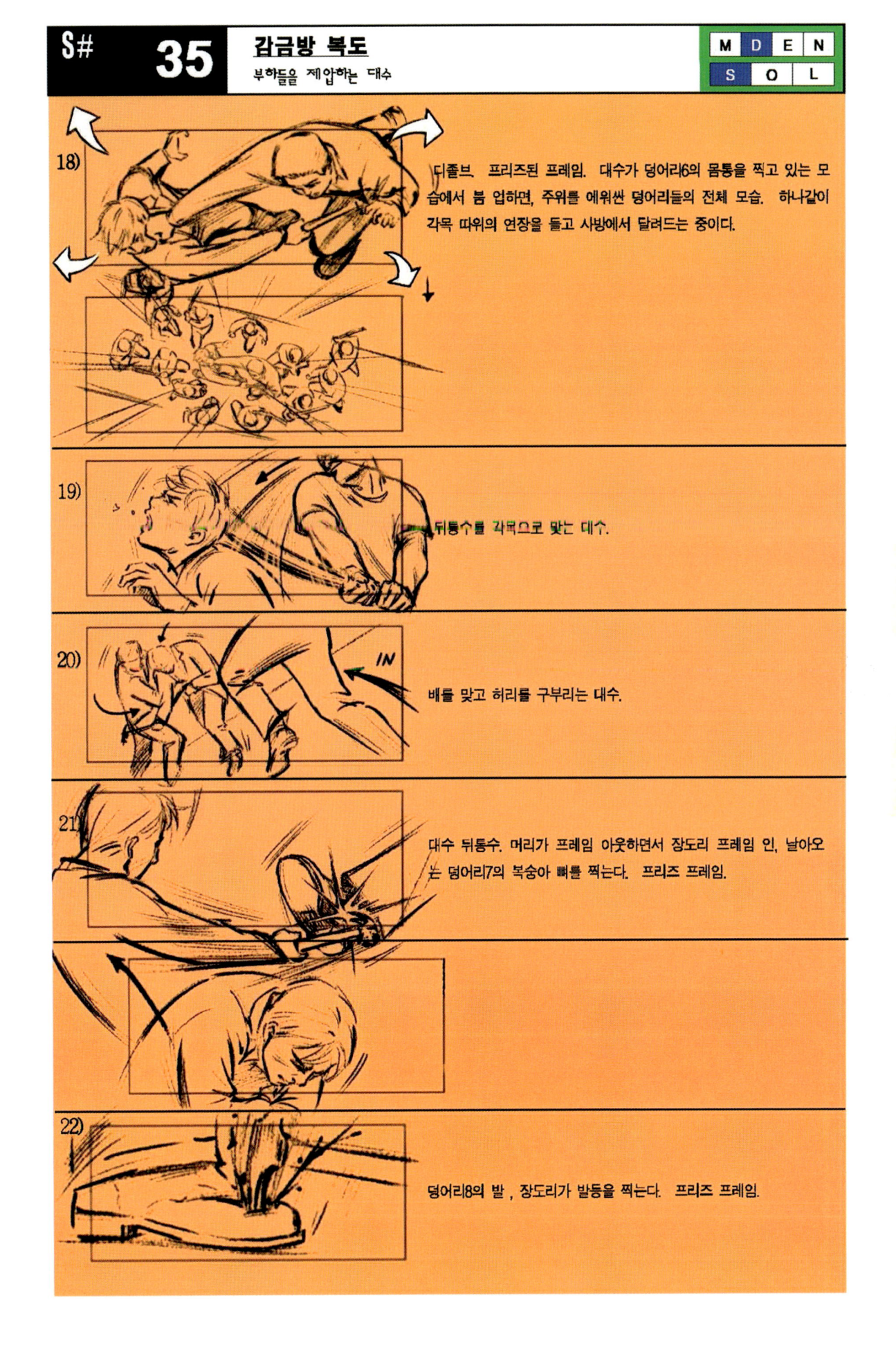

S# 35 감금방 복도
부하들을 제압하는 대수

18) 디졸브. 프리즈된 프레임. 대수가 덩어리6의 몸통을 찍고 있는 모습에서 붐 업하면, 주위를 에워싼 덩어리들의 전체 모습. 하나같이 각목 따위의 연장을 들고 사방에서 달려드는 중이다.

19) 뒤통수를 각목으로 맞는 대수.

20) 배를 맞고 허리를 구부리는 대수.

21) 대수 뒤통수. 머리가 프레임 아웃하면서 장도리 프레임 인, 날아오는 덩어리7의 복숭아 뼈를 찍는다. 프리즈 프레임.

22) 덩어리8의 발, 장도리가 발등을 찍는다. 프리즈 프레임.

OLDBOY 187

Pan's Labyrinth 2006

DIRECTOR Guillermo del Toro
STORYBOARDS Raúl Monge

The influential Mexican director Guillermo del Toro has turned to Spain for some of his more haunting creations, using the sinister, authoritarian backdrop of the Spanish Civil War to reinforce the gothic horror of his two Spanish-language films, *The Devil's Backbone* (2001) and *Pan's Labyrinth*. Both were produced by del Toro outside the studio system where he has made larger-scale dramas such as *Hellboy* (2004), *Hellboy II: The Golden Army* (2008), and *Pacific Rim* (2013), his first film as a director in five years.

Both of the Spanish films have enticed critics and audiences alike; the dark fantasy of *Pan's Labyrinth* won three Academy Awards, for Art Direction, Cinematography, and Makeup—unusual for a film not in the English language. (Del Toro himself was also nominated for Original Screenplay.)

Del Toro's visual esthetic is intensely devised by the director himself, famously in his conceptual creature designs, which were created in a series of notebooks and sketches over twenty years. These also detail how to realize the more fantastical elements of his vision.

Page after page of sketches and notes lay down the groundwork for this haunting fairytale. The young Spanish storyboard artist Raúl Monge, working for the first time with del Toro, was charged with turning these elaborate plans into production storyboards for *Pan's Labyrinth*. Although the director clearly had the film in his head for many years before the cameras began to roll, these functioned as a communication device for the various departments and crew servicing del Toro's vision.

Del Toro and Monge have consistently worked together ever since, both on del Toro's films as director (*Hellboy II*, *Pacific Rim*) and on his numerous projects as an independent producer.

BELOW AND OPPOSITE The opening credits (following a fairytale prologue) set the scene and the mood of *Pan's Labyrinth*—Spain in 1944, as Franco's Falangists thuggishly hunt down the last of the Republican guerrillas. Ofelia, a young girl whose mother is pregnant with the son of the evil Captain Vidal, is visited by strange creatures from an underground world. Earlier, she discovers a stick insect—or something that looks like a stick insect—that she believes is a fairy: it leads her to an ancient labyrinth.

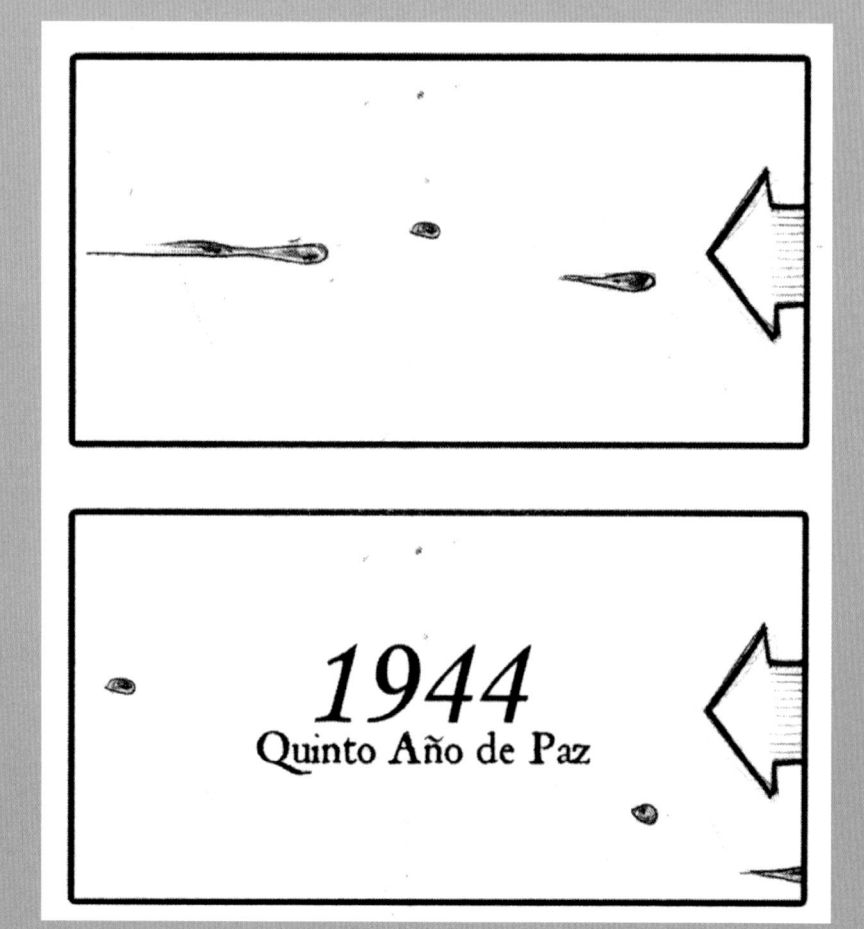

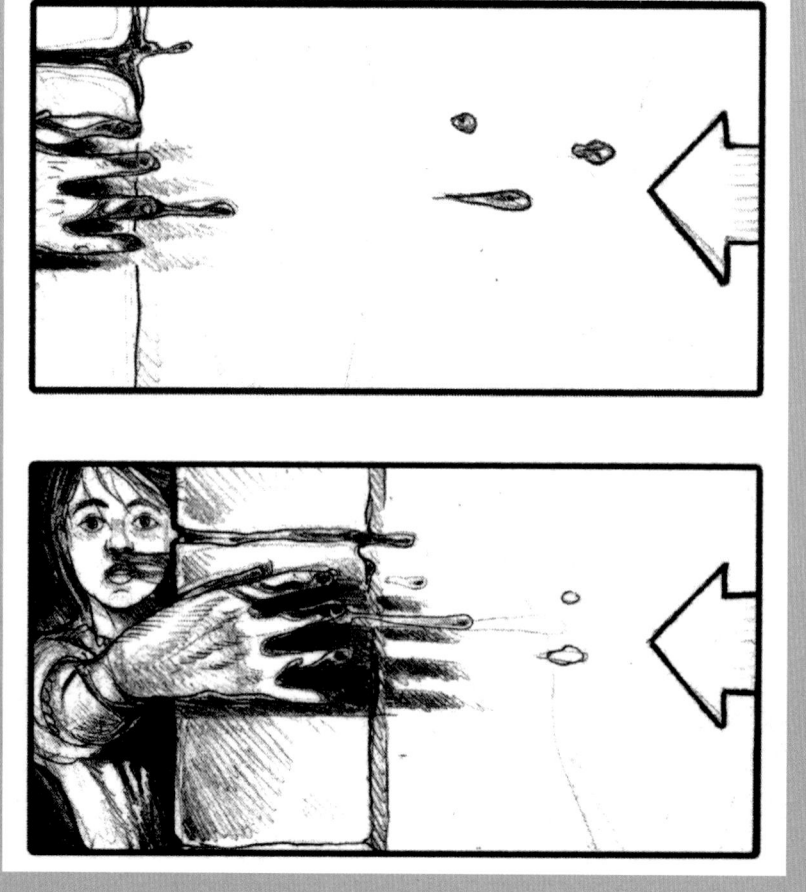

188 INTERNATIONAL PERSPECTIVES

PAN'S LABYRINTH 189

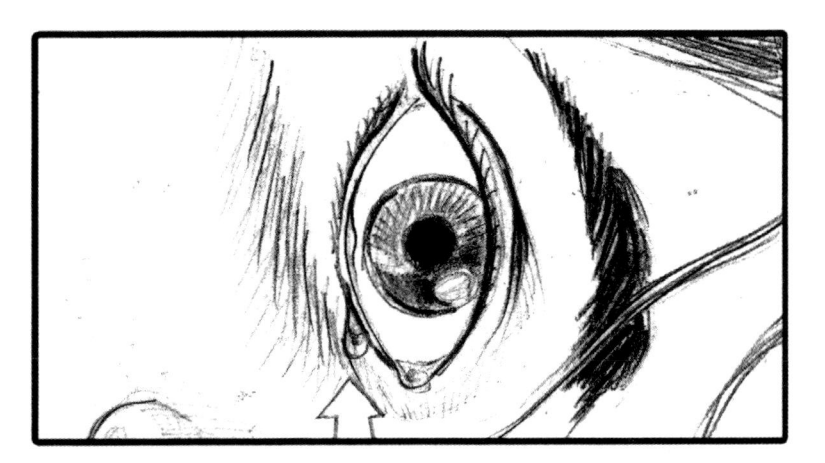

190 INTERNATIONAL PERSPECTIVES

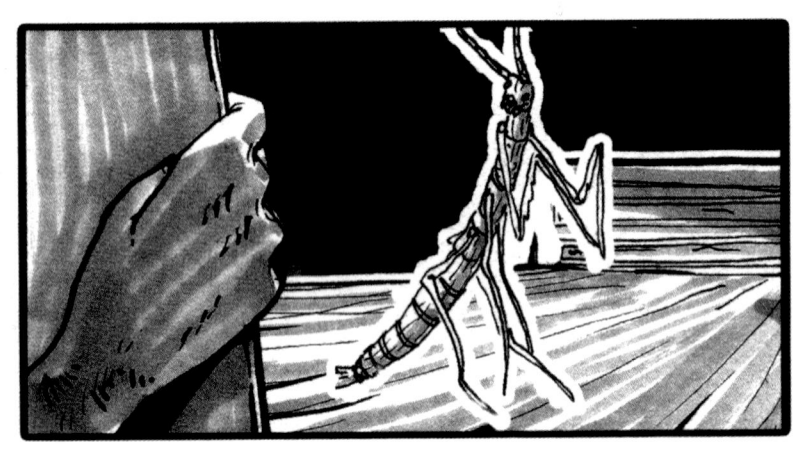

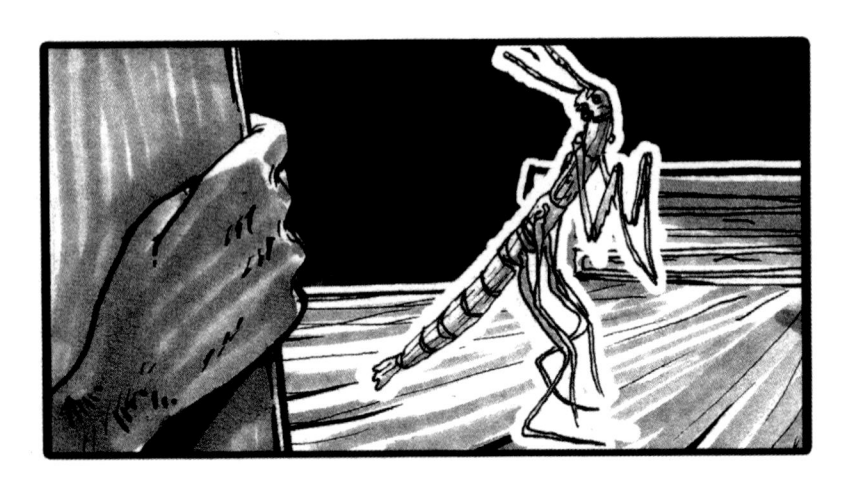

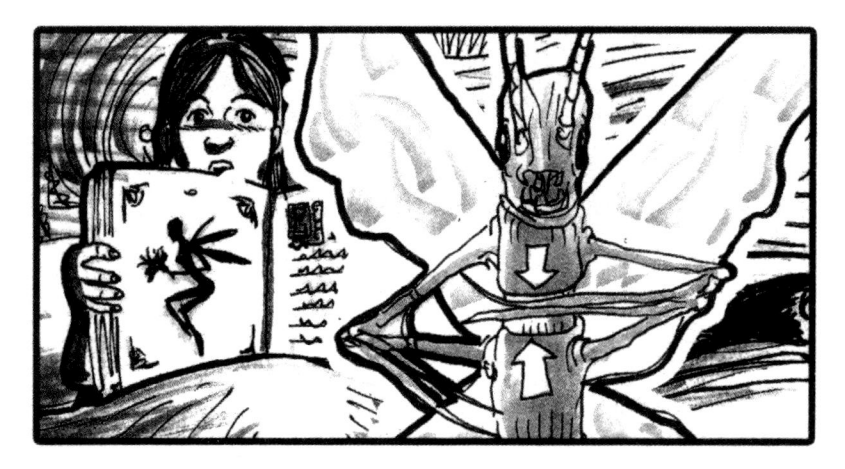

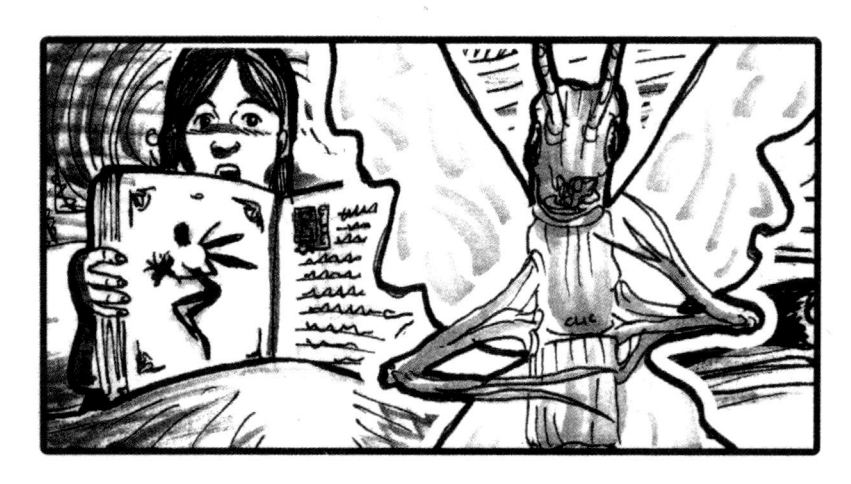

OPPOSITE AND LEFT This sequence shows the insect appearing again at night in Ofelia's bedroom.

PAN'S LABYRINTH 191

RIGHT AND OPPOSITE As Ofelia looks on, the insect turns into a fairy. It leads Ofelia back to the labyrinth and into her first encounter with the faun—Pan—who gives her three tasks to complete.

192 INTERNATIONAL PERSPECTIVES

PAN'S LABYRINTH 193

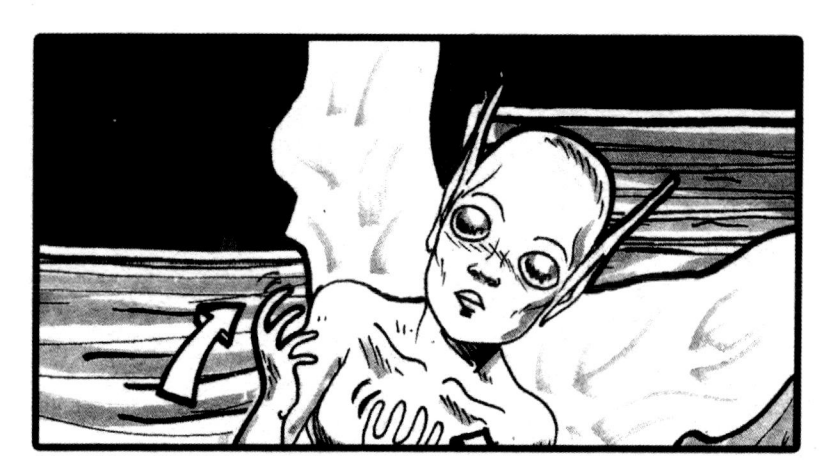

Drawing the Twenty-First Century

Technology has utterly transformed the film industry, and that process has accelerated exponentially since the turn of the century. It sometimes seems as though the film world has gone almost completely digital, from the first moments of storyboarding through to shooting and editing processes, distribution, and exhibition.

While many storyboard artists, particularly the more established ones, prefer the speed and subtleties of pencil and paper, ultimately those sketches will now be scanned into the computerized pipeline and manipulated online.

Storyboard artists tend to opt for tablets such as the Wacom Cintiq—which is a little like drawing on an iPad— and programs like StoryBoard Pro, SketchBook Pro, and, for animators, Toon Boom. Concept art is almost entirely computerized; some concept work is even being executed

This is by no means standard across the industry, however. Some storyboards in this section, particularly those for *Anna Karenina* (2012) and John Woo's 2014 Chinese Civil War drama *The Crossing*, have been entirely executed using computers and look markedly different from their compatriots.

Every style is equally valid, of course, and it all does come down to personal preference. It seems clear, however, that in years to come storyboards may no longer exist as the physical pieces that largely comprise the work on these pages, but as JPEG files.

OPPOSITE French storyboard artist Sylvain Despretz pictured with examples of his work at the Arludik Gallery, Paris, 2010.

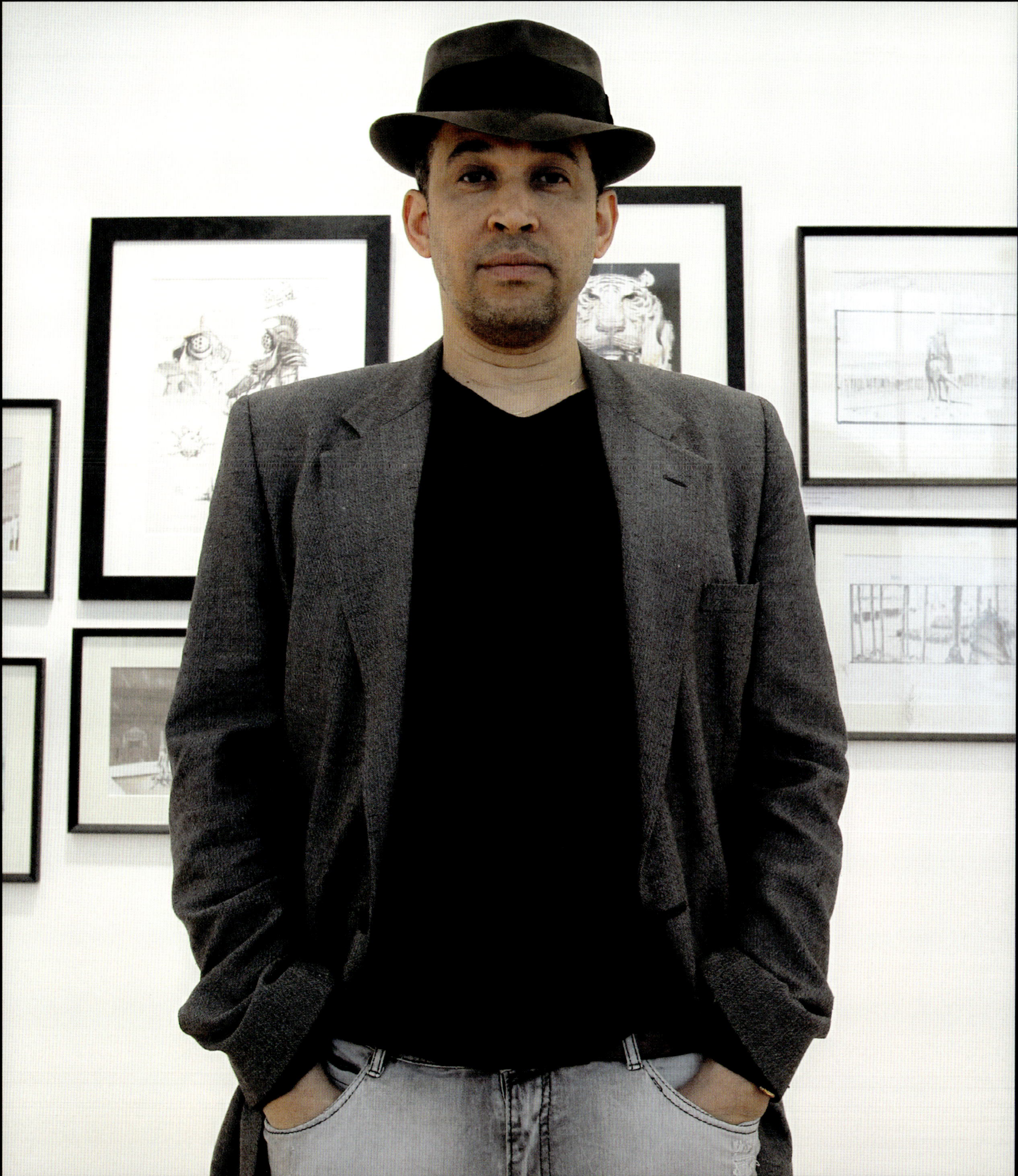

Gladiator 2000

DIRECTOR Ridley Scott
STORYBOARDS Sylvain Despretz

BELOW Russell Crowe and Djimon Hounsou in *Gladiator*.

French-born storyboard artist Sylvain Despretz has worked extensively in Hollywood, forming close relationships with the director Ridley Scott and the comics and conceptual artist Moebius (Jean Giraud), who provided the visual inspiration for many science fiction films including, perhaps most famously, *Alien* (1979).

Although not formally trained as an artist, Despretz remains reluctant to describe himself as self-taught, as he learned from his mentors on various jobs, from the advertising industry to working as an illustrator and on to Hollywood, which had always been his ultimate goal from a very early age.

Despretz recalls working for a full nine months with the director Ridley Scott on the multiple–Academy Award-winning *Gladiator*. Scott is, by reputation and by end result, a highly visual director and his films have always broken new ground. Having studied at London's Royal College of Art, Scott takes an extremely active role in the storyboarding of his films (his "Ridleygrams" are very fleshed out personal storyboards for his work, including *Alien*). Says Despretz, who has also worked on large-scale features, including *47 Ronin* (2013): "Most directors prefer telling a storyboard artist what goes into every frame of the film; Ridley Scott happens to be an excellent artist and can also draw it."

196 DRAWING THE TWENTY-FIRST CENTURY

RIGHT This page from Sylvain Despretz's *Gladiator* storyboards, depicting the gladiators emerging from the dark of the passageway into the glare of the open arena, also features a small note in the form of a diagram, lower right, demonstrating the layout of the arena.

GLADIATOR

DREAMWORKS
Director – Ridley Scott
Artist – Sylvain Despretz

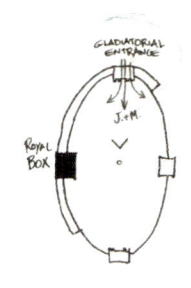

GLADIATOR 197

Cold Mountain 2003

DIRECTOR Anthony Minghella
STORYBOARDS Temple Clark

Following on from *The English Patient* (1996), *Cold Mountain* was another film on an epic scale from the late British director Anthony Minghella. Set during the American Civil War, it's about a battle-scarred Confederate soldier, W. P. Inman (Jude Law), who decides to desert the Army in order to reunite with his sweetheart Ada (Nicole Kidman) back home in North Carolina's Cold Mountain.

Minghella adapted the screenplay himself from the 1997 novel by Charles Frazier, and *Cold Mountain* was ultimately shot on location in Romania. The most visually arresting element of the film is its opening sequences, set during the brutal Siege of Petersburg in 1864. This is the prompt for mild-mannered Inman to make his decision to desert, so the believability of his character's entire journey depends on their dramatic effectiveness.

Two storyboard artists worked on *Cold Mountain*—Temple Clark and Tony Wright. Clark, whose boards are shown here, brainstormed with Minghella to execute "the pit"—the centerpiece of the real-life Battle of the Crater, formed after an explosion in Confederate-held territory during the Siege on July 30. With assault and counter-assault going on around them, the soldiers inside the crater—both living and dead—were buried in confusion on what General Ulysses Grant called "the saddest day of the war."

Calling his experience with Minghella "extremely collaborative," Clark worked hard to try visualize the Siege of Petersburg, which has been extensively documented and even photographed. He also drew on Brazilian photographer Sebastião Salgado's pictures of the Miners of Serra Pelada for inspiration. Most importantly, though, he had to break the sequence, in which further shells rain on the soldiers in the pit as the battle rages on, into separate shots.

Formally trained as an artist, Clark has been storyboarding since he got his break as a concept artist on Stephen Frears's *Mary Reilly* (1996). His almost twenty-year career has seen him work on major UK productions from the James Bond movie *The World is Not Enough* (1999) to *Lara Croft: Tomb Raider* (2001), from *Harry Potter and the Chamber of Secrets* (2002) to *Spider-Man 2* (2004) and *Sherlock Holmes* (2009), but his collaboration with Minghella on *Cold Mountain* still resonates a decade later. "I think it's some of the best work I've done," he says.

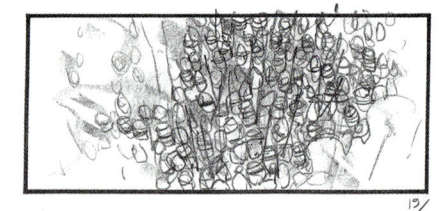

198 DRAWING THE TWENTY-FIRST CENTURY

Cold Mountain

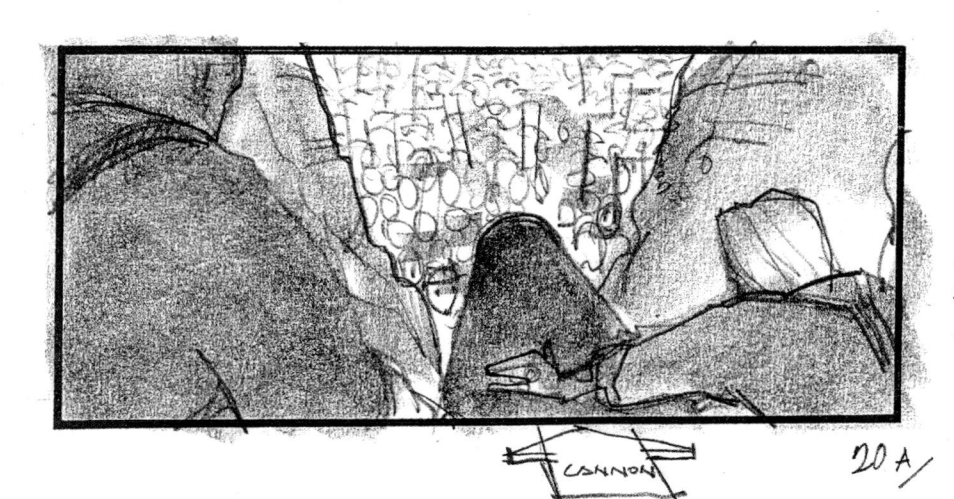

Sc: 11c.   (11A.)

SHOTS 20A-20E CANNON SQ.

A CANNON PUSHES FORWARD INTO FRAME

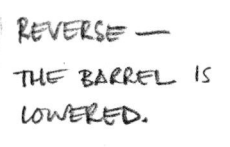

CANNON

20A/

REVERSE — THE BARREL IS LOWERED.

20B/

WE SEE TERRIFIED REACTION OF UNIONISTS — THEY TRY TO MOVE OUT OF THE WAY.

MEN   MEN

20C/

The sequence printed here (Scene 11c) places the main character, the Confederate soldier Inman, in the pit—the cavity at the center of the Battle of the Crater during the Siege of Petersburg. We witness, from his point of view, a mortar shell as it bursts above the tightly packed pit of living and dead soldiers. The Confederate soldiers fire down on the Unionists; but it's a scene of confusion and terror as they try to move out of the way (indicated by the large "men" arrows, below and overleaf), many suffocating amongst the dead.

Cold Mountain

Sc: 11C. (11B.)

Panel 20D (top): INMAN'S P.O.V. IT'S A HIDEOUS PANIC/CRUSH TO AVOID THE BLAST.

Panel 20D (middle): THE CANNON FIRES — THE UNIONISTS ARE SO PACKED THAT THEY DON'T DROP DEAD; — WE SEE A SORT OF "RIPPLE" AS THEY'RE HIT, BLOOD & BITS FLY UP.

Panel 20E (bottom): WE'RE IN AMONGST THE MEN — THE CANNON BALL PASSES NEARBY. WE SEE THE MEN KILLED, BUT STAY UPRIGHT.

Temple Clark used the photographs of Sebastião Salgado for inspiration as he worked to realize this sequence with the director Anthony Minghella. Although Tony Wright also worked on the storyboards for *Cold Mountain*, artists don't usually work on the same scenes. This time, however, when Clark showed his colleague the boards, Wright suggested the "chevaux de frise"—medieval anti-cavalry stakes that were used throughout the war. Clark added them to his drawings and instructions were rapidly relayed to the film's production designer Dante Ferretti and his team in Romania.

Cold Mountain

Sc: 11C

(12.)

21/

L/L CUT IN.

A SOLDIER HOLDS UP HIS HAND — HE CAN BARELY STAND AGAINST THE WEIGHT OF THE DEAD.

22/

L/L — A FACE COMES INTO FRAME & SHOUTS "SURRENDER!"

IN B/G — MEN START TO LOWER THEIR RIFLES.

23/

C/U — OUR UNION MAN WAVES A HANKERCHIEF.

COLD MOUNTAIN 201

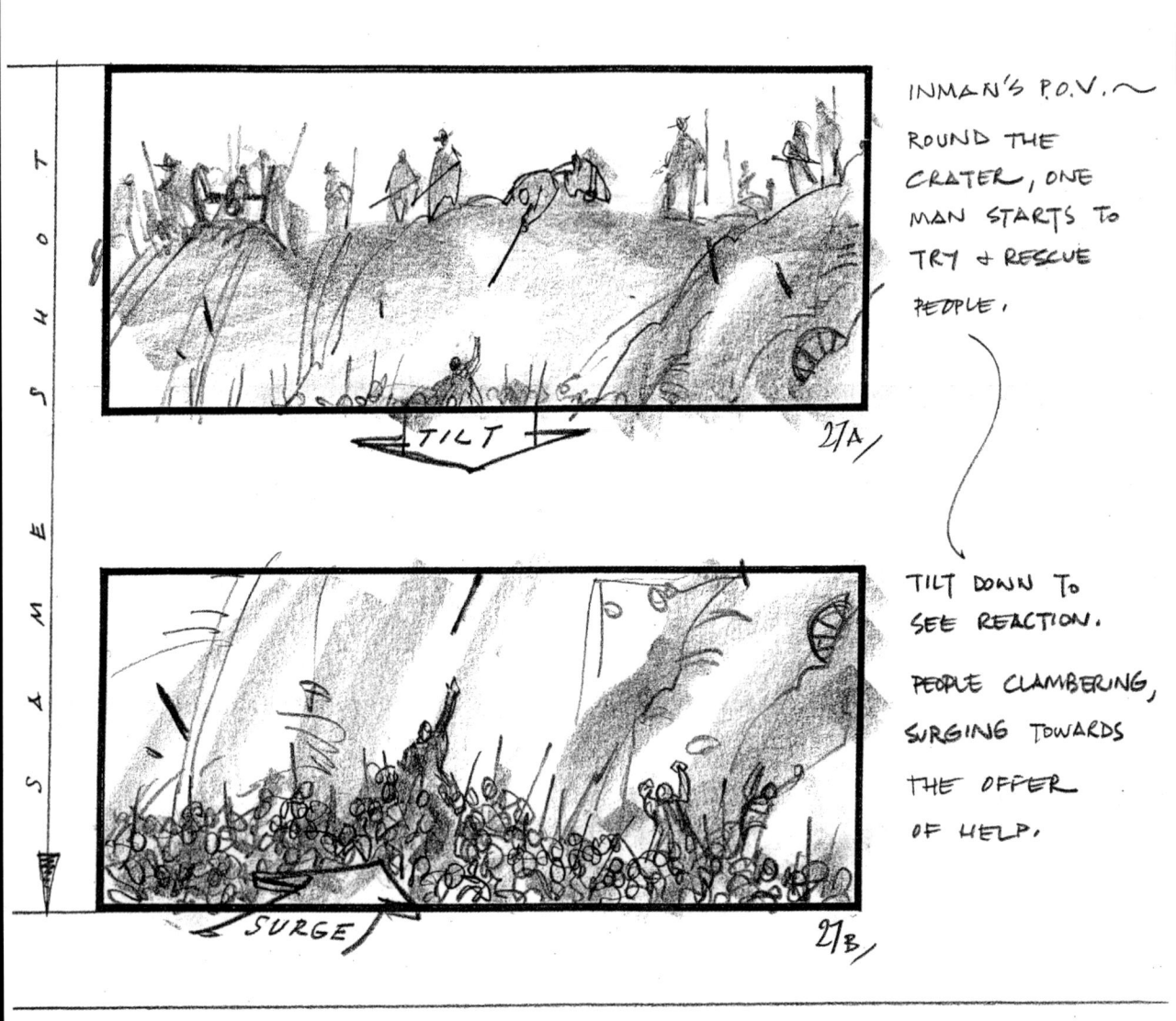

Cold Mountain

Sc: 11c

(14)

27A — INMAN'S P.O.V. ~ ROUND THE CRATER, ONE MAN STARTS TO TRY & RESCUE PEOPLE.

TILT

27B — TILT DOWN TO SEE REACTION. PEOPLE CLAMBERING, SURGING TOWARDS THE OFFER OF HELP.

SURGE

28 — INMAN WATCHES. WE SEE BUTCHER'S REACTION.

202 DRAWING THE TWENTY-FIRST CENTURY

OPPOSITE AND RIGHT A rifle is lowered to the trappped combatants as a way of helping them escape; the "surge" arrow indicates the direction of the crush of men toward the offer of help.

Cold Mountain

Sc: 11c

(27)

LOW SHOT OF THEM LEAPING OVER THE LIP.

52/

ANGLE—

THEY LEAP INTO THE PIT — SOME JUST PAST CAMERA.

ROCKS & RUBBLE TUMBLE DOWN.

53/

HIGH SHOT — THEY LEAP & SLIDE DOWN THE SLOPE INTO THE PACKED UNIONIST TROOPS.

54/

smoke booms — covers & reveals

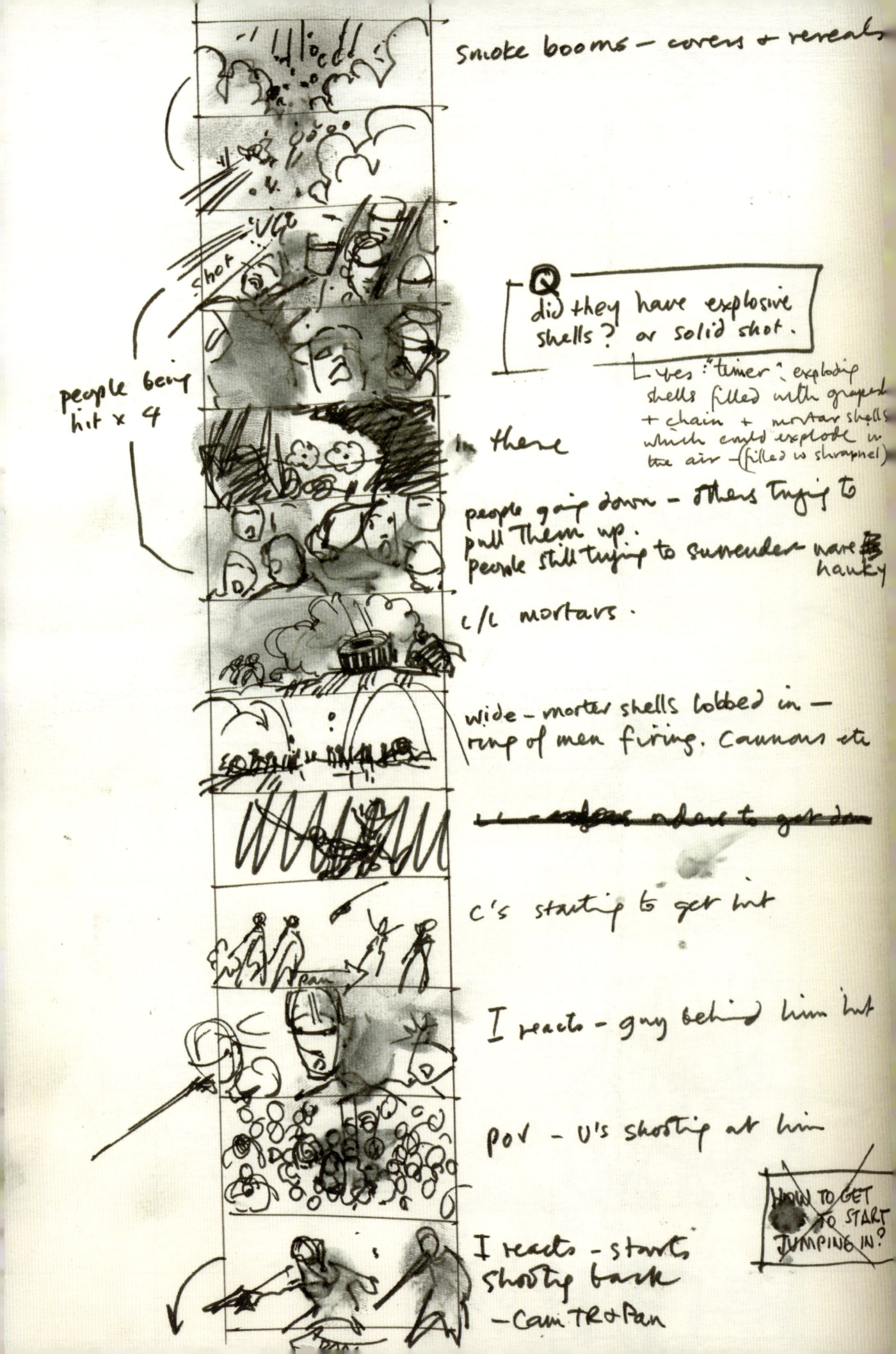

Q: did they have explosive shells? or solid shot.
└ yes "timer" exploding shells filled with grapes[hot] + chain + mortar shells which could explode in the air — (filled w shrapnel)

people being hit x 4

— there

people going down — others trying to pull them up.
people still trying to surrender — wave hanky

c/u mortars.

wide — mortar shells lobbed in — ring of men firing. cannons etc

~~others where to get down~~

c's starting to get hit

I reacts — guy behind him hit

pov — U's shooting at him

HOW TO GET TO START JUMPING IN?

I reacts — starts shooting back — cam TR & Pan

Temple Clark's sketchbook from *Cold Mountain* shows how he started to devise his work; the influence of photographer Sebastião Salgado is clear here. He also sketches images of soldiers on the side of the pit, inspired by documented incidents of how mortar explosions would blow the clothes off army fighters, leaving them naked apart from their gun belts. About five months of work went into Clark's boards and sketches for *Cold Mountain*, much of which was captured in the finished film.

COLD MOUNTAIN 205

Harry Potter and the Goblet of Fire 2005

DIRECTOR Mike Newell
STORYBOARDS Jane Clark

Experienced British storyboard artist Jane Clark worked on several *Harry Potter* films, from the third installment in the series, *Harry Potter and the Prisoner of Azkaban* (2004), through to the eighth and final episode, *Harry Potter and the Deathly Hallows, Part 2* (2011).

Her time on *Harry Potter* saw the artist working closely with several directors, from Alfonso Cuarón (*Azkaban*) to David Yates (the final four films). The head of her department, production designer Stuart Craig, was the key creative line through all eight films, and the storyboards shown here were drawn for the fourth film in the series, *Harry Potter and the Goblet of Fire*, directed by Mike Newell.

This film was darker and more urgent than those that had preceded it, and the underwater sequence in particular was exciting and dangerous, as these boards clearly demonstrate. On a film this size, several storyboard artists will be working on difference scenes at the same time.

Jane Clark started her career as a magazine illustrator before studying set design at Yale. She worked as a designer briefly before getting her break in storyboarding on *Prizzi's Honor* (1985), the great director John Huston's last film. "When [they] were filming a scene in New York, they asked me to come and storyboard it for them. So I followed them on a location walk and drew that up—work offers flowed in from there." Her other credits include films as diverse as *Bridget Jones's Diary* (2001) and the most recent James Bond movie, *Skyfall* (2012).

In *Harry Potter and the Goblet of Fire*, Harry is unexpectedly selected to take part in the Triwizard Tournament, which involves three tough challenges. The second task takes place in the black lake near Hogwarts, where merpeople live alongside small horned water demons called Grindylows, whose attack forces one of the competing wizards to retire from the challenge.

206 DRAWING THE TWENTY-FIRST CENTURY

UNDERWATER p. 3

④ CLOSE ON HARRY STRUGGLING, CHOKING, PERHAPS STILL TRAILING SOME GILLYWEED FROM HIS MOUTH. SCALES ARE STARTING TO APPEAR...

④ MORE ...AND DEPRESSIONS WHERE THE GILLS WILL BE.

UNDERWATER p. 4

⑤ ANGLE ON HARRY'S HANDS WITH PARTIALLY-WEBBED FINGERS — ADJUST TO PICK UP A HINT OF HIS REACTION

⑥ ANGLE ON HIS FLIPPERY FEET

UNDERWATER P. 5

Harry, however, has been provided with Gillyweed, which enables him to grow fins and breathe underwater for one hour. Jane Clark's exquisite sequence shows the moment when Harry and his two competitors first dive into the water. Soon, the Gillyweed starts to take effect on Harry. As she notes on Shot 5, the camera angles in on Harry's hands with partially webbed fingers and "his flippery feet," before he is clearly shown enjoying his new "piscine condition."

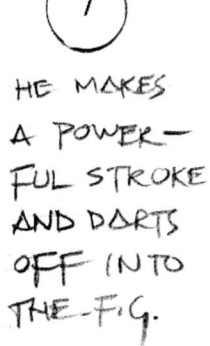

7 WIDER ON HARRY'S WONDERMENT

MORE 7 HE MAKES A POWERFUL STROKE AND DARTS OFF INTO THE F.G.

8 WATCH HARRY CAVORTING FISHILY — HE ENTERS A LONG...

HARRY POTTER AND THE GOBLET OF FIRE

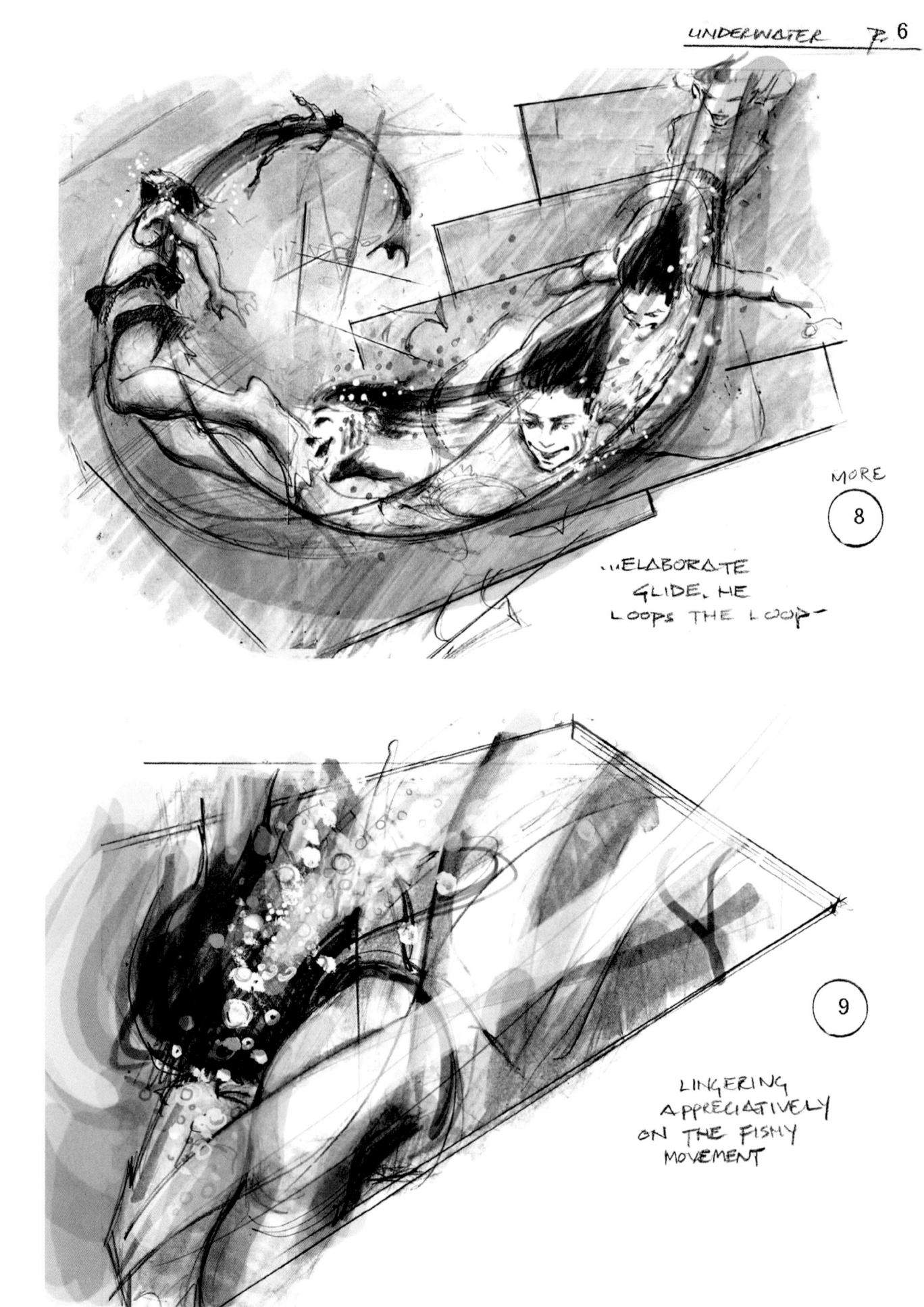

UNDERWATER p. 6

...ELABORATE GLIDE. HE LOOPS THE LOOP—

8 MORE

LINGERING APPRECIATIVELY ON THE FISHY MOVEMENT

9

UNDERWATER P. 7

The sequence will soon turn dark, however. Each competitor has been told they must retrieve something that has been stolen from them; this turns out to be their friends, including Ron and Hermione, who are tethered underwater in a state of suspended animation.

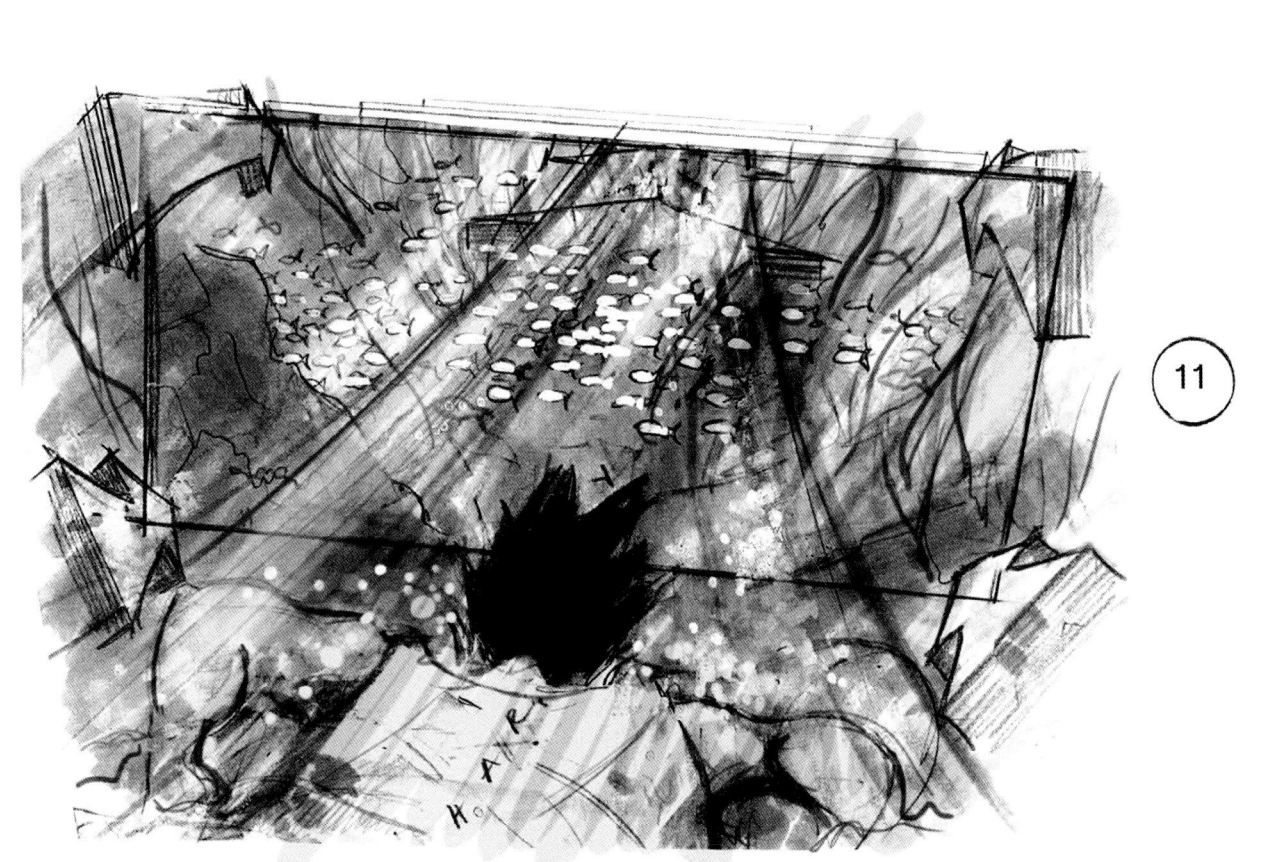

(10) CLOSE ON HARRY'S ENJOYMENT OF HIS PISCINE CONDITION

(11) TRAVELLING OVER HARRY AS HE SWOOPS DOWNWARD, HEADING FOR A PASSING SCHOOL OF FISH

HARRY POTTER AND THE GOBLET OF FIRE 211

Land of the Dead 2005

DIRECTOR George A. Romero
STORYBOARDS Rob McCallum

What book is complete without a reanimated corpse? George A. Romero's *Night of the Living Dead* introduced the zombie to modern cinema in 1968 (although Bela Lugosi played a zombie back in the 1920s, it wasn't the zombie as we know him/her/it today). Flesh-eating, brain-munching walking corpses, zombies are now a sizeable cinematic subculture and Romero ("The Godfather of Zombies") has continued to work within the genre. His fourth *Dead* film, *Land of the Dead* was released by Universal, with the largest budget of the series, at $16m. Dennis Hopper, Asia Argento, and John Leguizamo star in the story of a zombie attack on a post-apocalyptic Pittsburgh ruled by a feudal government (under Hopper). Survivors flee to the city, which is protected on two sides by rivers and on the other by an electric barricade.

The Scotland-born, Toronto-based storyboard artist Rob McCallum says he "likes doing monster films," and was a huge fan of Romero, "so this was a fun job to get." McCallum, a graduate of Glasgow School of Art, where he made short films as part of his degree, started out as a comic book artist but later transitioned to film. Moving to Toronto twelve years ago with his wife proved fortuitous, and McCallum has worked steadily on big-budget films there, including the 2014 *Robocop* reboot and nine months on Guillermo del Toro's *Pacific Rim* (2013).

This sequence of McCallum's storyboards features the rise of "Big Daddy" (Eugene Clark), the zombie leader who—as a gas station owner in his previous life—is a smart zombie, capable of understanding and revenge. He perceives that the river is not an obstacle and leads his zombies to attack the city, although he himself is hell-bent on finding the leader, Kaufmann (Hopper), and destroying him. "While I do like drawing monsters and sci-fi, it's always the storytelling that's the challenging part when it comes to storyboards," says McCallum. "Trying to find the best way to frame it, the least amount of shots. It's always a challenge."

Page_4

CUT TO.

Scene 112   Shot 5

CLOSER ON BIG DADDY

OPPOSITE AND LEFT "Big Daddy" is smarter than your average zombie and perceives that the water surrounding the city isn't really a problem for his armies of the undead. In Rob McCallum's storyboards, Big Daddy's head slowly emerges from the water; you know trouble is ahead.

Page 6

Scene 112 Shot 7
CUT TO

c/u HEADS BREAK SURFACE

Scene 112 Shot 8
CUT TO.

c/u MORE ZOMBIES BREAK SURFACE

LEFT AND OPPOSITE As McCallum notes, "more zombies break the surface," then "a *lot* of zombies rise up." The city is in trouble as they emerge from the water, intent on some flesh and brain-eating. McCallum recalls the shoot in a water park in Toronto in the middle of November. "It was very, very cold, minus fifteen," he says. "And even though the actors were in wetsuits, you had to feel sorry for them. This is one of the first sequences I drew and we knew who the actor was who would play Big Daddy, so that helped. I had to draw a few extra boards for the wide shots to show to the studio, so I'm pleased with this sequence. It ended up being shot pretty much as we'd conceived it, which is always nice."

Page 6A — Scene ___ Shot ___

Page 7 — CUT TO — Scene 112 Shot 9 
WIDER - ZOMBIES RISE

CUT TO — Scene 112 Shot 10 
MORE.

Page 8 — CUT TO — Scene 112 Shot 11 
WIDE - A LOT OF ZOMBIES RISE UP

Page 8A — Scene ___ Shot ___ 
REVERSE SCENE 112 - SHOT 11 - PAGE 8.

Page 9 — Scene 112 Shot 4
CU BIG DADDY - ZOMBIES BEHIND HIM.

Page 10 — SC. 113, Scene 113 Shot 1 
WIDE - FULL SCENE REVEALED

Page 11 — Scene 113 Shot 2
CUT TO
LOW - ON WHARF. BIG DADDY'S FOOT COMES IN.

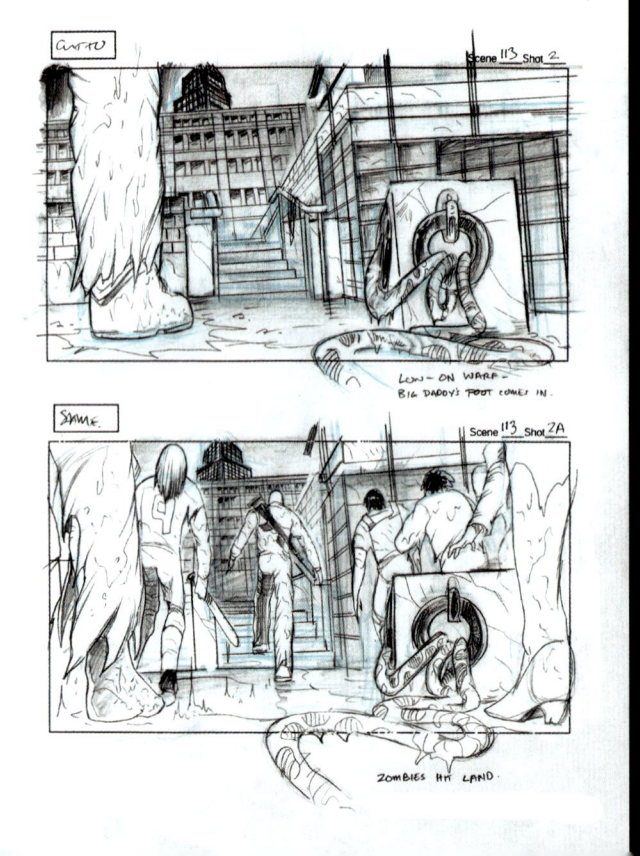

Scene 113 Shot 2A
SAME.
ZOMBIES HIT LAND.

Page 12 — Scene 113 Shot 3 
CUT TO
REVERSE - LARGE CROWD OF ZOMBIES COME OUT OF WATER.

Like many artists, McCallum prefers to work with pencil and paper, which he later scans. "The Cintiq [tablet and pen] is fast and I've done a few films where I've been happy with the results and it was quick," he says. "But there's nothing as fast and precise as pencil on paper."

REVERSE — PAGE 12 — SC 113 — SHOT 3.

The Chronicles of Narnia: The Voyage of the Dawn Treader 2010

DIRECTOR Michael Apted
STORYBOARDS David Russell

"The much-beloved Narnia stories had long awaited cinematic treatment," says artist David Russell, whose storyboards for *Who Framed Roger Rabbit* appear on pages 152–157. "I therefore leaped at the chance to work on *The Lion, the Witch and the Wardrobe* (2005), and, subsequently, *The Voyage of the Dawn Treader*."

This series of films (three to date) is a sumptuously mounted fantasy adventure adapting C. S. Lewis's wartime novels about British children who access the mythical land of Narnia through various portals, and, once there, become protagonists in the age-old battle between good and evil.

"I was initially called in to rework the storyboards of several preceding artists, as the studio felt that, despite their efforts, the film still lacked an epic feel. I also boarded many new sequences. I'm satisfied that the end result reflected my contributions," says Russell, whose participation in the Narnia films follows a lifetime love of classical fairytales and mythology. "The best fantasy films poignantly remind global audiences of our common humanity, and often postulate beatific concepts of the universe and our place within it," he adds. "I do feel the Narnia films gracefully achieved these laudable goals."

The Lion, the Witch and the Wardrobe, directed by Andrew Adamson, centers on the children's first visit to Narnia, where they encounter the faun Mr. Tumnus (James McAvoy) and the White Witch, played by Tilda Swinton. Later, Russell came back to work on the third Narnia film, *The Voyage of the Dawn Treader*, and his storyboards for an early sequence are shown on these pages. "It was a pleasure working with esteemed [director] Michael Apted on *The Voyage of the Dawn Treader*," says Russell. "Among other innovations, and following one of our discussions, Michael introduced black characters into the Narnia world. A small matter, perhaps, but one that seemed quite appropriate."

RIGHT AND OPPOSITE In Greek mythology, Naiads are nymphs made of water, and they appear frequently in C. S. Lewis's *The Chronicles of Narnia* series. This sequence from *The Voyage of the Dawn Treader*, storyboarded by David Russell, marks their cinematic debut. As Lucy Pevensie (Georgie Henley) waves from the deck of the Dawn Treader, the almost-transparent Naiads joyously beckon and dive.

218 DRAWING THE TWENTY-FIRST CENTURY

(4)

DOWNSHOT-(P.O.V. LUCY)-CLOSE ON SURFACE OF WATER- CAM. TRACKS DIAGONALLY AS UNDERWATER NAIAD #1 STREAKS INTO FRAME...

(4A)(CONT)

...NAIAD #1 SURFACES, SMILES, BECKONS TO O/S LUCY.

(5)

ANGLE ON LUCY - CHARMED - WAVES BACK TO O/S NAIAD #1.   CUT

(6)

EXTREME LOW ANGLE ON BOW OF DAWN TREADER - NAIADS 'SUBMARINE' GAILY AHEAD OF THE SHIP.   CUT

(7)

ANOTHER ANGLE ON THE NAIADS - LEAP OUT OF THE WATER!!!   CONT.

The sequence, one of the film's most beautiful, was complex to realize. Visual effects were created by London's The Mill, who utilized Russell's boards as a reference. The Naiad sequence underlines the fundamental position of storyboards in the filmmaking process: whether the sequence is live-action or digital, the boards come first.

220 DRAWING THE TWENTY-FIRST CENTURY

(7A) (CONT.)

|||CAM. DESCENDS WITH NAIADS AS THEY PLUNGE UNDERWATER|||

(7B) CONT.

|||CAM. ADJUSTS, RESTS AS NAIADS STREAK PAST CAM + O/S R...

(7C) CONT.

||| NAIADS O/S R.

CUT END SEQ.

THE CHRONICLES OF NARNIA: THE VOYAGE OF THE DAWN TREADER 221

Anna Karenina 2012

DIRECTOR Joe Wright
STORYBOARDS David Allcock

This dramatic sequence showing Anna Karenina's suicide in Joe Wright's highly artistic interpretation of Tolstoy's nineteenth century novel was drawn—digitally, in Photoshop—by storyboard artist David Allcock using a Cintiq tablet. ("How I work more and more nowadays; I still use pencil a lot because it's very quick, but if I've got time I'll do it digitally.") This was also used as a presentation storyboard, to communicate to the studio—as well as the production—Wright's imagining of Anna's dramatic end, so the images are more dynamic, with more detail in them (see also the boards for John Woo's *The Crossing* on pages 230–233). Allcock used splatters of red blood "to liven things up—whatever gets the message across," although color isn't normally used in modern storyboarding.

A comic book fan since early childhood, Allcock originally started out in the film business via a university degree in film and video, specializing in editing. But the loneliness of the edit suite was not for him, and he took an unpaid job as a gofer in a London Soho production house, all the time refining his drawing at home until the opportunity arose for him to step up to the plate and draw boards for a commercial. Allcock then worked as an assistant for the director Vadim Jean, drawing all of his storyboards, and finally went freelance a decade ago.

Allcock has worked closely with production designer Sarah Greenwood's UK-based team, on *Anna Karenina*, the two *Sherlock Holmes* films (2009 and 2011), and *Hanna* (also 2011); he has also worked on action spectaculars *World War Z* (2013) and *All You Need is Kill* (2014). "I have no training in art, not even a design course," says Allcock, who was mostly inspired by the boards drawn by Martin Asbury (whose credits include the Bond movies from *GoldenEye*, 1995, to *Skyfall*, 2012) and Mike Ploog (*The Thing*, 1982; *X-Men*, 2000) as he entered the business. "But I found my niche in storyboarding. You have to think like an editor when you draw. And a director. And a cinematographer."

Joe Wright's *Anna Karenina* was originally conceived as a "normal" period film, to be set partially on location in Russia, when the director radically reconceived it as taking place entirely within a theater, built in Shepperton Studios in the UK. Allcock worked through both visions of the film, and the "new" *Anna Karenina* was particularly difficult to explain to the outside world, requiring his full powers of visual interpretation.

222 DRAWING THE TWENTY-FIRST CENTURY

VER.2 9/5/12 | 2

D

...SHE IS HIT BY THE TRAIN'S UNDERCARRIAGE...

E

...AND SPINS...

F

...SHE TUMBLES TOWARDS CAM...

...CONT...

VER.2 9/5/12 | 3 |

G — ...HER FACE RIGHT INTO THE LENS...

H ...A BLUR OF MOTION AS...

I ...WE TILT DOWN TO THE TRACKS...

...CONT..

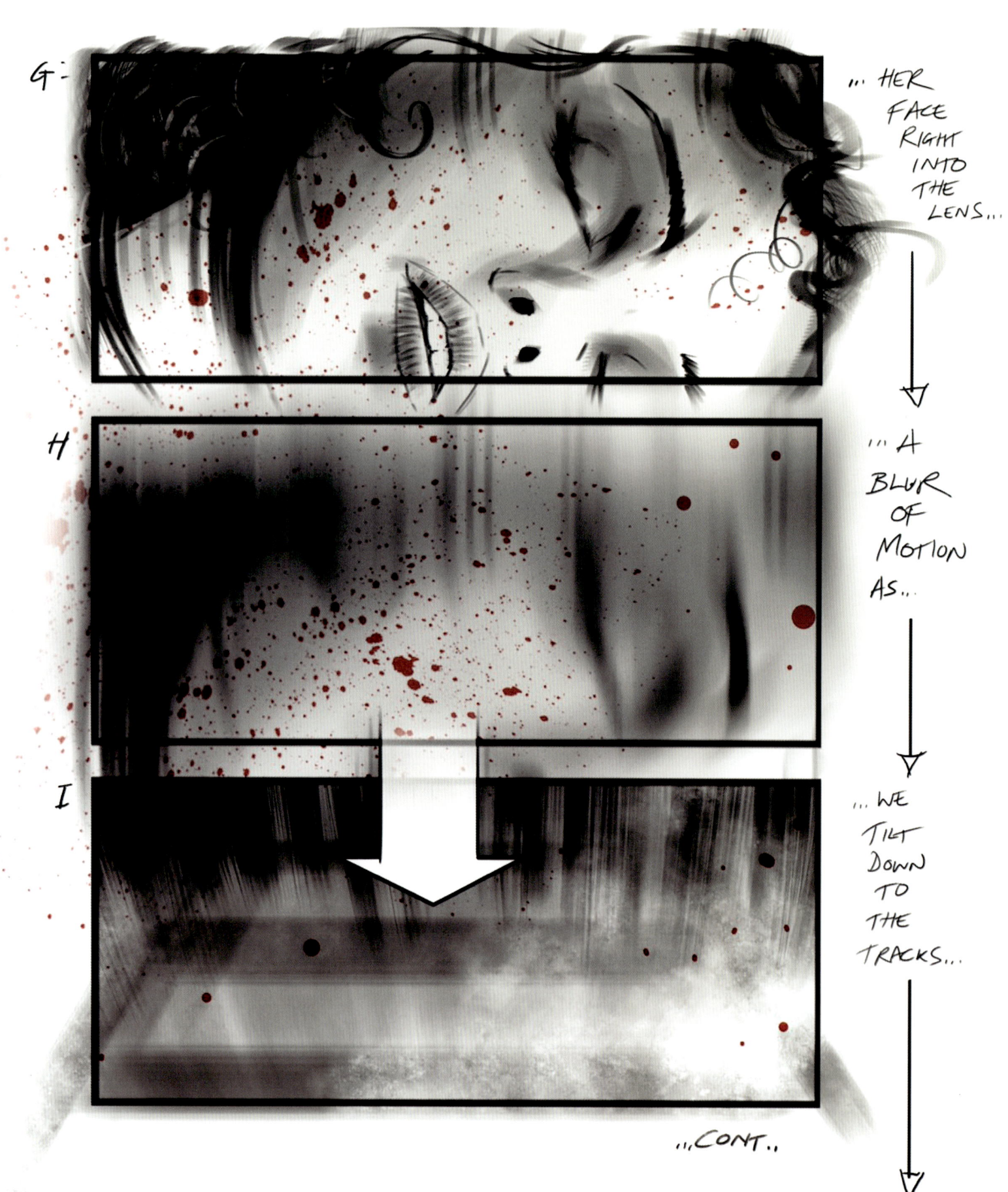

224 DRAWING THE TWENTY-FIRST CENTURY

VER.2 9/5/12   [4]

J ...LOOKING DOWN ON ANNA, DEAD...

K ...PUSH INTO HER FACE...

L ...END ON E.C.U

[CUT]

Anna Karenina was widely hailed for its visual excellence on release, with multiple, international awards nominations for the art department. These boards, which are "pretty close to what appeared," were produced for some reshoots, and thus Allcock was able to spend more time on them than is the norm.

The Invisible Woman 2013

DIRECTOR Ralph Fiennes
STORYBOARDS Temple Clark

BELOW AND OPPOSITE Here, Charles Dickens is seen at Kings Cross railway station in 1857, leaving his wife and youngest son (nicknamed "Plorn") on the platform. It's a happy scene, with young Plorn taking a marble from his father.

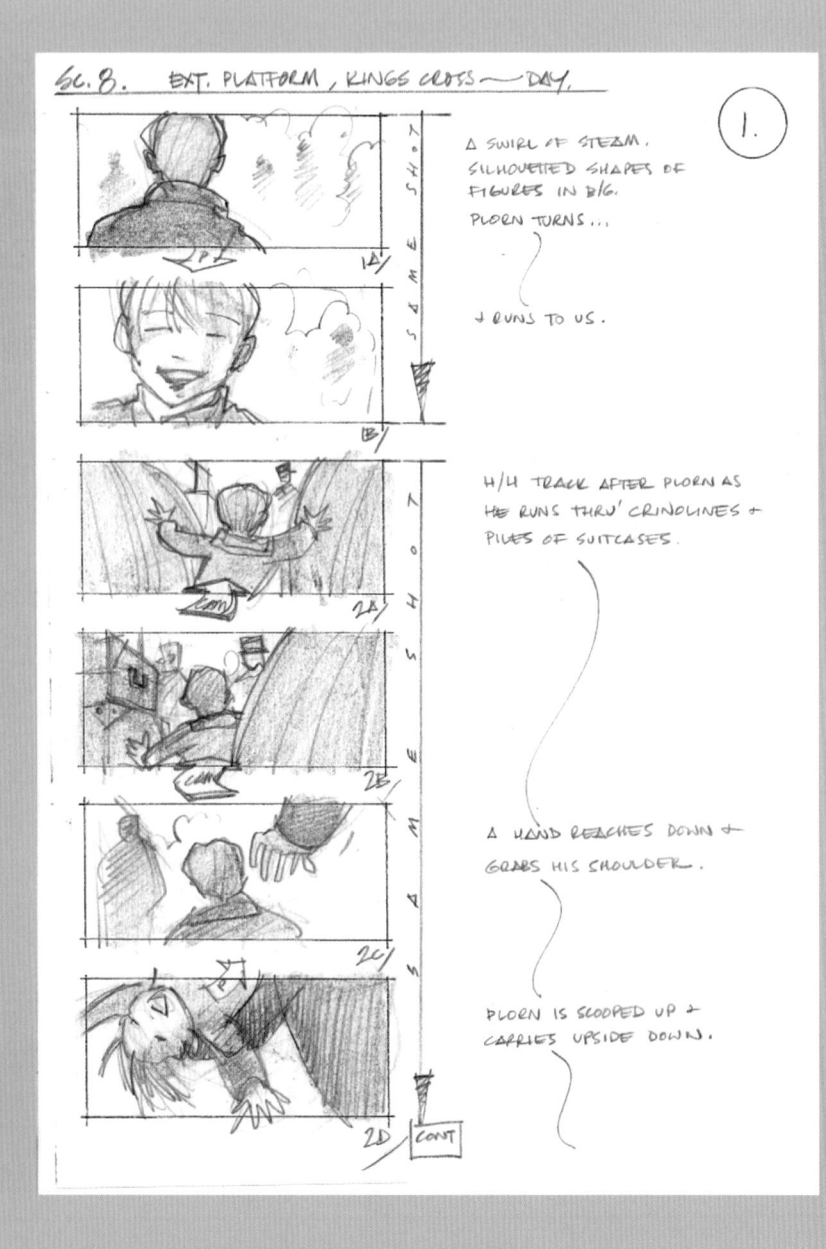

British storyboard artist Temple Clark (see also *Cold Mountain*, pages 198–205) worked with Ralph Fiennes on the actor's arresting directorial debut *Coriolanus* in 2011 and they came together again in the early stages of Fiennes's next film as director, *The Invisible Woman*. Set in Britain in the mid-nineteenth century, this period drama is based on the book of the same name by Claire Tomalin and focuses on the novelist Charles Dickens (Fiennes) and his lengthy affair with eighteen-year-old actress Nelly Ternan (Felicity Jones). The affair took place at the height of Dickens's fame as a writer when he was forty-five, more than twice Ternan's age, prompting him to abandon his wife Catherine and their ten children.

Clark worked closely with Fiennes, himself an artist (he studied at the Chelsea College of Art), with Fiennes providing preliminary boards. They first locked down the

226 DRAWING THE TWENTY-FIRST CENTURY

overall mood of the film with some concept storyboards before moving on to the more defined panels seen on these pages.

As a storyboard artist, Temple Clark has been most inspired by the work of Sherman Labby on *Blade Runner* (1982), and found a more personal mentor in the British artist Jane Clark, whose boards for *Harry Potter and the Goblet of Fire* feature on pages 206–211. Starting out after art school on pop videos and record sleeves, he has designed storyboards across multiple genres, from the stately *Elizabeth* (1998) to the action of *Entrapment* (1999), from extravagant family features like *The Golden Compass* (2007) to the epic science fiction of Alfonso Cuarón's *Gravity* (2013).

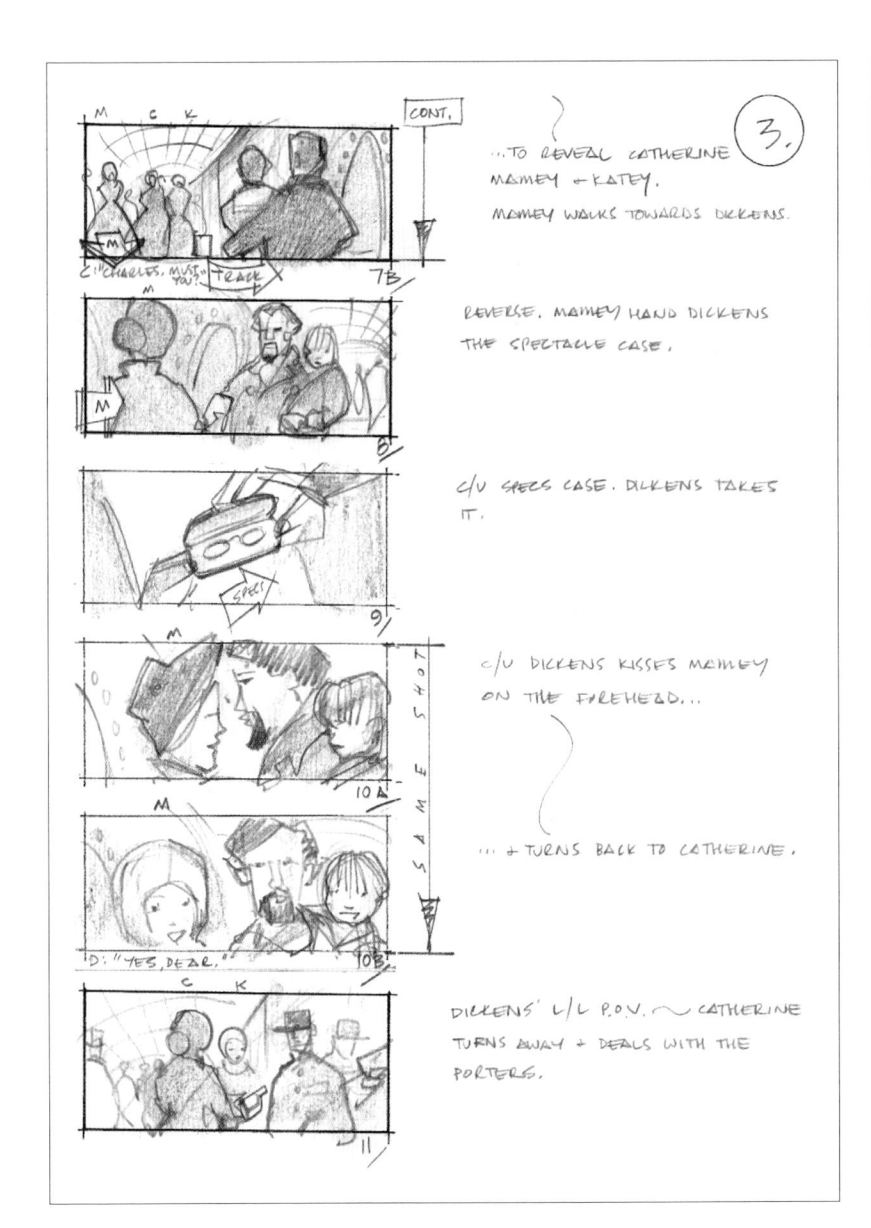

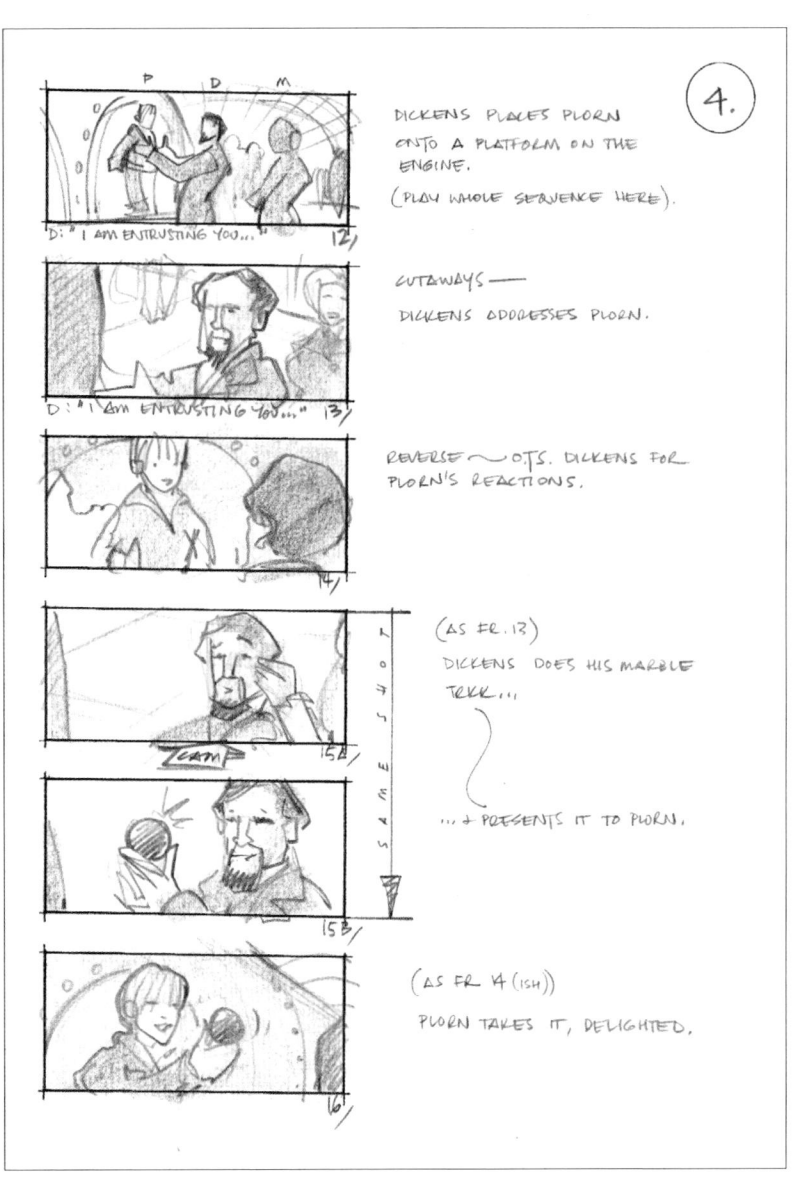

Sc.9. INT. CARRIAGE, TRAIN, KING'S CROSS—DAY 1857   12.

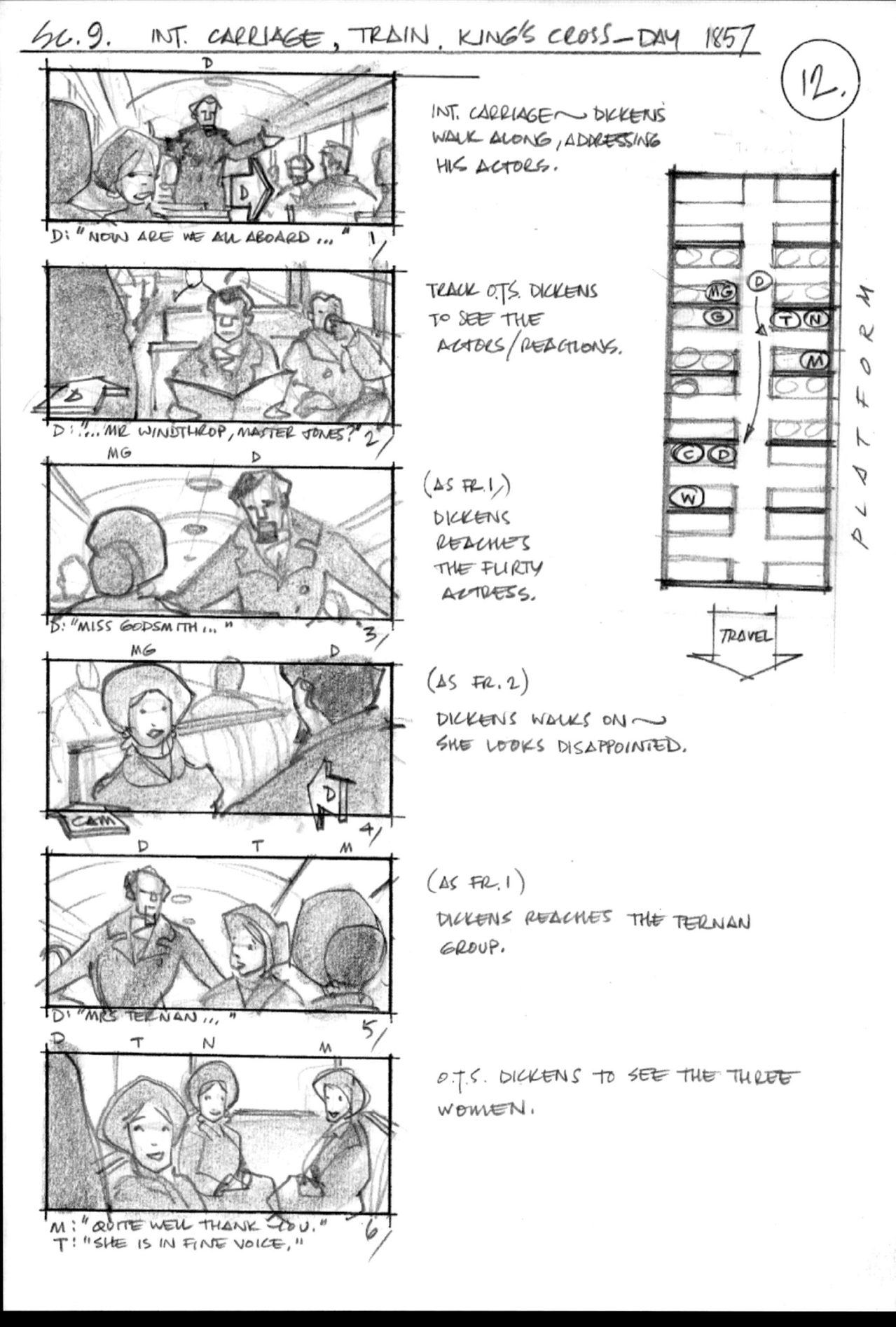

INT. CARRIAGE — DICKENS WALK ALONG, ADDRESSING HIS ACTORS.

D: "NOW ARE WE ALL ABOARD..." 1/

TRACK O.T.S. DICKENS TO SEE THE ACTORS/REACTIONS.

D: "...MR WINDTHROP, MASTER JONES? 2/

(AS FR.1) DICKENS REACHES THE FLIRTY ACTRESS.

D: "MISS GOLDSMITH..." 3/

(AS FR.2) DICKENS WALKS ON — SHE LOOKS DISAPPOINTED.

4/

(AS FR.1) DICKENS REACHES THE TERNAN GROUP.

D: "MRS TERNAN..." 5/

O.T.S. DICKENS TO SEE THE THREE WOMEN.

M: "QUITE WELL THANK YOU."
T: "SHE IS IN FINE VOICE." 6/

228 DRAWING THE TWENTY-FIRST CENTURY

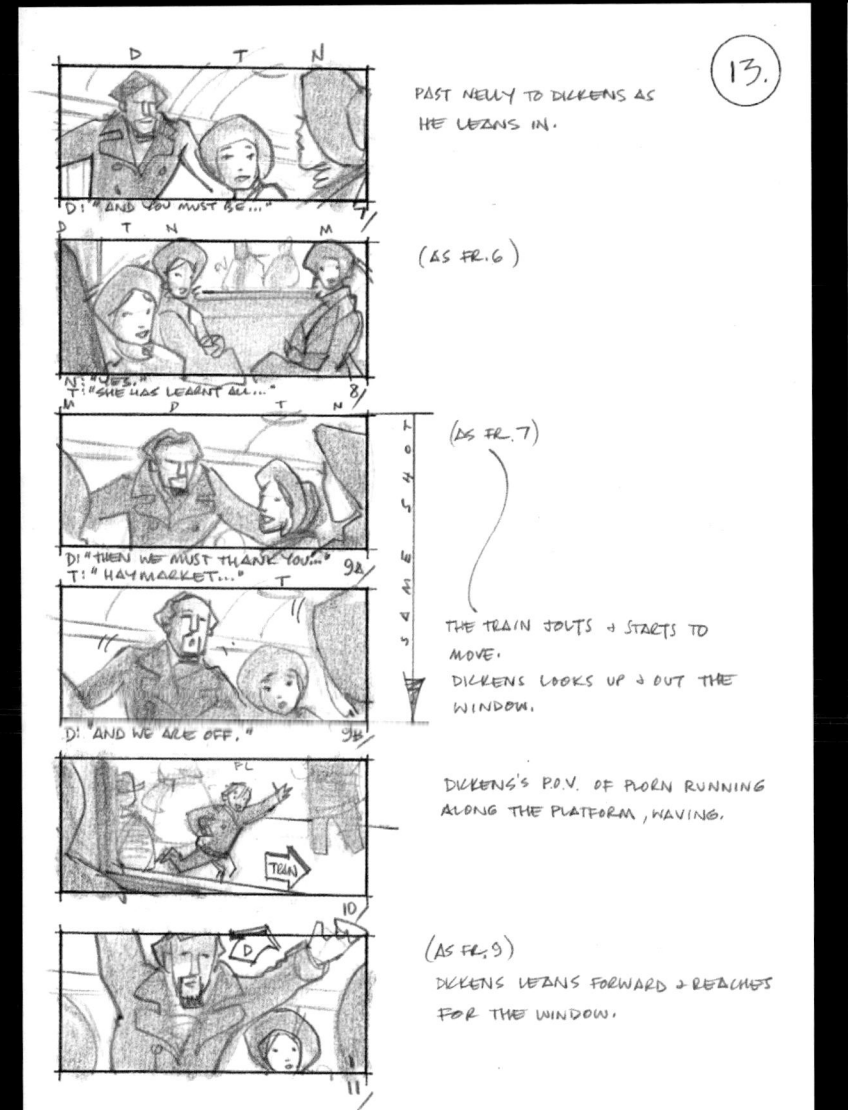

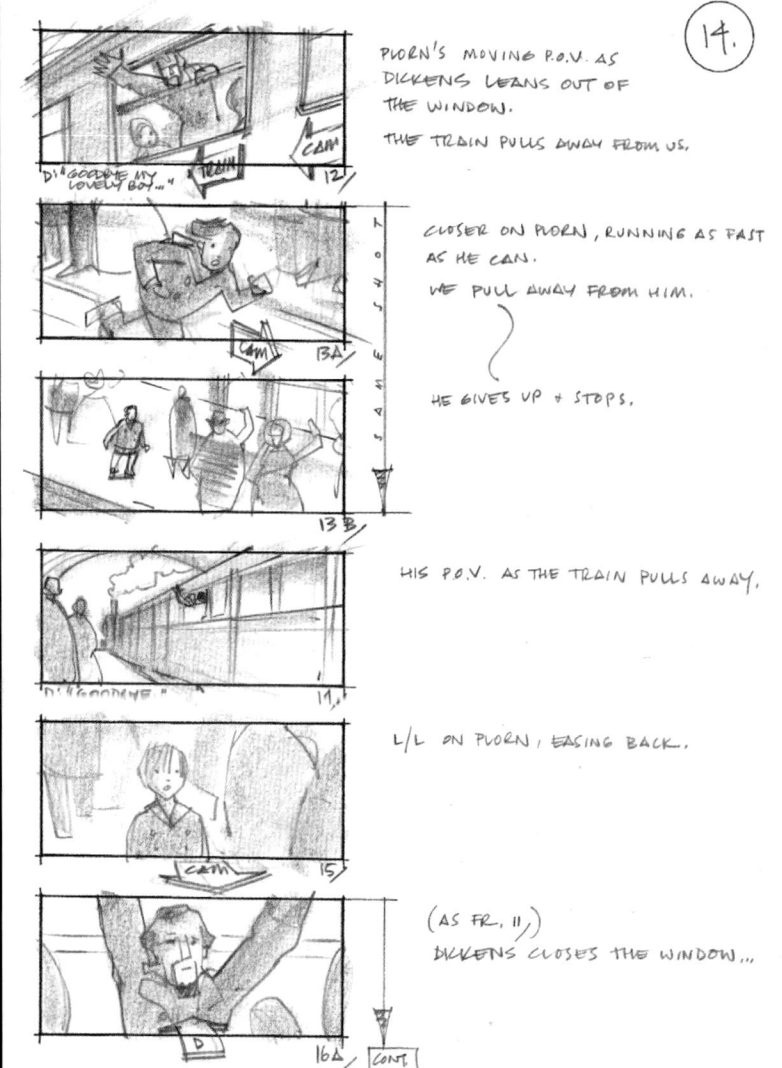

OPPOSITE AND ABOVE Scene 8 is immediately followed by Scene 9, the interior of the carriage train. On the top right hand side of the storyboard opposite, Clark has provided a seating plan of the carriage, where Nelly and her mother Catherine are sitting. Dickens passes a "flirty actress" to sit with Nelly, and they both—sequentially—watch Plorn disappear on the platform as the train pulls out. These scenes, when placed together, demonstrate Dickens's duplicity, and give a sense of the dark events about to take place.

The Crossing 2014

DIRECTOR John Woo
STORYBOARDS unattributed

BELOW AND OPPOSITE
The storyboards seen here were created digitally rather than with pencil and paper, lending them an almost photorealistic sheen in places.

The great Hong Kong director John Woo never once storyboarded a single scene from his classic high-octane Chinese-language thrillers, including *The Killer* (1989) and *Hard Boiled* (1992). He didn't even have a shot list. Woo liked to keep four cameras running and stage his famous action sequences like a ballet. The much-copied sequence in *Hard Boiled*, where he laid waste to a Chinese tea house (a real one, which was about to be destroyed), with the actor Chow Yun-fat sliding down the banisters with two guns blazing, was executed after a walk-through with the cast and crew.

That's unimaginable now, and was also impossible for Woo when he moved to the U.S. and began working with American crews on film such as *Face/Off* (1997), *Mission: Impossible II* (2000), and *Windtalkers* (2002). He started to work with storyboard artists there, and, when he went back to China to make *Red Cliff* (2008), the habit stuck, and he now uses storyboard artists extensively.

These scenes are for the two-part romantic-action epic *The Crossing*, slated to go into production in 2013, which sets intertwining love stories against the backdrop of 1940s Taiwan and Shanghai. At a cost of $30m and starring top Asian actors including Zhang Ziyi and Song Hye-kyo, it has taken Woo and his producer Terence Chang six years to pull the project together. "It involves recreating battles from World War II and the Chinese Civil War, along with an historical incident from the 1940s when a ship sunk off the coast near Shanghai," says Chang. Part one of *The Crossing* is tentatively set for release at the end of 2014, with the second part due in 2015.

SC. 43 平原/战场（日） 太平轮1949（第十五稿）

1. 
W.S. 战场上寒风忽忽，国共两军已激战多时，战地中央残缺的人体、车体满布，镜头缓慢升高并向左方移动……

1a. 
续：镜头升高，俯视山丘下的山谷，远处一片白烟弥漫的解放军据点，但见一排排来自排炮爆发的火光。镜头持续向左横移……

1b. 
续：镜头持续向左方横移中，无数炮弹射落至山头前小山丘脚下的战地中央。

230 DRAWING THE TWENTY-FIRST CENTURY

SC.43 平原/战场（日） 太平轮1949（第十五稿）

1c.

续：镜头跟着向左连环爆的炸弹落点持续移动。

1d.

续：镜头亦顺势跟着几个往山丘上窜的炮弹上摇，巨大火花及烟尘爆落山丘上国军的战壕周边。

1e.

续：镜头不停地向左横移，战壕内国军无目的地往下方放枪，一些士兵忙碌的边战边架设防御工事。

SC.43 平原/战场（日）　　　　　　　　　　　　　　　　　　　　　太平轮1949（第十五稿）　　3

1f.

续：镜头逐渐移向国军战壕后方，见国军炮阵亦发炮还击。

1g.

续：镜头渐加快速度，横推向战壕后方的排炮阵地。

1h.

续：镜头快速推近战壕的炮阵，猛烈发炮。

SC.43 平原/战场（日）　　　　　　　　　　　　　　　太平轮1949（第十五稿）　　4

1i.

续：镜头随连环发泡的火炮向右横移。

1j.

续：镜头随一个个连环发炮的火炮快速横移。

Apart from setting out the sequences for director John Woo's key technical team, boards like the ones shown here can be used as "presentation storyboards" to help raise financing, giving backers an idea of what the finished film will look like.

Glossary

8mm, 16mm, and 35mm
Film formats in which the filmstrip is either 8, 16, or, 35mm wide. 8mm is traditionally a home movie format: there are standard 8mm and Super 8 formats, the difference being that Super 8 has a larger image area. 35mm is the standard film format today; 16mm is more economical and favored in television.

Animatic
A series of still images (often storyboards) edited together and displayed in sequence with a rough dialogue added.

Art department
The crewmembers who work under the direct supervision of the production designer. Key roles include supervising art director, art directors, set decorator, scenic artists, construction coordinator, etc.

Art director
Formerly the head of the art department; now the person who works for the production designer to execute the design of the film.

Backlot
The outside area in a film studio used for set construction.

Blocking
The process whereby the director determines where each actor will be throughout the course of a shot.

Blue screen/green screen
See chroma key.

Camera angle projection
A perspective drawing from an architectural plan that views the set through a particular lens.

CADP
Computer Aided Design Programs.

CGI (CG)
Computer generated imagery.

Chroma key
A special effects, post-production technique for compositing or layering two images or video streams together, used widely to remove a background and also commonly referred to as blue or green screen. While chroma keying can be done with backgrounds of any color, blue and green are most widely used because they differ so distinctly from human skin colors and no part of the subject being filmed can duplicate the color in the background. Green screen is mostly used for film these days.

Color palette
The color range designed for the film by the director, production designer, cinematographer, and costume designer.

Composite shot
A single shot created from several separate elements blended together.

Construction coordinator
Oversees the set build to a schedule set with the art director.

**Concept artist
(also known as production illustrator)**
Renders the production designer's ideas for a set or moment in a film in drawings or paintings (now mostly computerized).

**Construction crew
(including carpenters)**
The team responsible for the physical set build on a shoot.

Costume designer
The person who designs and makes the costumes for the film.

Diagonals
Diagonal lines that cross the frame, believed to carry more visual weight with the viewer than vertical or horizontal lines.

Diorama
A set miniature.

**DP or DoP
(also cinematographer)**
The person responsible for the photography and lighting of the film.

Dolly
A piece of equipment designed to enable smooth camera movements. The camera is mounted to the dolly and often placed on a track.

Drafting/draftsman
Technical drawings for the film's sets.

Dress
To decorate the set with furniture/paintings/ornaments ready for shooting.

Elevation
A drawing that shows one view of a building.

Exterior
Outdoor location.

Façade
Front of a building.

First AD
Floor manager on a set, charged with making sure all departments are ready for the director.

The frame
The portion of the scene that will be captured on film, as seen through the camera's viewfinder.

Gaffer
The head electrician on a film shoot, reporting to the DP.

Interior
Indoor location.

In-betweening (or tweening)
The process of generating intermediate frames between two images, which gives the appearance of smooth motion; used in animation.

LAV
Live Action Video.

Lead man
The assistant set decorator.

Location
The exterior space used to shoot a scene in the film.

Location manager
The person responsible for finding locations.

Matte painting
A painting used to produce a visual unobtainable naturally in the set of filming circumstances. Can be a landscape, or a set. Previously executed on glass (AKA "glass painting") it is now created digitally.

Miniature
An identical small-scale model of the set, object, or location.

Model
A 3-D representation of a set or an object used in the film.

Pan (horizontal)
Rotation of a fixed camera on a horizontal plane.

Plan
The technical drawing used to create a set.

POV
Point-of-view.

Post-production
The process after the last take has been printed, including editing, sound mixing and Foley (everyday sound effects), dubbing and looping, music and music scoring, special effects, color timing, and printing the film.

Practical
Something that does work, as opposed to many props, which don't.

Previz (previs, previsualization, pre-rendering, preview, wireframe windows)
A computerized way of visualizing complex scenes in a film before production, usually combining digital video, photography, hand-drawn art, clip art, and 3D animation.

Production designer
The person responsible for creating the look of a film.

Production manager (unit production manager or upm)
Responsible for the budget and schedule of a film on a day-to-day basis.

Prop master
Person responsible for the props handled by the actors.

Rear screen projection (also known as process screen)
Process used to project film from behind a screen to create a background on set.

Shooting schedule
The order in which scenes will be shot in a film.

Shot list
A list of all the shots necessary for a particular scene or for an entire screenplay.

Stage
The area in a studio used to build sets.

Shot (establishing, long, medium, extreme long, medium long, full body, waist, close-up, etc.)
Indicates the position of the camera. A crane shot is shot from a camera set on a frame; a dolly shot is shot from a camera set on a dolly.

Standing set
A permanent indoor or outdoor set.

Storyboard
A series of images that tell the story frame by frame from the camera's perspective.

Tilt
Rotation of a fixed camera on a vertical plane.

Track (tracking shot)
A shot in which the camera follows the subject within the frame, either using handheld steadicam or mounted as a dolly ("dolly shot," or to "dolly in/out/dolly with").

Value
Lightness and darkness of a color.

VFX (also known as FX)
The processes by which imagery is created and/or manipulated outside the arena of a live action shoot.

VFX supervisor/VFX creative director
Works closely with the director to make creative decisions for visual effects.

Wild
Parts of the set that can be moved.

Picture Credits

Thank you to the following individuals and organizations for providing images, permission, and support.

© Aardman/Wallace & Gromit Ltd 1993: 160–167.

Courtesy of David Allcock: 222–225.

Courtesy of American Zoetrope. *Apocalypse Now* © 2000 Zoetrope Corporation. All Rights Reserved: 96–103.

BFI National Archive: 9–11, 55–61, 63–67, 69, 133–137, 152, 153.

Courtesy of Terence Chang: 230–233.

Cinémathèque Française: 171–175.

Courtesy of Jane Clark: 206–211.

Courtesy of Temple Clark: 198–205.

Corbis/Martyn Goddard: 138; Hulton-Deutsch Collection: 21; Nik Wheeler/Sygma: 169.

Courtesy of Crowvision, Inc. © 1994 Crowvision, Inc. All rights reserved: 127, 128.

Courtesy of Guillermo del Toro: 12, 188–193.

© Disney Enterprises, Inc. & Walden Media, LLC.: 218–221.

Getty Images/Kevin Cummins: 131; Francois Guillot/AFP: 195; Brian Hamill: 87; Gjon Mili/Time Life Pictures: 71; Terry O'Neil: 151; Topical Press Agency: 132; Warner Bros.: 46.

© Terry Gilliam: 139–141, 148–149.

Courtesy of the Halas & Batchelor Collection Ltd: 152, 153.

Harry Ransom Center, The University of Texas at Austin/David O. Selznick Collection: 22–24, 27, 52, 53; Ernest Lehman Collection: 85; Nicholas Ray Collection: 48–51.

Margaret Herrick Library / Saul Bass papers: 31, 72, 73, 75, 76; Robert Boyle papers: 32, 33; Leo "K" Kuter papers: 47; Arthur Max papers: 197; Edward R. Pressman papers: 127, 128; Production Artwork Collection: 41–45; Production Design Drawing Collection: 124, 125.

Courtesy of Christopher Hobbs: 142–147.

Courtesy of Paul Huson: 63–67.

Courtesy of Wonjo Jeong: 184–187.

The Kobal Collection/20th Century Fox/Barbara Nitke: 19T; Clarence Sinclair Bull: 35; Davis Films/Jasin Boland: 19B; Dreamworks/Universal/Jaap Buitendjik: 196; Selznick/United Artists: 26, 28, 29; United Artists: 16; Walt Disney: 7; Warner Bros.: 84.

© Kurosawa Production Inc.: 176–179.

Courtesy of the Estate of Ernest Lehman: 85.

Courtesy of Lucasfilm Ltd/*Star Wars: Episode IV—A New Hope* ™ & © 1977–2013 Lucasfilm Ltd. All Rights Reserved: 88–95; *Indiana Jones and the Raiders of the Lost Ark* ™ & © 1981–2013 Lucasfilm Ltd. All Rights Reserved: 114–123.

Courtesy of Rob McCallum: 212–217.

Courtesy of MGM Media Licensing/*West Side Story* © 1961 Metro-Goldwyn-Mayer Studios Inc. All Rights Reserved: 75, 76; *Rain Man* © 1988 Metro-Goldwyn-Mayer Studios Inc. All Rights Reserved: 124, 125.

Courtesy of Miramax: 198–205.

Courtesy of Paramount Pictures. *Gladiator* © DW Studios LLC and Universal Studios. All Rights Reserved: 197.

Photofest / Twentieth Century-Fox Film Corporation: 36–39.

Courtesy of The Nicholas Ray Foundation: 48–51.

© Satyajit Ray Society/The Ray Family: 171–175.

Rex Features/Everett Collection: 15.

The Ronald Grant Archive: 78, 79.

Courtesy of David Russell: 154–159, 218–221.

Courtesy of Vicki Russell: 133–137.

Martin Scorsese Collection: 104–113.

© Selznick Properties, Ltd.: 22–24, 27, 52, 53.

Courtesy of Gabrielle Tana: 2, 226–229, endpapers.

Courtesy Tapioca Films and Luc Desportes: 180–183.

© Touchstone Pictures & Amblin Entertainment, Inc.: 154–159.

Courtesy of Universal Studios Licensing LLC/© 1960 Shamley Productions, Inc.: 31; © 1963 Alfred J. Hitchcock Productions Inc.: 32, 33; © 1960 Universal Pictures Company, Inc. & Bryna Productions, Inc.: 72, 73; © 1962 Pakula-Mulligan Productions, Inc. and Brentwood Productions, Inc.: 80–83; © 2000 DreamWorks LLC and Universal Studios: 197; © 2005 Universal Pictures: 212–217; © 2012 Focus Features: 222–225.

Licensed By: Warner Bros. Entertainment Inc. All Rights Reserved: 41–45, 47, 206–211.

Every effort has been made to contact copyright holders and acknowledge the pictures. However, the publisher apologizes for any unintentional omissions in this publication.

Index

A

Aardman 18, 160
Abbott and Costello 124
Abel and Associates 114
Academy Awards 21, 68, 74, 84, 88, 104, 124, 160, 176–177, 188, 196
Adam, Ken 55
Adamson, Andrew 218
The Adventures of Baron Munchausen 131, 138, 148–149
The Age of Innocence 70
Albee, Edward 84
Alien 196
Alien: Resurrection 180
All You Need is Kill 222
Allcock, David 222
Altered States 130
Amélie 180–183
American Civil War 198
American Zoetrope 86
Anderson, Hans Christian 55
Animal Farm 152–153
animation 150–167
Anna Karenina 194, 222–225
Annakin, Ken 78
Aparajito 170
Apocalypse Now 18, 86, 96–103
Apted, Michael 218
Apu Trilogy 170
Apur Sansar 170
The Archers 54–55
Argento, Asia 212
Around the World in Eighty Days 70
art deco 34
art departments 8
art house films 168
Asbury, Martin 222
auteur theory 9, 70
Aylward, Gladys 62

B

Bacall, Lauren 46
Badham, Mary 80
Ballets Russes 55
Barry Lyndon 55
Bartók, Béla 55
Basevi, James 20, 26
Bass, Saul 17, 21, 30, 70–74
Batchelor, Joy 152
Bean, Sean 142
Beatty, Warren 84
Beddoes, Ivor 54–56
Ben-Hur 21
Bergman, Ingrid 20, 26, 62
Berkeley, Busby 132
Bernstein, Leonard 74
Bicycle Thieves 170
The Big Sleep 17, 34, 46–47
The Birds 17, 21, 52–53
Black Narcissus 55
Blade Runner 117
Blu-ray 18
Bluebeard's Castle 55
Bogart, Humphrey 46
Bonnie and Clyde 86
Box, John 13, 62, 68
The Boy Friend 130, 132–137
Boyle, Robert 32
Brando, Marlon 96
Brazil 13, 131, 138–141
Bridget Jones's Diary 206
Briggs, Raymond 152
Bumstead, Henry 17, 80
Buñuel, Luis 26
Burton, Richard 79, 84

C

Campbell, Martin 154
Canemaker, John 14
Cape Fear 70
Capra, Frank 17, 34
Caravaggio 13, 130, 142–147
Cardiff, Jack 55
Carmen Jones 70
Caro, Marc 180
Casablanca 46
Casino 70
Chandler, Raymond 46
Chang, Terence 230
Chapman, Michael 105
Chelsea College of Art 226
Chicken Run 160
Un Chien Andalou 26
Chinatown 86
Chinese Civil War 194, 230
Choi Min-sik 184
Chow Yun-fat 230
CIA 152
Cinémathèque Française 170
cinematographers 8, 20, 55, 62, 105
Cintiq tablets 194, 222
Citizen Kane 34, 40, 84
The City of Lost Children 180
Clark, Eugene 212
Clark, Jane 18, 117, 206
Clark, Temple 18, 117, 198, 226
Cleopatra 21
Close Encounters of the Third Kind 86
A Close Shave 160
Cold Mountain 18, 198–205, 226
concept art 10, 13, 17–18, 194, 198
concept storyboards 117, 168
Conrad, Joseph 96
Cooper, Gary 52
Coppola, Francis Ford 86, 96, 177
copyright 9
Coriolanus 226
A Countess from Hong Kong 62
Craig, Stuart 206
Crater, battle of 198
The Crossing 230–233
The Crow 126–129
The Crow: City of Angels 126
Cruise, Tom 124
Cuarón, Alfonso 117, 206
The Cure 126

D

Dali, Salvador 17, 20–21, 26, 55
Dark City 126
Dauthuille, Laurent 105
De Niro, Robert 104–105
De Sica, Vittorio 170
Dean, James 48–49
Del Rio, Dolores 34
Del Toro, Guillermo 18, 188, 212
Delicatessen 180
Desportes, Luc 180

Despretz, Sylvain 196
The Devils 130, 132
The Devil's Backbone 188
Diaghilev, Serge 55
Dick Tracy 84
Dickens, Catherine 226
Dickens, Charles 226
directors 8-10, 17-18, 20, 88, 130, 206
Doctor Zhivago 62
Douglas, Kirk 72
DreamWorks 160
Dreier, Hans 34
DVD special editions 18

E
Easdale, Brian 55
École Nationale Supérieure des Beaux Arts 180
Edward II 131
Elizabeth 117
The English Patient 198
Entrapment 117
ET: The Extraterrestrial 86
Expressionism 22, 36, 55

F
Face/Off 230
Fairbanks, Douglas 22
Famous Players-Lasky 20, 22
A Farewell to Arms 52-53
Faulkner, William 46
Felini, Federico 168
Fiennes, Ralph 226
The Fisher King 138
Fleming, Victor 22
Ford, Harrison 114
Fox 17, 34, 88, 180
Frankenheimer, John 70
Frazier, Charles 198
Frears, Stephen 130, 198
Freeman, Paul 114
Freud, Sigmund 20

G
Gable, Christopher 132
Gable, Clark 17
Gandhi 130

Gibbons, Cedric 34
Gilliam, Terry 130-131, 138, 148
Giraud, Jean 196
Gladiator 72, 196-197
Glasgow School of Art 212
Godard, Jean-Luc 49
The Godfather 86, 96
The Godfather: Part II 86
Goebbels, Joseph 36
The Golden Compass 117
GoldenEye 222
Golino, Valeria 124
Gone with the Wind 13, 17, 20, 22-25
Good Morning, Vietnam 124
Goodfellas 70
The Graduate 21, 86
A Grand Day Out 160
Grand Prix 70
Grant, Ulysses 198
Gravity 117
Greenwood, Sarah 222
The Guns of Navarone 62

H
Halas, John 152
Hanna 222
Hard Boiled 230
Harry Potter and the Chamber of Secrets 198
Harry Potter and the Deathly Hallows 206
Harry Potter films 18, 206
Harry Potter and the Goblet of Fire 117, 206-211
Harry Potter and the Prisoner of Azkaban 206
Hawks, Howard 46
Hayes, Helen 52
Head, Edith 36
Heart of Darkness 96
Heavy Metal 152
Heckroth, Hein 13, 54-56
Helen of Troy 84
Hellboy 188
Hellboy: The Golden Army 188
Helpmann, Robert 55
Hemingway, Ernest 52
Herwig, Bill 46
Hickox, Sid 46

High Hopes 130
Hitchcock, Alfred 17, 20-21, 26-33
Hitler, Adolf 36
Hobbs, Christopher 13, 142
Hockney, David 131
Hoffman, Dustin 124
Hooper, Tobe 86
Hopper, Dennis 212
Hudson, Rock 52
Huebner, Mentor 9, 17, 78
Huston, John 52, 206

I
I, Robot 126
Ice Age 150
Ihnen, Wiard B. 36
The Imaginarium of Doctor Parnassus 138
Indiana Jones films 18
Indiana Jones and the Temple of Doom 88
Industrial Light & Magic (ILM) 18, 86, 88
The Inn of the Sixth Happiness 62-67
international perspectives 168-93
The Invisible Woman 226-29

J
Jarman, Derek 13, 130-131, 142
Jaws 18
Jean, Vadim 222
The Jesus and Mary Chain 126
Jeunet, Jean-Pierre 18, 180
Johnston, Joe 18, 88
Jones, Felicity 226
Junge, Alfred 52, 55
Jurassic Park III 88

K
Kagemusha 177
Kennedy, Kathleen 154
Kidman, Nicole 198
The Killer 230
King Lear 176
Klapisch, Cédric 180
Kline, Marty 154
Kubrick, Stanley 55, 72
Kuri, Emile 26
Kurosawa, Akira 13, 168, 176-177

238 INDEX

L
Labby, Sherman 9, 117
LaMotta, Jake 104–105
Land of the Dead 212–217
Lang, Fritz 36, 88
Lara Croft: Tomb Raider 198
Laurant, Guillaume 180
Law, Jude 198
Lawrence of Arabia 13, 62, 68–69
Lawson, Arthur 55
Lean, David 62, 68
Lee, Brandon 126
Lee, Bruce 126
Lee, Harper 80
Leguizamo, John 212
Lehman, Ernst 84
Lehmann, Olga 62
Leigh, Janet 21, 30
Leigh, Mike 130
Leigh, Vivien 17
Levinson, Barry 13, 124
Lewis, C.S. 218
Life of Brian 131
The Lion, the Witch and the Wardrobe 154, 218
Lisztomania 130
The Little Mermaid 150
Loach, Ken 130
Lone Ranger 152
The Longest Day 17, 78–79
Looper 114
Lubitsch, Ernst 22, 34
Lucas, George 18, 86, 88, 154, 177
Lucasfilm 88
Lugosi, Bela 212

M
McAvoy, James 218
McCallum, Rob 212
McDowell, Alex 126
McQuarrie, Ralph 18, 88
The Magnificent Ambersons 17, 34, 40–45, 84
The Man with the Golden Arm 70
Man Hunt 17, 34, 36–39
Mann, Anthony 72
Marcos, Ferdinand 86

Marnie 21
Marton, Andrew 78
Mary Reilly 198
Mather, George 88
Matisse, Henri 55
A Matter of Life and Death 55
Mean Streets 86
Menzies, William Cameron 9, 17, 20–26, 86
Merchant-Ivory 130
Metropolis 36, 88
MGM 17, 34
Michelson, Harold 9, 17, 21, 32, 84
Mineo, Sal 48–49
Minghella, Anthony 18, 198
The Mission 130
Mission Impossible II 230
Moebius 196
Monge, Raúl 188
Monty Python and the Holy Grail 131, 138
Moulin Rouge 154
Mulligan, Robert 80
My Beautiful Laundrette 130

N
Narnia films 18, 154, 218
Nazis 36, 114
New York Museum of Modern Art 170
Newell, Mike 206
Nichols, Mike 21, 84, 86
Nickerson, Jimmy 104
Night of the Living Dead 212

O
Ocean's Eleven 70
Oldboy 184–187
Orwell, George 152

P
Pacific Rim 188, 212
Pan's Labyrinth 188–193
Paper Dreams 14
Paramount 17, 22, 34
Park Chan-wook 184
Park, Nick 17, 160
Pather Panchali 168, 170–175

Peck, Gregory 26, 80
Peters, Brock 80
Petersburg, siege of 198
Picasso, Pablo 55
Pickford, Mary 22
Pidgeon, Walter 36
The Pirates! 160
Pixar 150
Ploog, Mike 222
Poltergeist 86
Popeye 152
Powell, Michael 13, 52, 55–56
Preminger, Otto 70
Pressburger, Emeric 13, 52, 55–56
Previz 13, 194
Prizzi's Honor 206
production art 10
production designers 20
Proyas, Alex 126
Pryce, Jonathan 138
Psycho 17, 30–31, 70
Pulitzer Prize 80

R
Raging Bull 18, 104–113
Raiders of the Lost Ark 18, 114–123
Rain Man 13, 124–125
Ran 13, 168, 176–179
Ray, Nicholas 48–49
Ray, Satyajit 168, 170
Rebecca 20
Rebel Without a Cause 48–51
Red Cliff 230
The Red Shoes 13, 54–61
Redgrave, Vanessa 130
Reed, Oliver 130
A River Runs Through It 154
RKO 17, 34, 40
Robbins, Jeremy 74
Roberts, Michael D. 124
Robinson, Sugar Ray 105
Robocop 212
Robson, Mark 62
Rochemont, Louis de 152
The Rocketeer 88
Romero, George A. 212

47 Ronin 196
A Room With a View 130
Rosita 22
Royal College of Art (RCA) 196
Russell, David 14, 18, 154, 218
Russell, Ken 130, 132, 142
Russell, Shirley 132
Ryan, Robert 79

S
Salgado, Sebastião 198
Salter, Michael 18, 160
Sang-yong Jung 184
Schindler's List 79
Schoonmaker, Thelma 104
Scorsese, Martin 70, 86, 104–105, 177
Scott, Ridley 72, 196
screenplays 8
Sebastiane 130, 142
Selznick, David O. 17, 20, 26, 52
Shakespeare, William 176
Shankar, Ravi 170
Shearer, Moira 55
Sheen, Martin 96
Sherlock Holmes 198, 222
SketchBook Pro 194
Skyfall 206, 222
Slade School of Fine Art 130–131
Smith, Webb 14, 17
sodium vapor process 32
Song Hye-kyo 230
Sony 160
The Sound of Music 84
Spanish Civil War 188
Spartacus 17, 70, 72–73
Spellbound 17, 20, 26–29, 55
Spider-Man 2 198
Spielberg, Steven 18, 86, 114, 154
Stapp, Philip 152
Star Trek: The Motion Picture 21, 84
Star Wars: Return of the Jedi 154
Star Wars: The Empire Strikes Back 55
Star Wars films 18, 88–95
Steamboat Willie 14
Sternberg, Josef von 34
story crunch 14, 150

storyboard artists 8–10, 13–14, 17–18, 21, 34, 78, 80, 84, 88, 114, 150, 160, 188, 194, 196, 198, 206, 222, 226, 230
StoryBoard Pro 194
Strauss, Hannah 126
Sturges, Preston 34
Swinton, Tilda 142, 218
Sylbert, Dick 86
Sylbert, Robert 84

T
Tautou, Audrey 180
Tavoularis, Alex 9, 86, 96
Tavoularis, Dean 86, 96
Taylor, Elizabeth 84
Technicolor 17, 20, 55
Technirama 72
The Ten Commandments 21
Terms of Endearment 21
Ternan, Nelly 226
Terry, Nigel 142
Thatcher, Margaret 130
The Thief of Baghdad 22
The Thing 222
Time Bandits 131, 138
To Kill a Mockingbird 17, 80–83
Tolstoy, Leo 222
Tomalin, Claire 226
Tommy 130, 132
Toon Boom 194
Twiggy 132

U
Universal 212

V
Valois, Ninette de 55
Van Gogh, Vincent 177
Verraux, Ed 114
Vertigo 21, 30
A Very Long Engagement 180
Vidor, Charles 52
Vietnam War 96
visual consultants 70, 72
The Voyage of the Dawn Treader 154, 218–221

W
Wada, Emi 176
Wall-E 150
Walt Disney Studios 14, 17, 86, 154
Ward-Jackson, Nicholas 142
Warner Bros 17, 34, 46, 84, 154
Wayne, John 79
Weir, Peter 154
Welles, Orson 17, 34, 40, 84
West Side Story 17, 70, 74–75, 84
Wexler, Haskell 84
Weyl, Carl Jules 46
When the Wind Blows 152
Who Framed Roger Rabbit 17, 150, 154–159, 218
Who's Afraid of Virginia Woolf? 21, 84–86
Wicki, Bernhard 78
Wilder, Billy 17, 34
Williams, Richard 154
Wilson, Sandy 132
Windmill Theatre 55
Windtalkers 230
Wise, Robert 40, 74, 84
The Wolverine 154
Women in Love 132
Woo, John 18, 194, 222, 230
Wood, Natalie 48–49
The World is Not Enough 198
World War Z 222
Wright, Joe 222
Wright, Tony 198
The Wrong Trousers 17, 160–167
Wyler, William 34

X
X-Men 222

Y
Yates, David 206
Young, Freddie 62

Z
Zanuck, Darryl F. 78–79
Zemeckis, Robert 154
The Zero Theorum 138
Zhang Ziyi 230
Zuberano, Maurice 84

SC.9. INT. CARRIAGE, TRAIN. KING'S CROSS — DAY 1857   (12.)

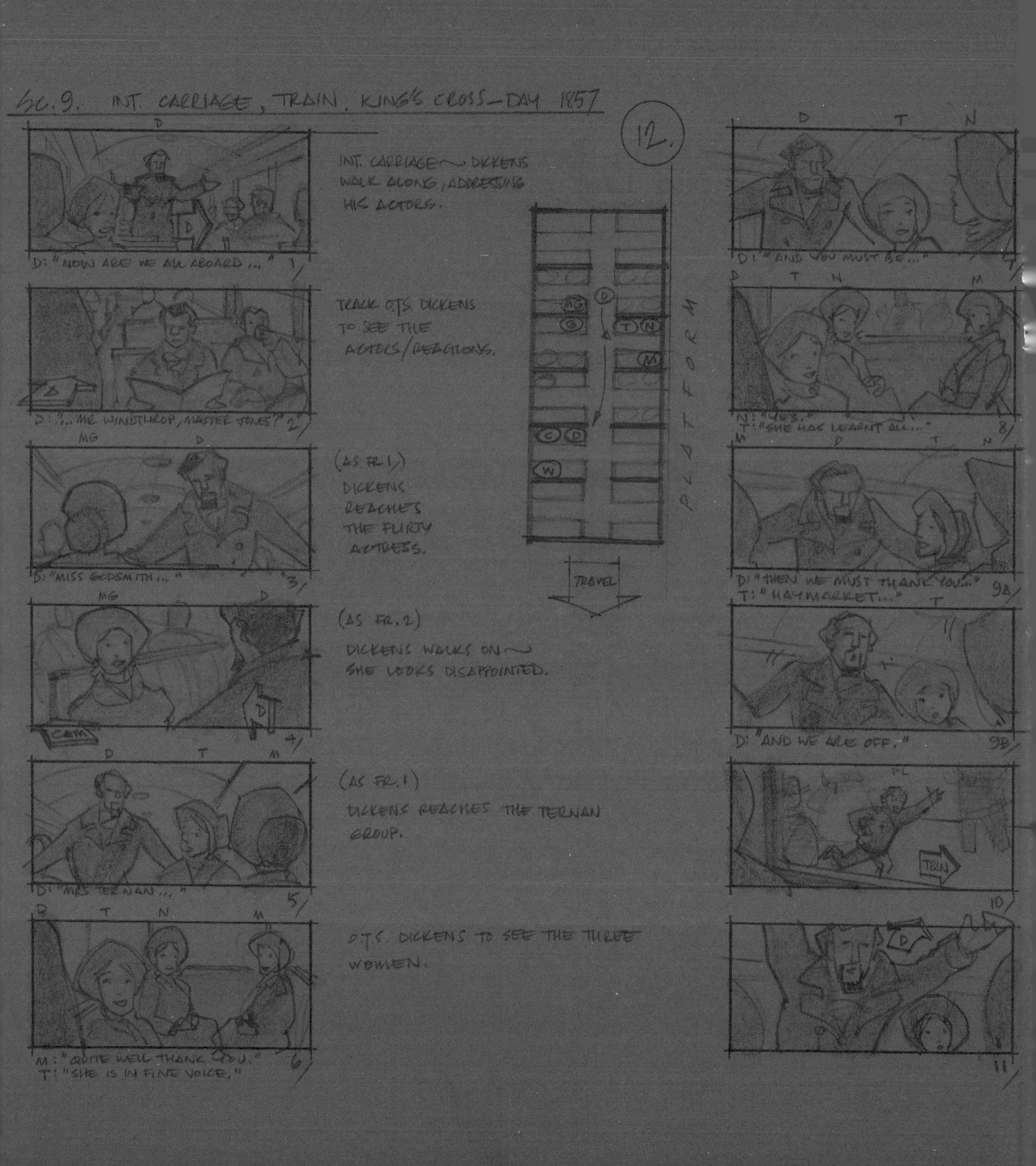

INT. CARRIAGE — DICKENS WALK ALONG, ADDRESSING HIS ACTORS.

D: "NOW ARE WE ALL ABOARD..." 1/

TRACK O.T.S. DICKENS TO SEE THE ACTORS/REACTIONS.

D: "...MR WINDTHROP, MASTER JONES?" 2/

(AS FR.1) DICKENS REACHES THE FLIRTY ACTRESS.

D: "MISS GOLDSMITH..." 3/

(AS FR.2) DICKENS WALKS ON — SHE LOOKS DISAPPOINTED.

4/

(AS FR.1) DICKENS REACHES THE TERNAN GROUP.

D: "MRS TERNAN..." 5/

O.T.S. DICKENS TO SEE THE THREE WOMEN.

M: "QUITE WELL THANK YOU."
T: "SHE IS IN FINE VOICE." 6/

D: "AND YOU MUST BE..." 7/

N: "YES."
T: "SHE HAS LEARNT ALL..." 8/

D: "THEN WE MUST THANK YOU..."
T: "HAYMARKET..." 9A/

D: "AND WE ARE OFF." 9B/

10/

11/